HOW TO
STOP CRIME

HOW TO
STOP CRIME

Chief Anthony V. Bouza (Ret.)

PLENUM PRESS • NEW YORK AND LONDON

Library of Congress Cataloging-in-Publication Data

Bouza, Anthony V.
    How to stop crime / Anthony V. Bouza.
        p.   cm.
    Includes bibliographical references and index.
    ISBN 0-306-44472-0
    1. Crime prevention. 2. Criminal justice, Administration of.
I. Title.
HV7431.B68   1993
364.4--dc20   92-43231
                                                           CIP

ISBN 0-306-44472-0

© 1993 Anthony V. Bouza
Plenum Press is a division of Plenum Publishing Corporation
233 Spring Street, New York, N.Y. 10013

Printed in the United States of America

To Virginia

PREFACE

Is the great American experiment dying?

Even a casual listener to the sounds emerging from the body politic during the 1992 presidential contest would detect deep, troubling rumbles of concern.

It is a fatuous conceit and a ridiculous presumption to assert that I wrote this book to save the Republic, yet the painful truth is that I must confess to this sin of hubris.

The Los Angeles riots of the spring of 1992 were wakeup calls that the nation was content to snooze through.

Our failure to address the issues of poverty and racism fuels levels of violence that produce such murder and mayhem tolls as would prove insupportable for any foreign war.

Riots are no more than rebellions, addictions are forms of escape, and muggings and graffiti are cries of protest and outrage.

Guns, drugs, and the body count become the artifacts of a domestic crisis that threatens the very existence of our nation.

Until the overclass of America can recognize its complicity in the lootings, pillagings, burnings, and killings flowing from the ghetto, any hope of stemming their flow will be dashed.

This book is offered in the fervent hope that Americans will wake up and deliver the social, economic, and racial justice needed to bring peace and progress and to move us to the realization of the American Dream.

Failure will turn it into the American Nightmare.

ACKNOWLEDGMENTS

For this book's existence, and whatever merit it may possess, I owe many debts to many people. Linda Regan conceived both the title and the idea for the book and its principal virtues— and guided the effort expertly throughout. Dave Doi helped with the section on guns and always offered useful, knowing advice. Larry Sherman taught me the importance of research and experimentation. Patrick V. Murphy was a tough, wise mentor. Constance Caplan and Anne Beller offered editorial help and valuable counsel. George Kateb filled me with utopian visions of justice. Carol and Ping Ferry, Mae Churchill, Gisella Konopka, and Fred V. Field taught me what the American Dream should look like. My wife, Erica, and sons, Tony and Dominick, always offered the support and encouragement these enterprises need. And the men and women of three police departments—the New York Police Department, the New York City Transit Police, and the Minneapolis Police Department— taught me how lucky had been my choice of a police career. Most of all, however, I must acknowledge my debt to this great country, which makes everything possible.

CONTENTS

Chapter One

CRIME

From a single crime know the nation.

—Virgil (70–19 B.C.)

Nobody knows what the actual crime rate is in America but everybody knows it's too high. The two principal ways of measuring crime are surprisingly flawed, yet we pay obeisance to the headlines trumpeting still another alarming increase, and we should. The rises are real even if the full outline of crime's iceberg has yet to emerge. What we do know is alarming enough. America is frightened.

THE FACES BEHIND THE STATS

The numbing array of statistics proves incomprehensible even as the figures, ironically, become essential to any under-

1

standing. For a city to go from one murder a day to about six, during a thirty-five-year period that sees the officially counted number of people actually decline, is just an easily ignored abstraction. We look at the statistic, utter some ritualistic regret, and move on. There can be no understanding of the magnitude of the problem without data, but they are, by their nature, mere faceless numbers that can't convey the horror necessary to prod people to act.

The sheer volume of crime only serves to deaden us to the reality because of its very commonplaceness. A murder has to be exceptional to capture the media's attention when six are vying for our notice every day.

Every once in a while, a case we might call a paradigm of the age occurs that shakes the public. It has to have a number of features: It must be a stranger-to-stranger atrocity with which we can identify, and which occurs to us as being unavoidable because of the impeccably blameless conduct of the victim. If the crime somehow seems forestallable, because the system might have prevented it if it had acted more efficiently in an earlier case, a scapegoat is sought. Race becomes an important element as our unmentioned prejudices are pandered to and our silent suspicions confirmed. The case that jogs Everyman into hysterical calls for action, alternatively threatening retribution for officials who fail to heed the call, is the one in which he can see himself, or his loved ones, as the victim. When the image on the screen suggests it might have been you being wheeled off in a body bag, officialdom quakes.

Thus, when a young white woman is stalked by a black male, repeatedly stabbed, and murdered while thirty-seven citizens are certified as having heard her shrill and pitiful screams for mercy, and having done nothing—not even called the police anonymously—the case becomes a terrifying emblem of the age.

Kitty Genovese, thirty-five and eager for life, was repeatedly pursued and stabbed by Winston Moseley, twenty-nine, in the early morning hours of March 13, 1964. It was a chance urban encounter, of the sort that haunts our dreams. The case might have lapsed into insignificance were it not for a snoopy reporter's casual question about the reactions of the neighbors who heard the shrieks and the police commissioner's fatalistic response that they hadn't even bothered to call. The case struck a nerve in the body politic, setting off an introspective debate about the sort of people we were becoming.

A similar case, on June 8, 1991, set off a different response by a community that came to the aid of another white woman attacked by a black male. The result, in this instance, was to ignite a discussion of official breakdowns.

Around dawn that Saturday, a vivacious thirty-year-old woman was stabbed in the neck and had an eleven-inch carving knife buried in her back by a deranged thirty-four-year-old homeless man.

This time, however, neighbors poured out to help the stricken woman, whose screams of "I don't want to die" "curdled the blood" of listeners. The killer was pointed out to the police and arrested.

Alexis Welch, a successful dancer, advertising agency employee, student, and wife, whose life seemed the stuff of Hollywood scripts, died five hours later in an emergency ward. She'd been on her way to meet other early-morning dog walkers in the park with her cocker spaniels, Pizza and Pepperoni.

The attack was apparently the result of the suspect's snatching the victim's purse and her feisty resistance. The initial account, in the June 9, 1991, issue of the *New York Times*, never mentioned the race of either victim or suspect, presumably using the logic that it wasn't germane to the story.

The next day's *Times* described Welch's happy life and the suspect's sad one, again without reference to race. This time, however, it furnished the eloquent message of photographs of the victim and suspect.

On June 11, the *Times* described the suspect's background and his mirror-image previous assault, on another woman a year earlier, for which he'd drawn a mere thirty days in jail. In that case, the victim had, either fortuitously or through the cunning of the people of the street, escaped death. The newspaper meticulously adhered to its silence on the race of the victim and the attacker.

The accused assailant, Kevin McKiever, was an unemployed and homeless wanderer, who had acted "like a vampire" according to a tenant in his old building. He'd hang around the stoop, continuously singing the blues and telling people he was a writer. He was described as "tall and spooky and he was always leaping around like a bat."

Tenants called him an erratic, sometimes violent man. One displayed an order of protection naming him as a threat to her safety. She'd been stabbed by him and he'd set her apartment door on fire. The police had been called on at least nine occasions to respond to his threats to her but had done nothing.

The thirty-day jail term and officialdom's lack of effective response provoked a harried official to lame excuses about trying to figure out "who's dangerous and who's not," and about there being no place to put "all the potentially dangerous people" out there.

The sentence had been a plea bargain because the prosecutor hadn't felt comfortable relying on the testimony of only one witness, the victim, who had herself been convicted of manslaughter in 1975. It isn't hard to imagine the references to "piece-of-shit cases" in the prosecutor's office.

There had been 157,160 felony arrests in New York City in 1990; 42,714 had resulted in plea bargains, and the state prisons were crammed with 56,037 inmates.

No doubt the *Times* editors had concluded that race had not been a relevant factor in the cases involving the suspect and that citing it would play into the hands of racists. Yet how could the conditions that shaped McKiever's miserable life be improved if the racial plight of his existence continued to be ignored? Could anyone really hold that McKiever's being black was not relevant to the way he turned out? Who was creating such monsters if not us? The challenge of the age was to inspire the observer to see his or her own complicity in the shaping of these criminals. This task had not even been approached.

In this case, the people hadn't failed—but the criminal justice system had. It had utterly abandoned future victims through its unwillingness to meet the challenge that McKiever represented. There was nowhere to send him. The mental wards had been emptied. No one would follow up on a menace who'd repeatedly demonstrated the danger he represented and who was probably responsible for an undoubted number of other, unrecorded, incidents. Small wonder New Yorkers were giving up in droves. Small wonder the city was likely to have its socks sued off by the victim's survivors. What kind of stewards-of-the-people's-safety had the cops and prosecutors become?

The *Times*, on June 21, described how the suspect had attempted to secure help for his mental problems and how he'd been turned away. On June 23, the paper loosed a genuine salvo with a front-page story and another entire page devoted to a recitation of the system's failures.

The suspect had not struck without warning: His life was described as giving off shrill and repeated signals of his need for help and his threat to others. He had sought medical help and had clearly needed to be institutionalized or, at the least, medicated. He had committed a serious assault and had repeatedly demonstrated his dangerousness, but the system had let him off. All of the bureaucrats had excuses, but the inescapable reality was that they had failed to protect Alexis Welch and she was now dead as a result. The system had been unequal to the challenge McKiever represented. It was this bankruptcy that had shattered the people's morale and provoked flight.

Could this awful murder have been prevented?

The answer must be unequivocally yes.

An alert, efficient, and effective criminal justice system would have intercepted the suspect at any of a dozen warning stops along the way. He might have been treated, medicated, or institutionalized—voluntarily or otherwise—by a psychiatric system alert to the dangers to future victims. He might have been picked up at any of the dozen or so police responses to his attacks, if the police had cared. A judge might have insisted that an order of protection wasn't a scrap of paper, and the prosecutor might have invested more confidence in a victim who had narrowly escaped death at the suspect's hands. Although she did have a record, it's hard to escape the suspicion that her being black had a lot more to do with the prosecutor's response.

All of the above actions could have been taken well within the boundaries of the U.S. Constitution. All that was needed was a decent regard for the safety of future victims. The New York City criminal justice system, in 1991, clearly had no such concern.

And there was good reason to believe that the public, despite a lot of misinformation and a gargantuan tolerance for myths, nevertheless retained a pretty solid grasp of the complexity of the problems surrounding urban violence, and of the cost and difficulty of the solutions. But with no progress noted and the levels of violence rising, the temptations of Draconian solutions proved irresistible.

FEAR

Street crime is frightening enough as a reality, but the potential for large-scale urban violence—as occasionally foreshadowed by riots—adds immeasurably to the threat of street crime to society. Every urban police chief in the United States fears rioting more than any other danger. The chiefs share a sure sense that the kindling for such a conflagration is ever-present, just waiting for the spark of an incident to ignite it into a roaring flame. Los Angeles was just one of the more recent dramatic examples of the potential for large-scale disorders by our alienated, angry, and excluded citizens.

Fear of crime in America has strong elements of xenophobia. The viewer who can't figure out how to avoid a seemingly random attack by a stranger will be frightened enough to pressure the system to do something. The system's response is frequently to attempt prevention programs that don't, and can't, really work. Incapacitation, through arrest and warehousing, seems to the system a much more promising approach.

The criminal justice system recognizes the critical difference between crimes between strangers and crimes between those who know each other and treats the former far more seriously.[1]

Street crime, especially when defined as stranger-to-stranger assaults, robberies, and burglaries (the most numerous of the personal violence crimes, which include muggings, purse snatchings, and shootings), is probably the greatest crisis facing the Republic. But it is in the individual incidents, rather than in the abstractions of general descriptions, that the real horror resides.

Our nation's anguish and embarrassment became acute when a masked intruder burst into the sixteenth floor hotel suite of the seventy-two-year-old president of Chukyo University and shot him dead before the horrified gaze of his wife. The image of an out-of-control America was stamped on the faces of his grieving family. The message communicated abroad must have breathed life into every film cliché of urban decay. The president had been in Boston to formalize a student exchange program.

A few days later, another visitor, a twenty-seven-year-old student from Germany, was stabbed to death in a robbery attempt in the Bronx. He'd been studying at Columbia's School of Architecture, Planning, and Preservation. His mother had

---

[1] U.S. Bureau of Justice Statistics, *Criminal Victimization in the United States.* Technical Report, March 1983.

kept her fears for his safety to herself, not wanting to dampen his enthusiasm.

Both tragedies were certain to reinforce the stereotype of a dangerous nation among all observers.

Children sent apprehensively to "bad" schools in Brooklyn received a ghastly reminder of the risks when a fifteen-year-old shot and killed a sixteen- and a seventeen-year-old classmate in Thomas Jefferson High School only minutes before the visit of the city's mayor and only a few feet from security personnel. The school had experienced another murder in its halls only months earlier and had lost scores of its students to street violence.

The shooting of a subway conductor and the killing of a young woman in New York City on February 27, 1992, proved another reminder of the danger that accompanies every urban dweller pursuing routine activities.

Avoidance strategies seemed, in those urban settings, increasingly futile. Fear was leading to the fortification of homes, the purchase of handguns, and the pursuit of self-defense courses, in addition to a lot of handwringing.

FLIGHT

Despite the frantic transfer of residences, jobs, schools, and wealth from city to suburb, the major cities of the nation remain centers of our commerce and the linchpins of our economy. It is there that we have the concentrations of skilled workers, the transporatiton and communications centers, and the great buildings, services, and schools that a modern economy requires. Despite the flight, the fate of the nation is bound up inextricably in the fate of its cities. Even those who have flown to transient and unsure safety have been forced to commute back to the central concentration of goods and services that our cities have always provided, but these commuters have had to establish sanitary corridors, from home to workplace, to avoid the dangers lurking between these points.

STRANGER-TO-STRANGER CRIMES

Americans fear crimes by strangers most of all. A National Crime Victims Survey (NCBS) study from 1982 to 1984 indicated that 57 percent of selected violent crimes were committed by strangers. Murder was the least—and robbery the most—likely to be committed by strangers, and women (77 percent) were the more likely victims of attacks by relatives. Stranger-to-stranger crimes more often involved a weapon than nonstranger crimes, and in another study, it was found that resistance raised the odds of the victim's being injured, but it also improved the chances of arresting the criminal and warding off an attack successfully. Violence could be productive as well as counterproductive.

The increasing incidence of frightening stranger-to-stranger crimes is most evident in the most serious of street crimes: murder.

MURDER, THE WEATHERVANE CRIME

Murder is probably the most faithfully, consistently, and accurately reported of all street crimes, yet even here mistakes and evasions occur. Detectives spend a lot of energy trying to convince coroners and medical examiners that the deceased actually expired as a result of an accident, a suicide, or a "misadventure" (criminology has a fondness for archaic language that conceals hideous realities), rather than of murder. They've got enough work to do and don't need another mystery, so they fudge the report through inventive labeling. That these sleuths have succeeded from time to time, as periodic exposés of medical examiners' offices reveal, simply adds to the total of unreported homicides. Then there are the few police departments that don't report their statistics to the FBI at all, as well as a number of missing persons who may have been murdered and may never be found or recorded.

And there is simple police incompetence, as illustrated by a New Jersey case in which the police were summoned to investigate awful odors of two garbage bags full of bones and rotting flesh.

The cops said they were animal bones and advised the occupant to discard them in the trash.

Seven years later it developed that those were the remains of the occupant's father and stepmother, apparently killed by his wife, now, in 1992, charged with slaying her sister as well.

The deceased had been missing, but little had been done to locate them. The accused daughter-in-law had systematically drained $150,000 from the disappeared couple's book of brokerage accounts.

Still, the most cursory examination of murder statistics in New York City—which, probably because of its tough handgun laws, has never been the murder capital of the United States (defined as the number of homicides per capita)—reveals that, in the fifties, with a population of eight million, there was about one murder a day, or less. In 1990, with a registered population of seven million—and about an additional million uncounted illegal aliens—there were six a day. Nationally, the murder total went from 7,210 in 1952 to 23,438 in 1990. Even more troubling than this tripling of the total was the solvability ratio. Whereas 93 percent of the murders resulted in arrests in 1952, by 1989 the rate had declined to sixty-eight percent, as stranger-to-stranger killings increased. Drug shootings, street crimes, and the proliferation of deadly weaponry increased the killings and reduced the police agency's ability to solve them. More people were getting away with murder.

The record was again shattered in 1991, with over 24,000 murders, attributed to drug trafficking, gang warfare, and demographics, that is, a rise in the population of those in their late teens and early twenties. Poverty, racism, and the conditions of life in the ghetto weren't labeled as causal factors by such erudite observers as U.S. senators, despite the horrific totals involving impoverished black males.

That murder was mostly an urban problem was again

illustrated by the nine murders committed in all of North Dakota in 1991. Washington, D.C., with an almost identical population of 630,000, had 489 killings in that year.

The police in Philadelphia "modestly" attributed the decrease in the number of Philadelphia murders (from 525 in 1990 to 468 in 1991) to better enforcement of drug laws. Minneapolis police believed their new record of 62 for 1991 was due to easy access to handguns, increases in drugs, and the growing menace of street gangs.

The police are usually quick to point to external factors as being responsible for increases and to their efforts as driving any declines in murder rates.

New York City's total declined to 2,200 murders in 1991, explained, to some degree, by 1990's murder of 87 in the arson of the Happy Land Social Club. Removing these 87 killings in one event resulted in a total of 4 fewer murders in 1991 than in 1990, whereas the number of bystander killings rose from 22 in 1990 to 29 in 1991. There were, again, over 2,000 murders in 1992 (2020), with Queens, by itself, reaching a total, 357, that the entire city of New York would not have matched in most of the fifties.

It is not unreasonable to extrapolate from New York's statistics that crime in the cities has at least tripled, and probably more, over the forty-year period 1952–1992, the most dramatic rise occurring between 1963 and 1973.[2]

RAPE

Murder is, of course, the ultimate disaster, but few crimes produce the soiled and traumatic sense of violation that rape inspires.

Rape, since it is so infrequently reported, is one crime on

---

[2] Henry S. Shyrock, Jacob S. Siegel, and associates. *Methods and Materials of Demography* (rev. ed.), vols. 1 and 2. Washington, DC: U.S. Government Printing Office, 1975.

which surveys, such as the ones undertaken by the Bureau of Justice Statistics (BJS), are bound to provide more accurate data than the arithmetical totals of those who did report rape to the police.

The Bureau of Justice Statistics (BJS) estimated that 155,000 women were raped, each year, between 1973 and 1987; 4 of 10 rapes occurred in the victim's home, 2 in 10 at or near a friend's home, and 2 in 10 on the street. Again the victimization rate of blacks exceeded that of whites, being 2.7 per 1,000 black women versus 1.5 per 1,000 white women.

It is likely that no crime depicts the complexity behind criminal behavior more clearly than rape.

A 1992 *New York Times* review of several studies of rape revealed these major findings:

Date rape was more prevalent than commonly believed, with 15 percent of college women having been raped, and 8 of 10 knowing the rapist.

Anger at women and drinking may prompt sexual arousal. Many rapists are misogynists acting out their hostility.

At least five types of rapists were identified:

1. Opportunists, who strike on impulse and frequently against someone they know.
2. Sexual fantasists, who act out a fantasy with rape and who believe the woman will fall in love with them as a result.
3. Vindictives, who hate women and attempt to degrade and humiliate them.
4. Angry rapists, who are furious with everything and strike out violently in assaults and rapes.
5. Sexual sadists, who are obsessed with their fantasies and who are stimulated by the victim's fear.

Men's attitudes toward women frequently dictate sexual treatment, including their use of violence.

Men abused as children are more likely to rape as adults.

The reluctance of rape and incest victims to come forward reminds us of the opprobrium that society still attaches to these victimizations, and that societal attitude guides much of the action that follows. One of the great contributions of the feminist movement has been to prod women into greater assertiveness. Shocking disclosures, by prominent public figures, of early abuse, rape, or battering inspire others to come forward, thereby offering hope for real changes and reforms.

Yet many of the defenses involved in rape prosecutions center on attacking the victim's reputation and behavior. Victims of rape, incest, and child abuse, as well as victims of "gay bashing," can expect their sojourn on the stand to be a merciless ordeal of cross-examination. The abused frequently decline to testify, thereby fatally injuring most cases.

Every year brings trials of prominent figures charged with such atrocious crimes, which, as a result of the enormous resources brought to bear on the accuser, frequently result in a reversal of roles.

The silence of too many victims, though, has served only to perpetuate and extend these victimizations.

The plight of battered women and the silence of raped women, abused children, and battered gays offer eloquent testimony to the futility and frustration experienced by victims who perceive the system as insensitive and unresponsive. Highly visible victimizations, like the Central Park jogger's assault, marshal all the forces of the system smartly into the fray. The near-murder of a black female by her neighbor elicits the muted response of a thirty-day jail sentence and makes possible another atrocious crime. Societal pressure has to be applied to the criminal justice system, to make it more responsive to the plight of the victim.

Systems that are unsupervised, unmonitored, and unaudited will go their own way and accommodate their own conveniences. Scrutiny and accountability promote energetic and responsive behavior. New ways have to be found, like a Citizen's Court Watch (where citizen volunteers observe court proceedings and report on the performances of judges, cops, prosecutors, and other players), to make the system more responsive to the victim who has no leverage or power.

The temptation to blame the victim in sexual crimes and the stain still attached to such victimizations, by too many unthinking bigots, have impeded progress toward eradicating these outrages. Nevertheless it must be added that avoidance strategies, such as those that identify the riskier circumstances, people, and places, do improve the odds of preventing these attacks.

DANGEROUS PEOPLE AND PLACES

Despite our common fears of dangerous strangers and dark, ominous spaces, the greatest risks to our safety come from those near and sometimes dear to us and at the site where we feel safest: the home. Domestic abuse, incest, child abuse, and violence in the home make that sanctuary too often a chancy one.

We are right to worry about burglars, muggers, car thieves, serial rapists and killers, and other menacing predators in life's jungle, but the statistics point also to the dangers posed by familiar and familial sources.

A society that is flooded with guns and drugs, that sanctions wide income disparities, and that inflicts harsh conditions on its underclass creates rising levels of danger for all its citizens.

Assessing the precise level of risk, however, proves more difficult than we might anticipate.

THE MORES AND POLITICS OF CRIME STATISTICS

The Uniform Crime Report (UCR) guides our strategy on crime, but it is inaccurate, so its usefulness is limited. The reasons for the inaccuracy are both complex and unexpected.

Police chiefs, who might be suspected of inflating the

figures in order to maximize the threat and thereby strengthen their perennial appeals for more cops, actually and uniformly do the opposite: They underplay crime to avoid greater public pressures and to demonstrate the effectiveness of their approaches. They're going to get more cops anyway, as there's nothing as sexy as hiring more cops.

It is usually estimated that far fewer than half the rapes in America are reported. The reluctance of rape victims to come forward, as well as the fear of the homeless and other street people to report crimes, adds to the chiefs' temptation to fudge the figures. Thus, we can see why so much street crime goes unreported. Even motor vehicle theft—a crime one would expect to be reported faithfully, if only for insurance purposes— gets recorded only about three fourths of the time. When Junior takes off with the family chariot, when a boyfriend or girlfriend drives off with what is technically the other's car, when the vehicle is uninsured or otherwise not worth reporting, and even when the police recover the vehicle before its owner discovers the theft—in all these cases, an auto theft would go undocumented and not make it into the UCR.

Since most crime victimizations and perpetrations occur in the urban ghetto, it is the values and mores of that culture that must be understood if street crime is to be understood. Failing to debate the real issues means not only that nothing sensible gets done, but that myths about punishments and the criminal having freely chosen a life of crime get in the way of progress. One myth is prompted by the fears of citizens weakened by age. Seniors are the segment most frightened of, and least victimized by, crime—because of native caution and the avoidance of dangerous places, times, and situations. In crimes of violence recorded from 1980 to 1985 those aged 12 to 24 represented 67.5 per thousand of the victims; those 25 to 49 constituted 34 per 1,000; those 50 to 64 were 11.3 per 1,000; and those 65 and over a mere 6 per 1,000.

The Uniform Crime Reports offer a cautious and understated portrait of crime in America.

The FBI offers a very cautious and tentative appraisal of

factors which have been determined to affect the volume and
type of crime....
  • Population density and urbanization.
  • Population composition ... particularly youth.
  • Stability of community.
  • Modes of transportation and highway system.
  • Economic conditions ... destitution ... jobs.
  • Cultural, educational, recreational, religious factors.
  • Family—divorce and cohesiveness.
  • Climate.
  • Strength of law enforcement.
  • Focus of enforcement efforts.
  • Policies of other elements of CJS [criminal justice system].
  • Citizen attitudes towards crime.
  • Crime reporting practices of citizens.

Nothing very controversial, or even very helpful, here. Not
a word on how racism affects behavior, and only a very tan-
gential reference to "destitution."

It seems obvious that murder must be the most accurately
reported crime. Auto theft is second, and rape is probably the
least fully documented of the street crimes. Bodies are easy to
count and hard to hide, and society still snickers at a woman's
violation.

Robberies may be bank holdups, which will be meticulously and officially described and frequently are solved because of the filming of the event by security cameras, or they
may be struggles over loose change among the homeless, which
won't even be reported. Burglaries are faithfully reported by
middle-class victims and much more cavalierly treated in the
ghetto. The recording of an assault will depend on the circumstances, and many arsons are classified as accidental fires. The
reporting of thefts depends on the policies of major retailers,
like department stores, toward shoplifters. Numerically, shoplifting is by far the most frequently occurring of all crimes.

Overlying all of this is every chief's temptation to reclassify crimes out of the Part I Index (the street crimes), which invariably gets a heavy press play, and into the much less regarded Part II, which encompasses a great range of minor violations. A robbery may be classified as lost property or a petty theft, so that it moves from Part I to Part II (from the more serious to the less noticed category). The same happens when a burglary is classified as malicious mischief. Classifying crimes downward affords the agency the protection of having recorded the event and thereby avoiding the charge of "canning" (failing to record a crime by throwing the report into the trash can), while avoiding inflating Part I UCR crimes. The result of such fudging may be a favorable, or at least a less damaging, news story.

Why, then, not simply poll citizens about the crimes they or their households have experienced over the past year?

As we've seen, the Bureau of Justice Statistics does just that, but it has sparked a lively controversy over the usually widely disparate findings between the Bureau of Justice Statistics' survey and those of the UCR.

How can this discrepancy be explained?

The root of the problem lies in people's memories. They simply forget about crimes that occurred to them or their family members over the course of the past year. The phenomenon is best explained by the fact that America's decennial census used to contain a question about how many members of the household had died during the past year. Some of these may have been stillborn illegitimate babies, many of which would have been concealed from official knowledge anyway at a time when these births carried the stigma of social disapproval. This question was asked from 1850 to 1900 and abandoned because the number of deaths reported underestimated the official total by over 50 percent.[3] Still, the National Crime

---

[3] The Vera Institute of Justice, *Felony Arrests* (rev. ed). New York: Longman, 1977, 1981.

Survey of the BJS routinely reports more than twice as many crimes as have been recorded by the UCR.

Crimes between consenting participants (such as prostitution, drug sales, and proscribed sex offenses such as sodomy, and gambling violations) are seldom reported. Suburban cops are more tolerant of the misbehavior of white middle-class kids than ghetto cops are of the activities of poor black youngsters. Surveys consistently show fairly similar rates of criminal behaviors among suburban and ghetto youngsters—and wide variations in how the police handle them. The differences extend up the criminal justice ladder, even to judges, whose biases have led to the adoption of sentencing guidelines that limit their discretion.

SAFETY

Our internal violence exceeds the cost, in dollars and human suffering, of any but the widest global conflicts, and it threatens to get worse. Our responses have been aggressive, lock-'em-up-and-throw-away-the-key approaches. They haven't worked. Legislative initiatives include subversions of the U.S. Constitution, usually centering on loosening restrictions on searches, seizures, voluntariness of confessions, access to lawyers, and so on, but these haven't worked either, and won't.

Americans are dramatically less safe than Europeans, Canadians, Australians, and any other nationality considering itself economically advanced. The Japanese would be appalled and dismayed by our crime rate. We ourselves would bridle at the thought of a war that took 24,020 lives and brought about the hundreds of thousands of assaults and the millions in thefts and muggings that street crime produces every year. We have overturned governments for failing to resolve external conflicts that caused a fraction of the annual toll that handguns alone produce here.

Every night, we are treated to whirling lights, bloody

scenes, manacled prisoners, body bags, sirens, smoke, and carnage as America takes its tally of the day's crimes. The images
reinforce racism, as the Willie Hortons are paraded before us.
The fears created this way fuel panic flights into simple answers, usually translated into calls for more cops, tougher
judges, and bigger jails, and all the while accelerating white
flight to the suburbs.

It is called *street crime*, because it occurs on the streets of
our cities. Part I crimes in the United States are centered in the
urban core and decrease dramatically as the map radiates outward to the suburbs and rural areas.

Such organizations as the World Health Organization, the
United Nations, and Interpol reported, in 1980, that the United
States had about 10 homicides per 100,000 population, whereas
Europe and Canada averaged 1.5 to 2 per 100,000. These figures
predated the upward spiral set off by the peaking of the crack
epidemic in the United States in 1985, which led to much
higher numbers of murders by 1991, as the effects of narcotics
trafficking in the ghetto spread. In a sense pandering to the
guilt of whites who have abandoned the core cities, headline
writers love to describe how crime in the suburbs and rural
areas is rising faster than in the central urban neighborhoods,
but they grasp at fallacious straws. Crime and violence center
in the urban ghetto. This fact is most dramatically illustrated by
the murder statistics of America's safest and most dangerous
communities: North Dakota, with 1.4 murders per each 100,000
citizens, and Washington, D.C. with 78 murders for each 100,000
of its population.

THE UCR AND THE BJS

Street crime is measured by the Federal Bureau of Investigation through the UCR, and in the annual polls of significant
samples of citizens by the BJS to establish victimization rates.

Since 1929, the UCR collected its crime data from the

monthly reports of the country's police agencies. Since 1973, the BJS polled 49,000 households (101,000 persons) every six months to get a valid statistical sample of the incidence of crime in America. The BJS survey discovers annually much more crime than the UCR, but the absence of murder, crimes against those under twelve, commercial burglaries or thefts, and arson tends to limit the survey's grasp. In the end, the two measures complement each other even as they provide an imperfect and incomplete picture of street crime in America.

In our statutory society, a crime can occur only when someone commits an act that is against a written law or fails to undertake an action required by a specific statute, such as filing a tax form. We have no such thing as common law, in which an act is treated as a crime because it violates a court decision or custom. In common law, a wife is frequently viewed as the husband's chattel and therefore cannot be raped by her spouse.

Street crime, as defined by the Uniform Crime Reports, consists of murder, assault, rape, and robbery (the so-called personal violence crimes) and the property crimes of burglary, theft, auto theft, and arson. In order to complete the circle, we need to add gun crimes and drugs, even though they are not included in the above categories, which are described in the FBI's annual report of crime as "Part I Crimes."

Part II is a potpourri listing of violations that might be conveniently described as "everything else," and it is more lightly regarded as an index of criminality.

THE UCR

The 23,438 murders of 1990 represented a 9 percent increase over 1989's 21,500. Of these 1990 murders, 12,847 were committed by firearms, 9,923 of them with handguns. More blacks were murdered than whites (9,744 vs. 9,724), an astonishing statistic when one recognizes that blacks make up only about 13 percent of the U.S. population.

Rapes increased 8.5 percent in 1990, to 102,555, the third

rise in a row. Robbery rose 10.5 percent to 639,271, also reflecting a rising trend that started in 1988. For the fourth straight year, assaults rose, this time 10.8 percent, to 1,054,863. Thus, we saw impressive rises in the personal violence crimes that frighten so many Americans.

Property crimes experienced lower rates of increase or declined.

Burglaries dropped 3 percent, to 3,073,909, and thefts rose only .9 percent, to almost 8 million. Car thefts rose 4.5 percent to 1,635,907.

In 1990, the overall crime rate increased 1.6 percent. This was the sixth year in a row of increases, and just under 14.5 million Part I crimes were reported to the police. The increase from 1986 to 1990 was 9.6 percent. In the first six months of 1991, Part I crimes rose 2 percent.

In 1990, law enforcement agencies reported an estimated 14 million arrests, for all criminal infractions except traffic violations. The highest total was for driving while intoxicated (DWI): 1.8 million. Next came thefts (mostly shoplifting): 1.6 million. These were followed by drug abuse violations: 1.1 million. The highest arrest rates occurred in cities with populations over 250,000. They had just under 8,000 arrests per 100,000 population for the year. The rate declined as the distance from the ghetto grew. Persons under twenty-five accounted for 47 percent of all arrests in the cities.

Of those arrested, 69 percent were white, and 29 percent were black.

There was an average of 2.2 cops for every 1,000 citizens, or a total of 523,262 officers, serving over 233 million Americans in 12,401 police agencies.

THE NATIONAL CRIME VICTIMIZATION SURVEY

The Bureau of Justice Statistics' National Crime Victimization Survey (NCVS) 1991 poll of 49,000 of the nation's 95 million households revealed that one fourth (24 percent) had been victimized by rape, robbery, assault, theft, burglary, or motor vehicle theft. The survey doesn't count multiple crimes, so that several burglaries may be counted as one, and it doesn't count other crimes, including murder.

The trend has been declining since 1975, when one third of America's households were victimized. Declines in thefts accounted for the drop from 1989 to 1990.

The National Crime Victimization Survey thus contrasts sharply with the Uniform Crime Reports, which have recorded an alarmingly ascending trend. The rise in murders probably indicates the truest movement in actual crime incidence. Motor vehicle thefts in the NCVS reflected the highest percentage of increase in 1990 over the past sixteen years, following a very flat trend. Recall that the UCR measures crimes reported to the police, whereas the NCVS polls a sample and elicits reports from memory of crimes that may or may not have been reported to the police.

In 1990, the NCVS revealed some expected trends (e.g., blacks and urban dwellers suffered disproportionately high levels of victimization) and some unexpected results (e.g., households with incomes of $50,000 or more experienced more crime than urban lower-income households; this statistic may be merely a function of the upper classes' greater likelihood of reporting, or even remembering, crimes against them).

The NCVS cited the following factors as affecting the trend in crime:

- The mobility of Americans.
- The flight to the suburbs.
- The increasing number of one-person households and the reduction in household size generally (six or more in a household declined from 7 percent in 1975 to 3 percent in 1990). Many criminals live alone, and persons living alone tend to be more vulnerable to crime, thereby frequently creating the anomaly of criminal as victim.

Nothing more clearly illustrates the slippery slope of crime statistics than the confusing contradictions reflected in the UCR and NCVS. What seems clear, however, is that the few facts we can rely on, such as murder rates and the rates of motor vehicle thefts, as well as the evidence of our senses and the reports of sociologists and other trained observers, clearly point to enormously high, and rising, levels of crime and violence.

We have seen in earlier statistics that except for societies suffering war dislocations, insurrections, or other serious, although temporary, spells of instability, the United States has hugely higher numbers of homicides per 100,000 population than other nations. America has far and away the highest number of rapes; only Chile surpasses *half* our rate. Our culture, addictions, and available weapons make our country an unsafe place for women.

In a survey it conducted of 1983 crimes, the NCVS revealed that the crimes least likely to be reported were household larceny (thefts by a family member, 25 percent); personal larceny without contact (shoplifting or theft from an auto, 26 percent); and pickpocketing (29 percent). The highest reported rates occurred for auto theft (a surprisingly low 69 percent) and aggravated assault (58 percent). The overall estimate was that, of the 37,115,000 estimated victimizations in 1983, only 35 percent had been reported to the police.

The NCVS approximated 34.4 million personal and household crimes in 1990, down from the 41.4 million estimated for 1981, and judging by the trends in the Uniform Crime Reports, very likely lower than the actual number.

Males, youths, blacks, Hispanics, the poor, and inner-city residents had the highest victimization rates.

Although many prefer not to report crimes to the police, many others simply forget past—even recently past—victimizations, skewing both the UCR and the NCVS statistics. Nevertheless, the criminogenic nature of our society can be easily inferred from what is known.

ARRESTS AND CONVICTIONS

Mind-numbing bits of data are essential simply because crime and its treatment are shrouded in so many myths, such as that everybody's getting away with murder and that we're a negligently merciful people. The fact is that, as murder clearances decline, our penalties are longer and more severe than those of the rest of the industrialized world, and that even those who got away with murder are likely to have been arrested and imprisoned for other crimes.

In a study of five states (California, Minnesota, New York, Pennsylvania, and Virginia) from 1983 to 1986, it was found that, as a result of the 1.9 million arrests that occurred, 1.6 million of those arrested were prosecuted and 1.2 million (62 percent) were convicted of a felony or misdemeanor. The number of felony arrests increased 18 percent from 1983 to 1986, and the number of incarcerations rose 28 percent. Drug offenses produced increases in arrests of 52 percent; convictions rose 71 percent; and there was a whopping 104 percent rise in incarcerations.

How many crimes have been reported? This study failed to consider the reported incidence of crime as if these crime statistics were irrelevant to the number of arrests and prosecutions in those five states. In fact, this turns out to be largely true. Arrests are driven as much by public pressure as they are by rising or declining levels of crime. We've all seen demands for action result in sweeps and roundups that have stuffed our courts, jails, and prisons with the little fish of the narcotics pool.

THE PUBLIC'S VIEW

There is every reason to expect that the public would accept a complex, long-term, and thoughtful program of crime prevention.

A qualitative analysis of public opinion undertaken by the Edna McConnell Clark Foundation ("Crime and Punishment: The Public's View") revealed a surprisingly sophisticated grasp of the issues by focus groups of plain citizens who looked at the crime problem in 1986. There did surface, to be sure, a number of popular myths and errors that have remained obstacles to reform, but these may well be seen as evidence of the system's utter failure to educate the public on some complex realities. The public has been ill served by pandering politicians and secretive police agencies; the people clearly have a hunger for hard facts and a willingness to consider painful solutions.

Using a racial, educational, economic, and geographic mix of ten groups, consisting of citizens not connected with the criminal justice system, the researchers found these prevalent opinions: Americans are frightened of crime; the goal of the system should be to prevent future crimes; criminals are the products of such remediable conditions as poverty, environment, and the values in their homes; drugs and the absence of effective deterrents to crime (lack of punishment) feed more crime; the cops are doing a good job, but the courts are lenient and inept; sentencing should be uniform for similar crimes; the criminal's record should be considered when the punishment is set; the prison system isn't working to rehabilitate criminals or deter crime; the public doesn't understand the impact of prison overcrowding on the system's effectiveness; and there is a lot of wishful thinking among the public about solutions for curing crime (e.g., military service for young offenders, deportation, and more responsibility by churches).

Furthermore, Americans see prison overcrowding as directly related to the rise in crime and don't accept the view that the crush is due to mandated stiffer sentences or the roundup of low-level drug users and dealers. The public wants prisons to be tougher and more self-sufficient by manufacturing items, growing crops, and so on. Alternatives to incarceration received wide support.

The discussions revealed that the public has some very

sensible and some rather insensible views, but that it is educable and concerned, and that it mostly takes a realistic approach. A corollary is that the people are eager for the truth, however unpalatable it may turn out to be. Chances are good that politicos and public officials underestimate the public's receptivity to harsh truths.

Nevertheless, the appalling levels of crime continue and escalate, driven by factors of poverty, racism, addiction, and hopelessness that have remained untouched. The likelihood of victimization has also increased for the young, the male, the black, and the poor urban dweller.

CRIME IN 1990 AND 1991

The facts and figures compiled in the Uniform Crime Reports for 1990 are carefully labeled as including only those crimes that have been reported; yet they reflect widespread and growing lawlessness. The hysterical cries for action in the mid-1960s produced a President's Commission on Crime, and it may be fair to ask if we haven't become so inured to today's appalling levels and so fatalistic in our acceptance of all this violence that we've become incapable of even such modest responses as once created that commission.

It now takes a wild and celebrated incident to rouse us from our torpor. On closer inspection, the riotous and unstable America of 1968 looks like a pretty tame period—one for which we might nostalgically yearn.

1968

The President's Crime Commission issued its report in 1967; the Omnibus Crime Bill that it inspired—the action program following the commission's study—came in 1968. That year also saw the Report of the National Advisory Commission on Civil Disorders, which offered the central conclusion that "our nation is moving toward two societies, one black, one white—separate and unequal."

Both reports were calls for action that went unheeded, with fateful consequences for the nation.

The watershed year of 1968 brought such national traumas as the assassinations of the Reverend Martin Luther King, Jr., and presidential candidate Robert F. Kennedy; student unrest was symbolized in the shootings at Kent State University by the National Guard and the bust, following the takeover of the campus buildings, at Columbia University. San Francisco had its Haight-Ashbury and drugs, and Chicago had a police riot during the Democratic Convention, which helped put Nixon and his law-and-order images into the White House. The irony of the predilection of these Nixon law-and-order types for dispensing their own versions of peace and safety resulted in over twenty years of dependence on Draconian measures that jammed our prisons and made our nation's capital the most policed city in America, without delivering anything remotely resembling domestic tranquility.

The Vietnam War was going full blast, and our streets were battle zones for cops and demonstrators. The Woodstock generation dropped out, and blacks rioted. In the end, the whites at the rock festival opted in, and many became yuppies, while the blacks' plight continued to deteriorate.

It looked a lot like Dickens's opening of *A Tale of Two Cities*: It was the best and worst of times; a time of hope and despair; a spring and winter. Yet beneath it all remained the vestiges of faith—as symbolized by the two reports—in the importance of having thought and study precede action.

Both reports represented thought, analysis, research, discussion, and debate, followed by plans for action flowing from the deliberations. The Report on Civil Disorders reflects a confident grasp of the War on Poverty policies then in full flower and assumes their continuance, yet decries the paucity of the effort. Little did those scholars know that 1968 would constitute the effort's high-water mark. Their demands for more social programs were met with stony silence, as existing efforts were dismantled.

Even amid all the claims for their attention, Americans were appalled by 1968's levels of criminality. The promise of achieving just such levels would, today, sweep aspirants into high elective offices. Yet, in 1968, these levels were decried as intolerable. In the 1990s, we must remain content to hire more cops, apply tougher penalties, build more jails, and reelect those who deliver such tarnished goods.

Only a very few of us, or our children, will escape crime victimization in our lifetimes—and the odds are worsening.

The National Institute of Justice conducted a survey of victims, starting at twelve years of age, from 1975 to 1984. The survey revealed that there was an 83 percent chance of being victimized by a violent crime over one's lifetime and a 99 percent chance of being the victim of a property crime like a theft. The odds on the violent crimes of rape, robbery, and assault were, as one would expect, much higher for blacks than for whites.

No understanding of crime is possible without the facts and figures. Yet they pack none of the emotional wallop likely to stir us to action. It is impossible to see the tears, blood, anguish, loss, pain, and horror behind the cold, dead numbers.

A young man from Utah was stabbed to death in New York City's subway by thugs attempting to rob his mother. In Central Park, a female jogger was set upon by a band of boys from the ghetto and atrociously assaulted. The event was labeled a *wilding* and linked by commentators to the horror movies then in vogue.

We now live in a society in which the reality of a Jeffrey Dahmer overshadows the vivid imagination depicted in *Silence of the Lambs*. A berserk gunman in Kileen, Texas, could mow down more citizens faster than any Rambo on the screen.

Crime encompasses the same inequities that attend the rest of life in our society. Some crimes are more important than others.

The murder of a wealthy or powerful citizen becomes more publicly significant than an assault on a ghetto resident. There is little doubt that black women were raped, atrociously assaulted, or cruelly murdered the same day as the attack on the woman who walked her dogs to Central Park, but their reports, if included in the newspapers, would be blurbs on page 37. These cases don't make it to our front pages, nor do they get first-class treatment by the criminal justice system.

No one speaks of street crime as a black problem, but we are treated to TV images and offered sacrificial symbols whose meaning is only too clear, even without explicit descriptions. "Wilding," "Willie Horton," and the images on the screen convey unmistakably clear messages. They pander to our basest instincts on race, without offering a clue to the white responsibility for the conditions that make depredations, victimizations, and riots acts of protest.

CAUSES OF CRIME

Americans are desperately anxious for simple answers about the causes of all this crime, but none will suffice. Street crime is rooted in poverty, but not all poor people are criminals, and many poor areas are safe. Relative poverty—where sharp and inequitable contrasts exist and where values have gone awry (as, for example, where rock stars and athletes are lionized, and ministers and teachers scorned)—creates tensions and jealousies that wind up with kids killing for a pair of sneakers or a leather jacket. Crime is a class struggle.

Racism produces an excluded and oppressed minority that suffers from low self-regard, instilled by the dominant class, and fierce inner tensions that seek outlets. Crime might even be described as an act of protest against oppression, yet it is essential, for the psychic well-being of the overclass, that crime be seen and described as malevolent individual actions. An unwillingness even to discuss the history and experience of

blacks in America precludes the development of a sound national approach. We continue to insist on treating blacks as if
they were another piece of America's polyglot mosaic, rather
than as a people who have had the unique experiences of
slavery, Jim Crowism, dependence, and exclusion. Crime is a
race struggle.

The rise of street crime in the United States can be at least
partially attributed to the selfishness of our people, whose
views were reflected in, not created by, the policies of the
Reagan presidency. We will explore how divisive economic
policies reversed a trend of diminishing poverty and greatly
widened the disparities between the haves and the have-nots.
The result was the creation of a Third World culture in which
the notions of an over- and underclass no longer inspired
raised eyebrows. Crime is rooted in selfishness and hedonism.

White-collar crime affects the equation in terms of the
punishments meted out to affluent white defendants who've
stolen thousands of times more than any mugger and destroyed infinitely more lives—even if the victims don't appear
in the hospital emergency rooms, or at least not right away.

The images of a U.S. president's son being involved in
"significant conflicts of interest" in the operations of a bank
(and its effect on investors and taxpayers), of five U.S. senators
intervening on behalf of a savings-and-loan operator who created enormous financial ruin, of the fraudulent televangelists
who have bilked gullible believers, and of billionaires who
speak contemptuously of those who pay taxes as if they were
suckers—all confirm the suspicions of the poor that the odds
are stacked against them. Crime is, above all things, an economic problem.

The ability of organized crime to hire the brightest legal
talent and thus gain advantages not available to impecunious
defendants also skews the vision of "equal justice under law."
Scandals involving defense contracts, U.S. Treasury certificates,
high government officials, and medical frauds—and the relatively light penalties given the offenders—work to undermine

faith in the system and to engender anger and frustration. Crime is fueled by society's double standards.

In Chicago, an alderman called for the National Guard to be brought to his community to combat crime. In New York, a senator offered a bill to federalize many crimes and possibly overwhelm the federal courts and wreck the one system that seems to be working fairly efficiently. In Minnesota, a legislature worked tirelessly to turn drug misdemeanors into felonies and, tempted to impose stiffer sentences, was held back by sentencing guidelines they'd reluctantly but wisely adopted more than a decade earlier, which prevented them from stuffing the prisons. As a result of this rare restraint, the state has the forty-ninth per capita incarceration rate, a statistic no public figure dares mention. Crime is furthered by political demagoguery.

On the streets, kids kill because of hostile stares and for jazzy outfits, and only the intrepid flaunt their fashionable clothes in order to make an impression. It seems a latter-day version of *Les Miserables* and the stealing of bread, which had at least the virtue of necessity as an excuse. Today, lives are extinguished over fashion whims.

Stability, social controls, strong family ties, an influential church, a sound educational plant, and all of the invisible social glue binding a community into a coherent neighborhood result in a safe area. Transition, mobility, rapid social change, and a transient population result in an unsafe area. Crime is a social struggle.

The role of movies and TV in inuring us to violence or inspiring criminal acts is still in question, although evidence of their powerful impact continues to accumulate. America believes strongly in the efficacy of violence, and its cultural expression in movies, on TV, and even in such national adventures as the Gulf War or the invasion of Panama reflects this view. Surrendering to feminist pressures, Indianapolis passed an ordinance linking pornography to rape—civilly. A rape victim could sue the publisher of a pornographic publication that the rapist had read and been excited by, the supposition being that the pornography had inspired the rape. The link proved too tenuous, and the courts threw the law out. It added up to a silly attempt at censorship that ignored both the real causes of such crimes and the U.S. Constitution. Crime, though, may well be a cultural problem.

Demographers will warn of doom when they spy a boom of males in the fifteen to twenty-four age group coming through, but the fact is that what matters most, demographically, is the number of "at-risk" males, who usually turned out to be poor, black, and from dysfunctional families.

If the typical criminal is born to a teenager, if no father is present, and if the living conditions are of squalor and brutality, what does this tell us about the wisdom of making contraception and voluntary abortion available to these young women? Crime is a problem of demographics.

A broken-down criminal justice system that cannot provide the consequences needed to deter crime—swift and certain apprehension and punishment—will not do what it *can* do, in the short run, to control its criminal population. The criminal justice system can focus on serious recidivists and the higher-ups in the drug trade, but it prefers sweeps and roundups. Crime is a criminal justice problem.

Our frontier tradition of violent expansion and reliance on force, coupled with capitalism's aggressiveness and the disparities it produces, as well as the apologetics for violence offered by Western religions—all combine with a shifting value system, changing families and neighborhoods, and the dynamics of a polyglot, heterogeneous population that has always loved guns, to fuel violence. Crime is a historical problem.

Some will aver that we've always been a lawless people. They cite the excesses, in the name of religion, of Puritan America, culminating in witch hunts and floggings. Abuses against Indians; expansions in the name of Manifest Destiny; the depredations of the robber barons; the political thefts of such as the Tweed gang and the corruptions of such presidential regimes as Grant's and Harding's; the lynchings of blacks; the lawlessness and violence of the West; street crime and draft riots; murderous urban gangs and the wildness surrounding Prohibition; war profiteering; Dillinger and the Mafia; corporate criminality; Watergate and the excesses of child labor—all attest to our history as a violent and aggressive nation.[4] In 1991, we had the Gulf War and, before that, Grenada and Panama. Crime and violence are woven deeply into America's social fabric.

Americans' search for drugs that bring euphoria without consequences and the availability of unimaginable weaponry fuels levels of criminality and violence that touched 29 percent of Americans in 1988, while only 9 percent of Japanese citizens were victimized. Crime is a problem of drugs and guns.

Even such unexpected addictions as gambling fuel crime's rise, even as they reflect our tireless search for pleasure. Inveterate gamblers frequently resort to crime to subsidize the action.[5] Crime is rooted in our hedonism.

Crime is probably most heavily influenced by the social problems encompassed by racism and poverty. But there is enough evidence relating to the role of biological and psychiatric factors to warrant their inclusion in any consideration of causal factors, if only as minor participants. Crime may be caused by social, biological, and/or psychiatric factors.

In the succeeding pages, we will explore these issues in detail as we try to arrive at some possible short- and long-term solutions to America's crisis of survival: street crime.

Street crime appears to be a uniquely American problem. Where other nations suffer insurrections and terrorism, and some the horrors of really pervasive organized crime, the peculiar aberration of widespread assaults, robberies, burglaries,

---

[4] Frank Browning and John Gerassi, *The American Way of Crime*. New York: Putnam, 1980.

[5] Anthony V. Bouza, *Gambling in Minnesota*. Minneapolis: State of Minnesota, 1991.

and shootings that touched over 40 million Americans in 1990 can safely wear the label "Made in the USA."

What is going to become abundantly clear is that simple and simpleminded notions, whether liberal or conservative, aren't going to stem the tide.

Chapter Two

THE CRIMINAL

There are a thousand hacking at the branches of evil to one who is striking at the root.
—Henry David Thoreau (1817–1862)

We are all criminals.

If a crime is an act punishable by a fine or imprisonment, or both, and if a criminal is anyone who has committed such a crime, it would be hard to find someone who hasn't, at one point or another in his or her life, engaged in a legally prohibited act. Most people have either taken some stationery home from the office, smoked a weed, fudged a tax return, or committed any of a host of other infractions forbidden by our statutorily puritanical society.

Although ours is a system of mostly voluntary compliance with the tax laws, estimators conclude that there is a good deal of evasion and, additionally, point to a large and growing underground economy based on cash and barter that avoids payments altogether. The Federal Reserve estimates that $100 billion in taxes is lost each year to this cash-and-carry black market.

Millions of workers are kept "off the books" and thus evade payments of taxes. Priests have shaken their congregations with sex scandals and fiscal irregularities, and presidential candidates have regularly titillated us with their peccadilloes. It comforts us excessively to witness their imperfections as we ignore our own. And the State sometimes creates hordes of criminals by criminalizing behavior that cannot be effectively controlled because too many seek to engage in it. Prohibition and the outlawing of abortion are good examples, as is the criminalization of prostitution and other "vice" operations. We need look no further than the large numbers of defaults on federal student loans to find an entire class of white-collar criminals who are emulating the conduct of some national figures.

It is helpful to remember the words of Michel de Montaigne (1533–1592): "There is no man so good, who, were he to submit all his thoughts and actions to the laws, would not deserve hanging ten times in his life."

Our common complicity in crime forces us to define our terms more clearly as we focus on such "simple" concepts as identifying who the "real criminals" are.

The center of our concern here, however, is the street criminal, the predator who routinely and relentlessly commits muggings, burglaries, and thefts and who endangers the public peace.

CREATING CRIMINALS

We harbor endless delusions about criminals, reinforced by movies, TV, and public figures who hurl monsters like Willie Horton or events such as "wildings" at us. Concepts of good versus evil and free will further cloud our understanding. It is little wonder that the citizen-on-the-street is confused when such preeminent authorities as criminologist James Q. Wilson can say "Wicked people exist. Nothing avails except to set them apart from innocent people."[1]

But do they exist? Are Willie Hortons born evil, or are they shaped? Does James Q. Wilson, or President Bush, for that matter, ask himself whether he may have contributed to the conditions that have created these monsters?

Cops very quickly discover that all of us are born with incredible capacities for doing either base or noble things. Genetics certainly plays a part, but so do conditioning and societal structure and expectations. Germany's zeitgeist in 1938 was certainly different from Sweden's in 1990, or from Germany's in that year, and the behavior of the people adapted accordingly. Humans are malleable creatures who are largely formed by the circumstances of their lives, times, and experiences. *—struggle*

The available evidence points strongly to the power of the environment, which includes the family, the neighborhood, and all the factors that go into the creation of the person's universe and that ultimately determine behavior. The child molester and the rapist are frequently the product of abusive relationships during their childhood. The batterer often emerges from a battering home. The street criminal recidivist is shaped in the ghetto.

This does not mean that poverty necessarily and invariably spawns crime, but it does mean that alcoholism, brutality, neglect, abuse, addiction, homelessness, and similar disabilities will dramatically shift the odds against a productive life. A society has the obligation of nurturing its citizens, at least to the point where it becomes clear that wickedness has been freely chosen and that there have been other viable options. A society like ours, with its economic disparities and racial injus-

---

[1] Alfred Blumstein, Jacqueline Cohen, Jeffrey A. Roth, and Christy A. Visher (Eds.), *Criminal Careers and Career Criminals*. Washington, DC: National Academy Press, 1986.

tices, cannot lay claim to the existence of such a social contact. Still, we are left with the necessity of coping with the immediate threat, even as we contemplate the upstream questions.

Arrest rates reveal that the overwhelming majority of property crimes go unsolved, and that the personal violence offenses have a higher clearance rate (are solved through arrests) only because of the confrontation between predator and victim.

DO WE KNOW WHO THE STREET CRIMINAL IS?

Wouldn't it be logical to ask, then, whether we even know who the criminal is, as he gets caught so rarely?

Even an unsolved rape, robbery, assault, or some such personal-contact-requiring crime produces a lot of information about the predator, such as a physical description, a method of operation, the presence of associates, and the method of escape. Additionally and surprisingly, we can confidently assert that all street criminals get arrested, mostly because of the repetitive nature of their crimes and the normal human propensity to make occasional mistakes. Although criminals are known to commit many crimes for which they are not caught, all of them trip up and do get caught—although usually later rather than sooner. The criminology literature is no longer dotted with references to the "smarties who never get caught," which were, in the early days of the street crime explosion in the fifties, pretty much a staple of the commentaries offered.

We will see that even following the strictures imposed by the Earl Warren Supreme Court, the police became so adept at capturing the street criminal that they were able to flood the criminal justice system with the volume of their arrests and to more than triple the prison population between the mid-1970s and the early 1990s. By then, nobody was saying that the cops were catching only the dummies. The questions now center on what to do with these criminals once they're caught, and the answers can be troubling.

American criminology is subject to the same liberal–conservative swings as attend our political, economic, cultural, educational, and social practices, and with the same results. Each end of the swing has its moment in the sun, and each suffers its inevitable overload and breakdown. The shifting balance of power permitted by the flowing tides of democratic debate is probably the accidental genius behind the success of the Great American Experiment. Its polarizations, however, often preclude adopting the eclectic approach so clearly needed.

THE CRIMINAL IS ORDINARY

Our mental image of the street criminal is of a monster, but the reality of the ordinariness and indistinguishability of the criminal would shock us. In person, he has as much chance of being a "regular guy" as any of us. While others wait on tables, drive trucks, or hammer nails, the criminal does drugs, holdups, and thefts—and also walks his kids to the school bus in the morning. This shock of recognition is one of the subtle factors leading juries to the finding of innocence. The accused just doesn't "look or feel like a criminal"—or fit the prepackaged mental image we have of one. "The banality of evil" Hannah Arendt called it. We are always disappointed and shocked when our villains lack horns, and many of us are led to think they must be innocent.

As we've seen, within the general offender population are persistent predators who commit disproportionate numbers of crimes. Identifying career criminals requires distinguishing those who commit crimes from those who do not, and then discerning the persistent from the occasional predators, establishing the seriousness of the offense, and determining the length of the career.

Real criminal careers vary in length, but most tend to be short, around five years. In that time, the crimnals either die, wind up in prison, drift into employment, get married and "go straight," or simply lose the energy that criminality requires. There's a kind of elephant's graveyard mystery to the vanishing criminal. No one quite knows where he goes, but all the charts indicate that he does go. The peak ages of activity are between seventeen and twenty-one and involve mostly males (usually arrested at a rate five times that of women, for street crimes) and a disproportionate ratio of nonwhites.

In a 1983 study of criminal careers, the FBI's statistics showed that robbers and burglars tended to reach their peak of activity at seventeen, and those engaged in assaults at twenty-one, with a very sharp and dramatic drop off after that. Every study of the street criminal confirms the finding that street crime is a young man's game.

As the criminal is studied, the preferred mode is to have him served up to us as a monster to be destroyed—much as presidential candidate George Bush's campaign served up Willie Horton in 1988. But the more we analyze the Hortons of the world, the further back we have to go to find the causes of their behavior.

SHAPING THE CRIMINAL CAREER

In searching for reasons for criminal behavior, we must focus on the criminal's development. From early childhood, parenting shapes the child's actions. A united, wholesome family that provides discipline, supervision, structure, permanence, communication, and the other artifacts of positive child–parent relationships is critical to healthy psychological development. Studies have demonstrated how the absence of these factors leads to criminality. Divorce, family disruptions, and instability are consistently related to criminal actions. Another factor consistently associated with criminal behavior is criminal actions of the parents.[2]

---

[2] Marvin Wolfgang, Robert M. Figlio, and Thorsten Sellin, *Delinquency in a Birth Cohort.* Chicago: University of Chicago Press, 1972.

In early 1992, the U.S. Justice Department disclosed that more than half of all imprisoned juvenile delinquents, and more than a third of adult criminals in jails or prisons, had immediate family members who had also been incarcerated. The implication seemed to be that criminal behavior was family-centered and family-transmitted, but was this transmission genetic or environmental? Then came the question of how to separate family influences from those of the neighborhood and the surrounding conditions of life.

In the end, the analysts were left with the central causal factors of poverty, drugs, family stability, and the neighborhood. The search for the magical virus of crime causation would have to continue, but the evidence gathered continued to point to what was happening to the family, to the cities, to the poor, and to those victimized by racism.

Our passion for action has mostly precluded the sort of research and study that understanding such complex behavior as repeated criminal acts demands; yet the recidivist must be understood if we are to entertain any hope of deflecting his attacks.

The Rand Corporation developed a scale that contained these criminally predictive factors[3]:

1. A previous conviction for the same charge (robbery or burglary).
2. Incarceration for more than 50 percent of last two years.
3. A conviction before age sixteen.
4. Serving time in a state juvenile facility.
5. Using drugs in the preceding two years.
6. Drug use as a juvenile.
7. Employment for less than 50 percent of preceding two years.

---

[3] Peter Greenwood, *Selective Incapacitation*. Report R-2815, National Institute of Justice. Santa Monica, CA: Rand Corporation, 1982.

Not included were such roots-in-the-community factors as stability of residence or family problems with alcohol or illiteracy. The scale is retrospective, although it attempts to predict future actions. The human's infinite variety continues to confound any attempt at convenient compartmentalization. Yet jurisdictions such as Iowa's have adopted similar keys to evaluate their suspects, and Minnesota and the federal government have implicitly adopted these views by incorporating many of these values into sentencing guidelines that are intended to act as filters for identifying the dangerous predators.

The fact is that studying crime and its disposition is an art, not a science. It is a subjective attempt to understand a complex human and his actions and to prescribe a sanction that deters, rehabilitates, or incapacitates. Studying the event is an attempt to deal with an act that has been committed, as well as an effort to affect future behavior. In assessing future prospects, we are forced to acknowledge the fallibility of the process, even while we work mightily to reduce the margin of error. It has to be said that mistakes can and very likely will be made. It also has to be acknowledged that society is going to have to risk making such occasional mistakes as incarcerating some who might not ever repeat a crime. Creating mechanisms for review and appeal in order to mitigate the damage provides a safety valve.

At this moment, the system's failure to predict and interdict criminality is enormous.

A study by the National Institute of Justice of state prisoners released in 1983 who were rearrested, reconvicted, and reincarcerated showed that 40 percent were rearrested within a year of release and over 60 percent after three years, most of them being convicted and imprisoned.

There is a predictable pattern that establishes a consistency between prior activity and the future prospects of an arrest. The more adult arrests in a prisoner's record, the greater the likelihood of rearrest and reincarceration, following release from state prison. A prisoner with eleven or more prior arrests is almost 80 percent certain of being rearrested within thirty-six months of being released from prison.

THE RECIDIVIST

Having targeted the street criminal, we are led to the discovery that, even among prison populations, there are gradations. We have the casual, occasional criminal and the "violent predator" who routinely commits the overwhelming majority of crimes and who constitutes only 10 percent of the incarcerated and clearly identified "criminal population."[4] Developing a filtration system that separates the persistent violator from the much less dangerous casual criminal is one of the daunting yet critically important tasks of the system.

This phenomenon of a violent minority among the larger criminal population was also found to exist among juvenile delinquents, 18 percent of whom were found to be chronic, in that they had had five or more contacts with the police. Recidivism was found to be connected with lower income, lower IQ scores, failure in school, and being a nonwhite male.[5]

That a small minority of the criminal population commits about two thirds of the crime and that perhaps about 5 percent of a city's locations ("hot spots") account for two thirds of the police calls argues potently for the development of techniques for identifying, analyzing, and responding to the challenges posed by the few people and sites that create a vast preponderance of the police problems in a city. The challenge is, of course, to identify the predators before, not after, the fact. This course raises delicate and difficult ethical and juridical ques-

[4] David P. Farrington, *Further Analyses of a Longitudinal Survey of Crime and Delinquency.* Final Report to the National Institute of Justice. Washington, DC, 1983.

[5] Mary Toborg, *Preliminary Findings on the D.C. Urine Testing Experiment.* Paper presented at a meeting of the American Society of Criminology, Cincinnati, Ohio, 1984.

tions. What seems clear is that there are a few specific sites and persons who spell trouble for society, and it seems equally clear that diagnosing the problem and prescribing a solution become essential to the society's well-being. A neighborhood will be improved through the closing of a bucket-of-blood bar, and a community will be made safer through the interdiction and warehousing of a serial rapist. Even a block will achieve peace through the expulsion or reform of a troubled family. These actions also transmit strong signals of society's determination to safeguard itself, while showing that it retains a rational sense of priorities and is not responding in panic.

⚓ A study of released prisoners indicates the importance of sex, race, and prior number of arrests in establishing what might be described as the factors predicting a return to prison. In an eleven-state recidivism study, the National Institute of Justice found that over 94 percent of recidivists were male, 45 percent were black, and the median age on release was twenty-seven. Just over a third were in prison for a violent offense; almost half were there for property crimes; and because the study focused on those released in the pre-drug-peak year of 1985, only 9.5 percent had been in prison for drugs alone. The prisoners had an average of 8.4 prior arrests each, with a median number of 6, and over two thirds had been incarcerated previously.

Certainly not all, nor even most, of a city's poor are criminals, but we will see that all of the street criminals are poor, and that many of them share identifiable characteristics, whether it is diplomatic to speak of these or not. These include being addicted, nonwhite, unemployable, and afflicted with disabilities that make criminal careers the inevitable, and perhaps even the logical, course.

We are mainly concentrating here on the criminal who strikes randomly—depending on presented opportunities—and at strangers. The areas of principal concern are robberies (holdups, muggings, necklace snatchings, and other such personal confrontations); burglaries (breaking and entering to commit a crime); and assaults (e.g., inflicting injury or threatening with a gun or other weapon).

COMPULSIVE RECIDIVISTS

There are limits on any supervisory program that envisions the offender's freedom. These center on the risks and on the prospects of success. The criminal must be both motivated, positively, to work, go to school, stay sober, repay his victims, attend treatment, and such, and he must be sufficiently frightened of the consequences to work to avoid failure.

Criminals acting out of compulsions are poor risks for monitoring. Child molesters, serial rapists, serial killers, and other repeaters of that type should simply be warehoused for very long periods. If they are medicated, there must be frequent verifications. Voluntary castration or a similarly disabling procedure ought not to be precluded in extreme cases. This is an issue that requires more research and discussion.

There is an extremely high probability of relapse among compulsive recidivists because they can't or won't control their own actions. There is an urgent need for monitoring and verification in these cases.

There is the additional need to attack the protective instincts of organizations, such as churches, to avoid scandal and suppress information about violations by their members. Despite understandable reluctance, there is an inescapable duty to uncover and confront such betrayals of trust. Failure to do so simply ensures the perpetuation of victimization.

The intervention of the National Baptist Convention USA, Inc., on behalf of convicted rapist and former heavyweight champion Mike Tyson split the black community. Because both the victim and the accused are black, the controversy proved divisive on feminist and even fiscal grounds as well, and some critics raised questions about a large pledge made by Tyson to that church. To complicate things further, both Tyson and his accuser are Baptists.

THE PSYCHOTIC MURDERER

It may be easier to devise interceptors for recidivists who are, after all, acting from rational, easily comprehended motives relating to profit, pleasure, and the like, than it may be to prevent the attack of the mentally disturbed offender.

A star of a television sitcom inspired an obsessive interest in a viewer, who tracked her down, stalked her, and finally murdered her on July 18, 1989. He'd been able to devote every waking moment and every erg of energy to this single-minded pursuit. A defense psychiatrist described him as schizophrenic, and his lawyer pleaded for his commitment to a prison for the criminally insane. Yet we must be wary of tempting killers to take grotesquely cruel measures to convince juries that they must have been crazy to do what they did. The defense of insanity should be strictly limited to those who are certifiably and obviously unable to understand the nature of their actions.

Intercepting such criminals requires the creation of a system of identifying such menaces early and committing them, through court processes that are assisted by competent medical authorities, to secure mental institutions. Our society is moving in the opposite direction and putting everyone at risk by tolerating a population of dangerously demented persons who do not take the medicines that enabled them to be released.

Most murderers are shaped by conditions of deprivation and racism, by the little-understood effects of malfunctioning body chemicals or traumatic conditioning experiences, and by such quotidian factors as greed or lust.

The criminal in America has many faces and different motives. He represents a challenge of both variety and difficulty. How can we identify the recidivist and set him apart from the other 90 percent of the accused criminals? The search for a simple answer will be undone by the unlikely semblance of the specific criminal.

Today's street criminal is spawned in the urban underclass of the excluded, the impoverished, and the racist-victimized and would—but for the carnage he causes—be readily forgotten by the rest of us. But crimes and riots do force us to search for answers, whether we want to or not.

A POSSIBLE APPROACH TO RECIDIVISM

Criminality is behavior, and like much that falls under that description, it is learned, practiced, and repeated. Recidivism thus becomes a key factor in understanding crime.

A Bureau of Justice Statistics study of young parolees (seventeen to twenty-two) showed that 69 percent had been rearrested within six years of their 1978 release from custody. Approximately 10 percent accounted for 40 percent of the arrests, and length of prior confinement was not a factor in whether there would be another arrest. Recidivism rates were highest in the first two years after release, and among males, blacks, and high school dropouts. The longer the prior record, the higher the prospect of rearrest: 90 percent of parolees with six or more previous arrests were rearrested, as opposed to 59 percent of first-time offenders. The earlier the first arrest, the likelier another would follow (79 percent of those arrested before seventeen vs. 51 percent of those first arrested at twenty or older).

The experience argues for the lifting of the protective veil of secrecy from juvenile criminal records. It is becoming increasingly clear that a criminal's record as a juvenile offender is critically important to assessing the risks he represents to the community, and this record is usually not legally available at an adult's sentencing. Recognizing the need to provide protection to the nonrecidivist, legal provisions could be made to

expunge or suppress the record of an offender who has demonstrated a determination to stay straight and clean.

Imprisonment helps reduce recidivism by incapacitating
the criminal during the years of high crime productivity, by
discouraging the criminal through the punishment of incarceration and the fear of returning to prison, and by providing an
environment in which rehabilitation, education, or treatment—
such as to divert the returning offender from a life of crime—
are at least theoretically possible.

There is a sameness in the profiles that suggests a societal
cookie cutter that stamps criminals out at a fantastic rate. The
ingredients of the matrix are race, poverty, ignorance, and
general hopelessness. The result is the recidivist, revealed in
every study, including one of persons arrested in America's
most populous seventy-five counties, which produced almost
half of all reported crimes in the United States in 1985.

A 1988 study of felony defendants reveals that defendants
with prior records were hugely more likely to be rearrested and
that the probability increased with the number of prior arrests.
Again, the figures illustrated how much more prone to property crime or personal violence is the person who has been
previously accused.

Such studies demonstrate that criminal behavior is just
that: behavior, a learned and repeated mode of responding to
the world. Behavior implies a measure of choice, and criminal
behavior should be seen as a succumbing to what is perceived
as a rational or inescapable option.

The striking question hinges on the unfairness of labeling
someone by punishing him for future conduct, but it cannot be
forgotten that the criminal justice system informally and implicitly makes such decisions every day, under other labels.

Actuarial tables are established not to predict specific outcomes for specific individuals but to determine the statistical
probabilities affecting large samples. The dilemma of recidivism can be likened to trying to apply an actuarial table
individually.

Predicting future conduct requires a careful professional analysis of past behavior and an assessment of the circumstances of the life of the accused. Recent actions need to be weighed for signs of a determination to reform. Developing a formula not only involves the accumulation of many facts relating to the life history of the accused but requires weighing the importance of those factors, so that a useful, if fallible, predictive table can be devised.

Investigative agencies have profiled major cases by systematically analyzing a crime and extrapolating, from the evidence (in emulation of the Sherlock Holmes method), characteristics of the criminal that may assist them in finding him. Such profiling causes patterns to emerge that may reveal the existence of a serial criminal at work.

The risks of error, and injustice, are enormous. The stakes are high. A friend once joked, early in my police career, that I should lock everybody up and release only those who could give a satisfactory account of their lives. In the cynical world of the police, there are no innocents.

This joke has assumed some ironic value, and we may now be in a position to exploit its grotesque promise. Having stuffed the prisons and generally become almost as Draconian as my friend's fanciful humor suggested, we might undertake programs for observing, evaluating, and commenting on prisoner behavior. Marrying this in-prison analysis to the factors pointing to lower recidivism risk may lead to the release of those who can be controlled in other ways.

A 1986 Bureau of Justice Statistics survey of prison inmates found that over half (53 percent) had been charged with violating prison rules. Those who were at higher risk of committing infractions, it was found, were younger inmates with more extensive criminal records or drug histories, as well as those housed in large or maximum-security prisons and those who had been incarcerated previously.

The infractions ranged from minor actions, such as smoking, horseplay, bad language, and infringement of sanitary regulations, to more serious actions: assaults, extortions, and even murder. Punishments included loss of privileges, restrictions on movement, solitary confinement, and transfers, among others. Evaluating in-prison conformity with rules ought to assist us in assessing the prospects of responsible behavior in freedom.

Such a radical winnowing as would result from freeing the huge number of prisoners who could be otherwise, and far more cheaply, controlled would free up a lot of prison space, thereby enabling the system to cope with the current volumes of arrests, and perhaps even to increase capacity; would save money; and would enable the system to concentrate on, and incapacitate, the most serious risks to public safety. It would also provide prison administrators with a powerful tool for controlling inmate behavior more effectively. Prisoners could be released to halfway houses, could work or participate in educational or treatment programs, could be fined or required to make restitution—any of a host of innovative possibilities, all of which must include control and observation, as well as sanctions in the event of failure. And the system would have to learn to live with the statistical certainty that there will be such failures as Willie Horton and to have the courage to confront such consequences.

In a logical extension to sentencing guidelines, the program could be labeled *incarceration guidelines* and could be administered by corrections officials or parole boards. Making the issue explicit would remove a great deal of the hypocrisy and unevenness driving the current approach. Even considering such a proposal would at least ensure some informed discussion of a subject that legislatures are currently ignoring as they ratchet every crime upward and mandate ever harsher sentences, without regard to the consequences or the effectiveness of the legislation, seeking only to be "tough on law-and-order issues."

A useful predictive dossier could be developed from a description of the crime for which the offender is currently

incarcerated; his prior record; a comprehensive probation officer's report (including a personal, work, educational, and related background-factor history); and documented analyses of
in-prison behavior.

The statistics demonstrate the utter failure of mindlessly
harsh policies that have left the underlying causes of crime
untouched. The numbers offer an image of the breadth and
scope of events, without conveying the blood, sinew, bone, and
flesh feel of the individual tragedies behind the criminal's
façade. Statistics provide the facts, but anecdotes demand the
vivid reflections we need. The awfulness of the Holocaust is
made vivid not by the fact that six million Jews were extermi-
nated, but by the diary of a heroic and doomed adolescent
whose agony touched every heart.

Symbols, though, can be used for other purposes. We were
offered Willie Horton not with a plea to understand his origins,
but as a symbol to feed our prejudices. He became the embodiment of an inexpressible image: the black predator feasting on
white womanhood. His name became, as "law and order" had
before it, a code term for the racist feelings that so many
shared, but that they couldn't explicitly express. Just as blacks
had to adopt codes and church rituals to communicate within
the slave-master's alert earshot, whites adopted codes to communicate their fears and hatreds of blacks. The key challenge
was to identify, segregate, and incapacitate the recidivist and to
safeguard future victims from his attacks.

TARGETING THE REPEAT OFFENDER

The implications of a formula that defines and identifies
the dangerous predator are that a program that targets the
persistent, serious recidivist holds the promise of suppressing
crime while reducing the prison population by making incarcerations far more selective. This goal is possible through the
adoption of strategies that incapacitate the repeater, while con-

trolling through alternative sanctions those who are casually involved.

Drugs produce many crimes in different ways: they alter behavior to induce violent acts; they promote drug traffic turf wars and battles for control; and they create the economic dilemma that forces the addict to commit crimes to support the habit. The connection between drug use and crime, prominently featured in the Rand scale previously described, was established through urine tests of suspects in Washington, D.C., and New York City: it was found that well over half the suspects had illegal drugs in their systems at the time of their arrest.[6]

Vicious competition among narcotics traffickers has resulted in the explosion of assault weapons and sophisticated semiautomatics on the streets, raising the murder toll—of both participants and innocent bystanders—appallingly.

The involvement of alcohol in all this violence is also apparent from the statistics and the individual histories of street criminals, even if its total effect hasn't been precisely measured.[7] And some estimate that another addiction—gambling—has been responsible for perhaps as many as 13 percent of the crimes committed by our prison population. The connection between addictions and criminality is inescapable.

NO OBVIOUS ANSWERS

Sparked by a spate of highly visible sex crimes, the Minneapolis *Star and Tribune* investigated 767 Minnesota rapists and child molesters in 1991 and found that those who had received treatment in exchange for shorter prison sentences had been

[6] J. Roizen and D. Schneberg, *Alcohol and Crime*. Report of the National Institute on Alcohol Abuse and Alcoholism, Social Research Group. Berkeley, CA: University of California, 1977.

[7] James Q. Wilson, *Thinking about Crime* (2nd ed.). New York: Basic Books, 1983.

rearrested more often than those who had simply been imprisoned, for longer periods, without treatment. The rapists who had completed psychological treatment programs were 40 percent more likely to be rearrested for sex offenses within four years of release than those who hadn't been treated. The child molesters were also found to be more likely to recidivate after seven years of freedom, an outcome suggesting the depth of the roots of their maladies.

Minnesota spends $6.3 million annually on treatment and is notably conscious of the need for a variety of approaches, including prevention, education, and treatment, as well as incarceration.

The rearrest figures were sufficiently troubling to cause the newspaper to conclude that the state's "much-praised treatment programs don't work."

In another study of the impact of increased penalties passed in 1989, the paper found longer sentences for murderers (18.9 years in 1990 vs. 13.2 years in 1988); rapists (11.1 years in 1990 vs. 7.4 in 1988); assaulters (7.5 years in 1990 vs. 5.5 in 1988), and robbers (4.6 years in 1990 vs. 4.1 years in 1988) but still found that the really serious threat of overcrowding the prisons came from the increased penalties for drug offenses.

These two studies, once again, illustrate the complexity of criminal behavior and emphasize the importance of intercepting the shaping of these criminals upstream, as well as the great challenge of separating the repeat from the occasional offender. A caution must, however, be added: Such recidivists as child molesters and similar criminals sometimes go undetected for years and surface either by chance, as a result of good police work, or through the appearance of complaining victims who may have been silent for years.

Although most Americans would doubt it, we've been on a Draconian binge of repression since at least 1972. The Warren Court's decisions simply made the police more professional and legalistic, not less effective or even less aggressive. We will see just how severe we Americans can be, even while we entertain the fanciful conceit that we have a fuzzily liberal approach to criminals and allow them to get away with murder. Many do get away with it, not because of any gentleness in our approach but because of the system's ineptness.

Richard Nixon, Ronald Reagan, and George Bush vigorously pushed and reflected the conservative lock-em-up agenda that Americans hankered for, yet they failed to deliver the promised levels of safety—or anything close to them. The rhetoric, however, continued to play beautifully in Peoria as these men converted the Republican Party into the vehicle of white suburban dreams. By 1992, Bush knew very well that his votes lay in California's Simi Valley, not in Watts.

In a very real sense, both liberals and conservatives are right and wrong. The answer may lie in an eclectric approach that holds out the promise of a better life to those who might otherwise be channeled into criminal careers, while delivering harsh sanctions to the transgressors.

It seems clear enough, after a long and fair trial of stern measures, that the conservative approach won't, by itself, work. The 1960s proved the liberal approach wrong, and being whipsawed from one to the other doesn't offer much promise of discovering lasting solutions. We continue, as a nation, to remain mesmerized by the images on the TV screen and eagerly embrace the view that the bums and criminals depicted there, every night, have nothing to do with us or our sins.

THE KILLER

We must look behind the veil of facts and figures if we hope to understand the nature of crime and its sources, and to do something useful about them.

Beeper Mike, twenty-nine, sold and rented the electronic paging devices that were the tools and emblems of the drug trade in Oakland. He pocketed the proceeds himself, and the electronics company shut off the pagers. The dealers were hurting and started to hunt for Beeper Mike. Finally found, he was cursed, pummeled, and chased. In broad daylight and before more than a dozen witnesses, a cool killer shot him in the back with a .22 caliber revolver. The killer had previously boasted of his prowess with the piece. This was a routine ghetto murder, typical of the leading cause of death of black males in that age group. The familiarity and predictability of the scene forces the drama into the background of the deadening realm of statistics.

As the curtain parts, though, to reveal the humans behind it, we see a new scene: The killer is a frightened five-foot two-inch, 125-pound boy who is, amazingly, twelve. He is a hardened street killer and dealer. He's lived on the streets, was taught to deal drugs by his older brother, and was left to fend for himself by a mother who is too preoccupied with surviving to give him much time. She has just broken up with a male whom our young killer admired, and this breakup has upset him so much that he has developed colitis. As the holder of an unexceptional school record, he had been engaged in the ghetto's routine mischief: arrests for battery, possession of a switch blade, and the surprisingly precocious driving without a license. Not a big-deal record. Then he started hanging out with the older kids and carrying a piece to make up for his youth and size. He learned to swagger and deal, like the big boys. With drugs, guns, and violence all around him, the models were inescapable. In the meantime, the powers that be were cutting back on school, job, and recreation programs.

This boy-soldier was so distraught following his arrest for murder that he tore out his hair, wept hysterically, and threatened suicide. He had to be placed in solitary confinement and monitored by a camera for his first ten days in detention.

Yet his mother had always worked and they even owned the bungalow they called home. She wasn't on welfare and they weren't homeless. The stereotypes don't always fit as snugly as we'd like them to.

Just another black kid lost to the ghetto's mean streets. What's his life going to be like over the next dozen years? We don't know his name, but wouldn't Willie Horton do as an alias?[8]

---

[8] *New York Times*, May 26, 1991, p. 11.

Chapter Three

JUVENILE DELINQUENCY, GANGS, AND YOUNG OFFENDERS

America's best hope for reducing crime is to reduce juvenile delinquency and youth crime.
—The Challenge of Crime in a Free Society (a government report), March 1967.

Street crime is mostly a black and poor young man's game. The most serious concentrations of these perpetrators fall in the fifteen- to nineteen-year-old age group. From a demographic perspective, plotting the course of the poor, black male cohort in this age group is as reliable a predictor of coming street crime trends as can be found.

Addictions offer the ephemeral hope of escaping the awfulness of the conditions of life into which these kids are born and in which they are raised. Alcohol and drugs then grease the skid into criminality. Guns facilitate the criminal process further.

DELINQUENCY AND ITS VARIETIES

Juvenile delinquency is generally defined as an act committed by a youth that, if committed by an adult, would be a crime. The legal definition of *youth* varies by state, from under sixteen to under nineteen. The special treatment juveniles receive is intended to spare them the stigma of a criminal conviction early in their lives. A prosecutor can usually take legal steps to have a juvenile delinquent adjudged an adult in particularly heinous cases that require a more severe prosecutorial approach. Usually, these cases involve youths at the upper age margins who have committed egregious offenses that have shocked public sensibilities. The option of prosecuting a juvenile as an adult is typical of the sorts of flexibilities that must be built into any system that hopes to cope with anything as complex and varied as criminal behavior—at any age.

In treating a young offender as a juvenile delinquent, the criminal justice system acknowledges that the State has taken the offender's tender age into account and has extended the prospect of mercy by promising to blot the stain of a lifelong criminal record. In exchange for this generosity, the delinquent is seen as a ward of the State, to be protected and sheltered while having diminished rights in the criminal justice process.

Youth also confers a status that sets kids apart in other ways—labeling acts that can be committed only by youngsters as *status offenses*. Among these are such items as truancy (if school attendance is compulsory up to a certain age, usually sixteen), purchasing cigarettes or beer, driving before coming of age, or running away from home. A status offense applies to classes of individuals who are able to be charged only because of their specific situation—typically, being too young to be permitted the act they're attempting to perform.

In criminological circles, there is a debate about the fairness of the State's punishing status offenses by criminal sanctions, while also depriving the juvenile delinquent of the full panoply of rights available to the adult offender. Criminally punishing juveniles for truancy, running away, driving without a license, or drinking alcohol—while depriving them of the usual array of defense weapons available to accused adults—is seen by some criminologists as being hypocritical and abusive.

Juvenile delinquency court proceedings are usually confidential, and the records are suppressed to protect the youngsters. Because assessing the dangers that criminal repeaters pose for the larger society has been assuming greater significance, a debate has begun over releasing juvenile criminal records to assist in the early evaluation of potentially serious chronic offenders. It is becoming increasingly clear, from crime statistics and studies of offenders, that the criminal predator is molded early in life; therefore, the humanitarian processes of juvenile courts are rendered largely a nullity. Intervention must be used earlier to deflect youngsters from a life of crime. Today's criminals are yesterday's delinquents, last week's battered and abused preschoolers, and last year's low-birth-weight and malnourished babies. They are the Lost Boys of our nation.

It is entirely possible that, by the time a boy becomes a delinquent, it may be too late to do much about it.

THE URGE TO CONTROL

The focus of the criminal justice system has not been to educate, entertain, employ, or include: it has been, instead, to control. No chamber of commerce calls the police chief to insist that the city's youth have wholesome recreational facilities, or that they be encouraged to stay in school or have jobs made available, although some have, to their credit, pitched in and helped solve problems that have been pointed out. A call to the police chief is usually made to keep the kids out of downtown shops and out of sight.

The growth of drug use and the availability of guns have contributed exponentially to the proliferation of violence among kids, as among adults. The factors that influence kids to become delinquent are dysfunctional or one- or no-parent families, media images that desensitize the public to violence, poverty and hopelessness, the availability of alcohol and drugs, and, of course, the mountain of guns that turns every minor encounter into a potential shoot-out. Trivial episodes thus escalate into deadly violence in our armed camp.

LIFE AND DEATH AMONG THE VERY YOUNG

The National Center for Health Statistics reported that 1,022 teenagers, fifteen to nineteen, were shot dead in 1984. By 1988, the figure had risen to 1,641. Predictably, young black males bore the brunt of this carnage, with 418 deaths in 1984 and 955 in 1988, which was more than half the total. The homicide rate among black teenagers was more than eleven times that of whites. In 1990, the number of blacks under eighteen who were murdered actually exceeded the total number of whites, 971 to 942.

The demographics point to a bleaker future as the general population of five- to seventeen-year-olds will soon rise a projected 7.7 percent with poor minority youngsters experiencing even higher growth rates.

On the basis of surveys, the National Schools Safety Center estimated that 135,000 students carried guns to school daily in 1987. Officials at that center believe the figure was higher in 1991.

A Seattle high school uses a breathalyzer to test students suspected of drinking, and Detroit passes students through metal detectors before they enter the school. Many schools have finally come to resemble prisons by developing security forces, adopting programs for safety, bolting doors, barring windows, and using camera surveillance.

In Minnesota, the 1992 legislature considered an antiviolence training program for schoolchildren that would focus on such negative acts as leering, mooning, grabbing, taunting, telling dirty jokes, and making obscene gestures.

The Dade County, Florida, schools have a gun-safety program intended to alert youngsters to the dangers of firearms.

In Boston, the Harvard School of Public Health conducts programs, in the high schools, on dealing with violence and how to avoid it through alternative strategies. The consequences of violence are analyzed in an attempt to reduce its allure. Ghetto kids are taught how to mediate, negotiate, and use violence-avoiding techniques in disputes.

Every Boston public-school student caught with a weapon is sent to the Barron Assessment and Counseling Center for five to ten days to undergo a psychological and educational assessment and to develop a plan for his or her future. The program features counseling, regular academic work, violence prevention classes, and trips to local detention facilities. The brief period provides an opportunity to reflect on past behavior.

In Oakland, California, student volunteers are trained in violence prevention tactics involving such ghetto staples as guns, drugs, and family violence and are returned to the schools to teach their peers.

The shifting tides of scapegoating lap up against parents, schools, peers, TV, and surrounding poverty or racism. The pressure of an atrocious incident creates a rush for explanations, which frequently disintegrate into accusations. The need to find a single answer is palpable, but a thorough search will reveal a number of possible causal factors that impinged on the principals with differential force.

In light of this complexity, we can see that simpleminded and unconstitutional efforts to legislate parental responsibility for a child's misdeeds are transparently demagogic approaches to relieve pressures without addressing the underlying problems.

Brooklyn's Thomas Jefferson High School has many needs, yet donors are asked to contribute to a burial fund to pay for the interment of kids killed by the violence in the surrounding streets. In November 1991, a sixteen-year-old was shot dead inside the school. The arrested suspect turned out to be a fourteen-year-old who was shooting at a youth fighting his older brother. He struck the sixteen-year-old bystander instead. The shooter's parents had worked hard to provide their three children a supportive, loving home. They had to wonder what it would have taken to defeat the surrounding mean streets.

This tragedy was followed by another tragic shooting, described earlier, in that same school. Following the later incident, which took two lives, a student shot and killed himself after leaving the terrible scene in hysterics.

A glance at the school, its neighborhood, the kids hanging out, the state of housing in the area, the proliferation of guns and drugs, and the social and physical disintegration would have offered many clues to the cause of all this mayhem. A glance at the ubiquitous, overworked TVs would have provided another answer to the frustration, anger, and sense of defeat and exclusion surrounding these kids.

The awful carnage and waste defined as juvenile delinquency have stimulated a search for approaches—from the predictably Draconian to the gentle, if simpleminded, humanitarian—that has thus far not provided the magical solution so widely sought.

DIFFERENTIAL TREATMENTS

An examination of any aspect of the street crime problem will reveal hideous complexities. In the field of delinquency, it appears, from famous studies in Philadelphia and elsewhere, that poor black males get formally processed as delinquents much more frequently than their overclass white counterparts in the suburbs. The cops in the inner city discharge the overclass's mandate to keep the underclass under control with no-nonsense law-and-order policing. As we've noted, in the suburbs the cops are more understanding, treat delinquents more generously and informally, and avoid stigmatizing them. The overclass resides in the suburbs, and it exercises greater informal control over the police—through votes, budgets, contracts, and contacts—than the powerless adults of the inner-city ghetto who have no leverage over the cops.

The result is the growth of a criminally labeled group in the ghetto that increasingly feels it has little to lose by further contacts with officialdom, while its suburban brethren proceed to college and the corporate halls, unblemished by any official—even suppressed—record of their malefactions.

A good example occurred in a suburban Minnesota high school that was found seriously vandalized. The community rose in outrage over the trashing of their facility, and in the fullness of time, the police discovered the culprits. The community now had its very sons, rather than faceless vandals, accused of what it had interpreted as vicious destruction by "outsiders." Understanding grew with knowledge. The kids received the support of their families and, ultimately, of the community, which ended up mitigating the charges. Hence, contrition and restitution carried the day.

One cannot help but wonder what reaction would have greeted vandals who turned out to be blacks from the inner city. In that case, one suspects that contrition would have been ignored and restitution perhaps not given a chance.

The challenge is to see the human behind the symbol that society is so quick to embrace, and to understand the complexities behind the mask.

TRACING THE APPROACHES TO TREATMENT

Juvenile delinquency inspires the same temptations to apply quick fixes—whether of the conservative right or of the liberal left—as all other forms of criminal behavior. The same pendulum swings repeat themselves: One view dominates, is widely adopted and generally supported, and finally, its flaws showing, is followed by a reaction toward the opposite pole. The perennial swings from permissive to repressive, and back, never strike a balanced middle course.

In 1847, Massachusetts introduced the first state-administered reform school, with a donation from Theodore Lyman, a philanthropist. Its purpose was to undertake "the instruction, employment and reformation of juvenile offenders." It would separate youthful from adult offenders and enable the authorities to treat kids more humanely. It would also have the unintended effect of promoting the lockup concept of dealing with delinquents. By 1985, there were 253 public reform schools and 428 detention centers for young offenders across the land, containing about five sixths of the children detained or committed. The other sixth were in halfway houses and other residential settings. These juvenile facilities have evolved into exploitive manufacturing enterprises, dreamy agrarian visions, or regimented and retributive centers where abuse is commonplace.

Jerome Miller, the head of the Massachusetts Department of Youth Services, closed the Lyman training school on January 17, 1972, and thereby launched a "deinstitutionalization" program that sought to eliminate the cruelties and abuses that had crept into the centers.

By 1983, Utah had closed its reformatory and replaced it with a varied menu of therapeutic approaches. Other jurisdictions seemed poised to follow suit. The punitive, controlling model gave way to a social service perspective intended to assist the child through therapy, counseling, education, treatment, and so on.

A few juveniles needed to be locked up because of the danger to society they represented, but they could be assigned to smaller secure facilities that held out the promise of individual care and attention. Even the most convinced humanitarians admit the need to closely control a number of violent and intractable youngsters.

Today, openness, trust, and a return to the community are the approaches and objectives of thinkers in the juvenile delinquency field.

DEINSTITUTIONALIZATION

The values and truths undergirding the deinstitutionalization movement are:

1. Children need love most when they deserve it least. A rehabilitation program has to be tailored to the child's special needs.
2. All children can be redeemed, even the "incorrigible."
3. Brutal treatment will engender a brutal response. Only the worst should be locked in.
4. Status offenders shouldn't be locked up.
5. Large institutions dehumanize; family-type settings nurture.
6. A diversity of programs and of providers should be sought.
7. Mechanical restraints (e.g., handcuffs and straitjackets) shouldn't be used.
8. The child's confidence and self-respect should be built up.
9. Children should be used to help their peers through such support mechanisms as discussion groups, friendships, and counseling.
10. Progress should be monitored.
11. Society will benefit through lower crime and violence rates, and treatment will be cheaper than incarceration.

The movement flies in the face of a frightened electorate anxious for repressive measures to ensure its safety. The prisons are bursting. The plight of the mentally disturbed on the city streets stirs suspicion of approaches that involve freeing inmates and trying to maintain them on medication. The institutions have created their own constituencies and pursue their instincts to survive. Occasional failures—frequently highly publicized—reinforce the "lock-'em-up" instinct of the body politic.

There is, among the new thinkers, a fundamental suspicion of bigness. Large institutions are seen as impersonal, bureaucratic, corrupt, brutal, and ultimately at the service of their operators. Small is beautiful, and big is ugly.

I became familiar with this school of thinking because one of its leaders, Ira Schwartz, taught and wrote at the University of Minnesota before becoming the Director of the Center for the Study of Youth Policy at the University of Michigan. I was then the Minneapolis police chief, and he was good enough to send me material and to invite me to symposia and lectures.

Frankly, I found this school altogether too sympathetic to youthful wrongdoers and too neglectful of regard for their victims—especially their future ones. In this view, delinquents had been wronged and abused by a Draconian system that had divested them of their rights. This school seemed to see its role as protecting kids accused of crimes from the vindictiveness of an unforgiving society and from the cruelties of this society's agents.

That this group has a point—in attacking the society's ever-widening penchant for harsher penalties—doesn't afford it the right to eschew punishments and restraints altogether. Young criminals, like their older counterparts, come in different shades, types, and levels of dangerousness and need to be handled accordingly.

Juvenile detention facilities are now also suffering from overcrowding, with its attendant abuses and inhumanities. Jamming kids into large facilities increases tensions, heightens opportunities for abuse (by both inmates and keepers), and diminishes opportunities for the sort of individual contacts that hold out the best hope for progress toward a better life.

The Youth Law Center in San Francisco sent observers into youth detention and training centers and catalogued a series of abuses for a congressional committee in Washington, including rape, beatings, torture, and treatment that made kids desperate enough to commit suicide.

As in adult institutions, remedies and reforms began to be applied only following lawsuits and court-ordered actions. There is little doubt that society's binge of punishments has forced many bureaucrats to cut corners, and worse. Such abuses tempt reformers to call for the abolition of segregations and punishments that may either act as deterrents or at least safeguard society for the period of incarceration.

On the basis of the abuses found and the corrections mandated, the deinstitutionalists broadly conclude that punishment doesn't work. This is the classic trap of having to choose between love and force. The fact is that both have their place, and either can be effective, given the right context.

England discovered that hanging for almost any crime proved no deterrent because the punishment was so disproportionately applied, frequently to minor offenses, as to have no logical force. America's cops found that deescalating their own violence, by severely curbing the circumstances in which cops were allowed to fire their weapons, led to a precipitous drop in the number of officers killed annually since 1973, when they adopted firearms guidelines that sharply reduced shootings, and killings, by the police.

Dramatic examples strengthen the arguments of the advocates on either side, without offering us useful evidence. The reality must include acknowledging the complexity behind human acts and motives and the need to develop a panoply of strategies—including both humanitarian and repressive measures, administered with a sense of proportion—to control criminal behavior.

A Harvard study that followed Jerome Miller's deinstitutionalization of the Massachusetts Youth Detention Centers produced mixed results that satisfied no one. It ushered in attacks and defenses that resulted in a cloudy assessment of the value of treating kids in ways that didn't involve locking them up. What the advocates sought was vindication, and the slippery human animal simply doesn't stand very still for categorization: It seems clear that a community-based program would work for some and that incarceration might work for others. In any case, the study found little divergence in recidivism rates between those not locked up and individually treated and those harshly treated.

In the end, the researchers concluded that the greater the choices, the happier the consequences. The kids needed a variety of programs in order to fit into one suitable to their needs. This means that relying on any single approach is likely to fail. What the follow-up studies revealed was that deinstitutionalization may be a workable strategy but that it is no panacea. Individual attention does help, but so does punishment. What works best is to have a wide range of options and a thorough diagnosis of the offender so as to match him or her with the program likeliest to work.

Deinstitutionalization, like decriminalizing hard drugs, will prove no panacea, but considering either possibility at least launches the discussion so desperately needed if we are to find solutions to the seemingly intractable problems of delinquency and addiction. Twenty years, or more, of reflexive and increasing repression haven't provided the answers.

Such factors as an organized school life (as opposed to unstructured time spent "hanging out") and strengthening the conventional community and family bonds, training for a legitimate occupation, and improving opportunities for economic self-sufficiency were found to be correlated with the absence of delinquency.

SOME APPROACHES TO JUVENILE DELINQUENCY

Different places have tried to develop innovative approaches to youthful misbehavior. On a rising scale of seriousness, the programs, across the nation, offered such services as these:

1. In one jurisdiction, runaway or ungovernable children are taken to a shelter where they are held for up to forty-eight hours. Efforts are made, through repeated calls, to get their parent(s) to respond and discuss why the kids ran away or acted up. The runaways are usually persuaded to give

home another try. "Host families" are used for up to sixty days while the family comes in for counseling. Parenting skills are taught; communication and listening skills are thus addressed. Peer groups, for the kids, give them insights into their own behavior.

2. A teenage burglar was brought to an unlocked, staff-secure detention unit that provides schooling and a homey setting where joint activities, like cooking, cleaning, and games, are encouraged by a caring staff. It is a residential setting in which the kids receive feedback on their behavior, attitudes, and progress. Bedeviled by escapes in its early years, this facility has, over its recent history, learned that placing responsibility on the youngsters mostly produces positive results.

3. In Utah, a more serious wrongdoer is taken to an observation and assessment center for up to ninety days, to be tested and scrutinized. There the child is exposed to high school instruction, individual counseling, and group therapy. The point is to appraise the child in order to devise a follow-up approach. Many of the kids come from dysfunctional (alcoholic, druggie, abusive, or criminal) families, use drugs or alcohol or both, have had trouble in school, and have committed more than one serious offense. Many have been brutalized or abused at home. About 10 percent are sent to secure facilities; the rest are sent either home or to a small group residence. Many take vocational tests, which may point the way to future employment.

4. The Northwestern Minnesota Juvenile Training Center is on the campus of Bemidji State University and services up to thirty-two boys and girls, aged twelve to seventeen, who have been committed by district court judges for nonstatus offenses. Presence on the campus enables the youths to use the facilities and to be a part of the college community. This is a nonsecure facility offering highly individualized treatment and school attendance. The aim is to raise self-esteem and facilitate a successful return to community life. The program takes place in a group-living educational environment. The counselors are drawn from among university students majoring in human

services, and supervision is direct and present twenty-four hours a day. Those who fail to perform positively are returned to court for more secure commitment. The center also operates four satellite homes in which up to five youngsters live with a family in a setting that offers affection, unity, and structure.

5. Pilgrim Center, in Massachusetts, serves forty boys who have committed grave crimes, such as assault, robbery, rape, or murder. The usual programs of schooling, counseling, and recreation are offered by a staff that functions as a family. The effort centers on working with the boys' real families in order to return them to their homes. They receive passes to visit home, and there is a gradual transition to graduation, lasting up to a year or more.

6. Key programs are for kids who are still in custody but out of detention. It is a transitional approach to reentry into society. The program monitors the daily activities of seventy adolescents. Whether the kids are at home or at the center, there is a daily accounting of their behavior and verification of their activities. The point is to shepherd these adolescents through the tough years between childhood and adulthood. This is a closely supervised probation program in which the staff personally checks on the kids to determine that they are where they're supposed to be.

7. Proctor living is residing with a paid person, one or two at a time, who supervises and monitors the behavior of young offenders on probation. Restitution, which serves as a form of atonement and which includes turning earnings over to the crime victim, is a feature of the program. A staff member visits and monitors the program and offers counseling to five to eight clients, affording the opportunity for frequent interventions. A long-term treatment program is developed, with the offender's participation, that features such items as getting a high school diploma, paying fines and reimbursing victims, staying drug-free, attending a support group program, and participating in family therapy sessions. Gradually, there is a transition to independent living.

In juvenile as in adult corrections, the same unhappy results have surfaced, from reliance on large, impersonal, overcrowded lockups. Individuals require individual attention, which is not to say it may not take the form of being locked in, but other approaches must be available as well. The deinstitutionalizers have provided us with a valuable model by centering their efforts on intense, personal approaches that treat the individual.[1]

The numbers of throwaway children this society produces, in terms of dropout rates, unemployment, and low prospects of a career, ensure a steady supply of delinquents. There is probably no city in the United States that is anything but highly nervous over its kinetic population of youngsters, loaded with energy and having no direction. That these kids almost always suffer the additional handicaps of being the victims of racism and economic inequities simply makes matters worse.

GANGS

Chicago and Los Angeles are the gang capitals of America. A recent study[2] in two Chicago high schools revealed the sorts of activities reflecting gang operations:

- Street gangs exercise control over individual schools, areas of the school, buildings, and/or particular classrooms.
- Gangs control the lucrative drug trafficking within the school.
- Students are actively recruited into gangs, in school or on the way to or from school.
- Students are intimidated and physically assaulted by

---

[1] Richard J. Margolis, *Out of Harm's Way: The Emancipation of Juvenile Justice.* New York: Edna McConnell Clark Foundation, 1988.

[2] R. Hutchison and C. Kyle, "Hispanic Street Gangs in the Chicago Public Schools," in *Gangs: The Origins of Impact of Contemporary Youth Gangs in the U.S.*, Scott Cummings and Daniel Monti (Eds.), Albany, NY: State University Press, 1990.

gang members in school buildings or on the way to or
from school.

- Students list street gang activity as the most frequent
  reason for dropping out of school. They are trying to
  escape the violence.

New York is not widely regarded as having a youth gang
problem at all, whereas Chicago and Los Angeles suffer notorious gang violence, yet all three cities host appalling levels of
violence, which include the young and the old and which are
apparently unrelated to the existence or nonexistence of gangs.

Whether gangs exist or not is not going to have an important effect on the levels of violence engaged in by ghetto
kids, although it may change the nature of that violence. The
permanence of the conditions promoting crimes is typical of all
urban centers.

Imagine the horror of Lorna Hawkins, whose twenty-one-
year-old son was killed by gang members in 1988 in a drive-by
shooting, and who thereafter channeled her sorrow into a
television program she organized to combat such tragedies. On
March 30, 1992, her remaining son, age twenty, was shot four
times, by suspected gang members, and was killed on a Los
Angeles street.

Those are the cataclysms behind the abstract figures and
slippery phrases.

In another city, these killings might have been non-gang-
related, individual crimes, but they would still have taken
place. The urban ghetto is merciless in its failure to make
distinctions between cities with gangs and those without.

Youth gangs institutionalize and perpetuate violence as
they continue feuds, battle over turf, squabble over girls, and
pursue actions and reprisals that endanger the gang members
and everyone in the area. Gangs are continuing enterprises,
with identifying labels, hierarchies, geography, and rules. Identifying graffiti carve out the turf, as gangs mark their areas
with symbols painted on walls and other surfaces. The groups

engage in illegal acts such as drug dealing, assaults, drive-by shootings, extortion, and other crimes. They are most visible in schools, where they are unable to slip into the cover of their familiar neighborhoods.

Every city in the United States lives by myths, such notions as that they have an extensive and growing gang problem and that they're being invaded by welfare cheats and hustlers from Gary, Indiana, or its equivalent. Labeling a group of restive, relatively hopeless, and increasingly angry and unprepared ghetto losers as a gang enables the overclass to objectify them and makes it possible to hate them. The value of a label, like *gang*, is that it permits the fears—and tremors of conscience—to be assuaged through actions against the feared and hated object.

In 1991, the Minneapolis *Star-Tribune* undertook a deep study of youth gangs in the city in response to years of alarms and media reports on the activities gangs, as well as on highly publicized actions that were often described as "gang-related." The newspaper found an amorphous mass of youngsters in trouble but deduced that much of the violence had more to do with personal feuds than with gang rivalries.

The newspaper concluded that there was a small group of violent criminals who attracted hangers-on, who were capable of horrific violent actions, and who used gang names, but that much of what was believed about street gangs in the Twin Cities was "questionable." The findings precisely mirrored and confirmed studies indicating the existence of a hard-core corps of recidivists, constituting about 10 percent of the criminal population, who represent the real threats to society's safety.

The reporters cited police overstatements, which too often described violence as being "gang-related." The reporters saw little connection between local gangs and Chicago or Los Angeles groups. They failed to detect discipline, in terms of orders obeyed or policies faithfully pursued, or tight organizational structures. Though individuals used drugs, this was a personal addiction rather than a group or gang activity. The reporters concluded that the theory of gangs with Uzis was purely a myth.

The writers described most gang members as "delinquent youths in uniform," yet cops and local minority leaders were quoted as raising serious alarms about gang activity. The article analyzed nineteen "gang-related killings" and found that the majority had to do with disputes over girlfriends or other fights and personal conflicts that had nothing to do with gang concerns. The creation of a police unit to monitor gang activities ensured the emergence of evidence pointing to a gang (including membership lists of the Disciples or Vice Lords) and organizational charts, geographic boundaries, telltale graffiti, and other accoutrements of gang life.

The issue transcends the simple fact that the police and society either choose a label (gang) or identify the kids as being excluded, in trouble, and in need of help. Calling them gangs invites repression, and seeing them as kids in need of help means social programs, including jobs, housing, and education, that benefit the underclass. Constituencies crop up. Cops see the gang scare as leading to more resources. Community leaders think that scaring Whitey will unloose purse strings. Frightened citizens can hide their prejudices behind calls for drastic actions against gangs.

A GANG MEMBER

As participants in a glamorous role in ghetto street theater, the kids strut, boast, and play into the hands of those screaming for the gang's blood as well as of the poverty pimps waiting with their paper programs in the wings. The seemingly intractable problems of ghetto youth need both money and dedicated, honest professionals working to resolve the difficulties. For some months, the *Tribune* reporters followed a Disciples gang member, Patrick Slaughter, who'd been involved in an incident in which a white cop shot and killed a seventeen-year-old black male named Tycel Nelson, in Minneapolis in December 1990. Patrick's father had been killed in a motorcycle crash when the child was eight. He had started as a truant at twelve, and his dossier had fattened, with references to drinking, disorderly conduct, possession of a small amount of crack, trespassing, and other minor offenses. But there was also a conviction for terroristic threats, as well as an incident involving a gun and references to gang activity. He became a father at seventeen. Many of his problems centered on tensions surrounding his girlfriends. He was turned in on failure to appear in court in connection with an arrest for a stolen car, because of jealousies involving his son's mother. Patrick had a long criminal record. He went on daily binges of drinking gin and malt liquor. He didn't see much point in school or in the counseling programs he'd been in. His mother spoke of the anger in him. Immediate pleasure—like girls and drink—were his objectives.

This was the heavy-duty gang member being served up to the frightened residents of Minneapolis by their police department.

Gangs frequently are angrily, defiantly black. They form as a way of expressing solidarity and defying a white society that excludes them. Los Angeles, of course, has many Latino gangs, but the cops' effort to create an image of white gangs, in order to legitimize oppressive techniques used against all gangs (the tactics can't be labeled racist if the ostensible targets are white as well as black), is mostly a figment of police creative thinking. The same is true of the organization charts and flowcharts that police gang units so love to produce. The amorphous, ad hoc and shifting reality belies the rigid rank-and-function models created by the police. White gangs do exist. They are frequently of the motorcycle or racist genre, but the ghetto spawns gangs among all of the underclass, and they are often white, as well as black or Hispanic.

The police themselves are frequently referred to as a gang, not only by gang members but sometimes by the cops themselves. In such references, we see the true psychic dynamics of the relationship, in this case, a group (ghetto kids) organizing themselves to defy another group (the cops). The propensity of cops to label their precincts "Fort Apache" and "The Alamo" and after other beleaguered fortresses among hostiles is a perfect corollary of this dynamic. The cops are seen, and see themselves, as an army of occupation, there to keep the hostiles under control, for a nervous overclass.

The *Tribune* study of gangs in Minneapolis, despite some easy rhetoric about "white gangs, too," almost immediately centered on the activities of young black males. The study reflected the racism, exclusion, and conditions of poverty that induced blacks to band together. When one has grown up amid violence and drug use, drifting into loose neighborhood coalitions becomes almost natural. What white gangs were found centered on menacing motorcycle bands and groups of racist skinheads who represented real dangers, but of sorts relating to actions (racial attacks) rather than turf (gangs in the neighborhood), and who, as a result, needed to be dealt with by different police tactics.

L.A.'s GANGS

In an interview in *USA Today* (June 25, 1991), Leon Bing, a white female author of a book on the Los Angeles Bloods and Crips gangs, described a world where the most powerful sense of self-importance emerges from violence. Her remarks indicated that kids see gangs as familial settings that give them a sense of power and belonging. Her life among the gangs convinced her that whites are mostly to blame for the conditions that have black kids killing each other.

Bing confirmed the findings of the Minneapolis *Tribune* study, that these gangs coalesce in an atmosphere devoid of structure, organization, or discipline. Moreover, the larger society's cold indifference to the plight of these kids permits gangs to thrive. She saw the gang members as failed humans, who have been programmed for those failures by an uncaring society. She spoke knowingly of the fear whites have of blacks and described black's evolution in America as going from slaves to scapegoats to threats.

Bing also predicted the spread of Los Angeles–like violence to the other cities of the nation. As if to echo her warning the *New York Times* reported, on October 15, 1991, how Hispanic kids fleeing the violence of Southern California and trying to break the cycle of ghetto life in the gang found they had only sped to reencounter their fate in Las Vegas. The report described the spread of gangs and violence to Phoenix, Portland, and Seattle. Another report described how nine innocent Buddhists were slain, in a temple near Phoenix in August 1991, by youngsters enraged by the absence of suspected riches they had hoped to rob. In the account, there were references to Crips, without any direct evidence of gang affiliation. Shootings, killings, and drive-by fusillades are the accompaniments of gang life, and the police have identified such groups as the rival black Crips and Bloods and several Hispanic groups in Las Vegas.

All of Bing's observations point to an oppressed underclass that acts out its anguish with violence that is almost exclusively directed inward—at the mirror image of another ghetto kid with a gun. Hers is not the simpleminded view of the many, who see these kids as monsters who must be destroyed.

Gangs do exist. Bing and others believe there are ninety thousand gang members in Los Angeles, and the Minneapolis *Star-Tribune* reporters did, for all their debunking of gangs, find gang members in Minneapolis.

A kind of culture lag attends every arrival of a new wave of immigrants, who bring with them the promises and problems of the culture they left behind. The Cuban wave brought the ex-convicts of Mariel, Sicilians brought the Mafia, and currently, Asian migrants have brought violent and extortionate gangs that abuse their countryfolk.

In such circumstances, the police have to race to understand and catch up with the challenges. In the gap between criminal acts and the police agency's development of coping strategies lies a handwringing no-person's-land of time during which a lot of victimizations go unaddressed and the criminal behavior is permitted to take deep root.

COMBATING GANGS

There seems little doubt that tough law-enforcement measures are needed to combat gang activities in the cities. Curfews, the creation of gang units, and vigorous enforcement all have their place.

In a dramatic shift in approach, the FBI announced in January 1992 that it was shifting 300 agents from counterintelligence operations against mostly formerly communist nations to combating street gangs. This historic reallocation mirrored the collapse of the external threat and the growing danger posed by internal forces. It also promised to plunge the Feds much deeper into the murky waters of street crime.

In Los Angeles, a clearly desperate sheriff's office began random car stops to obtain information from drivers in areas suffering gang violence. Pamphlets were distributed to inform drivers on how to report gang-related crimes.

At about the same time, the FBI announced the arrest of big-time cocaine dealers who were members of the Crips street gang, tying them to a Colombian cartel.

The emphasis continued to focus on toughness, despite the absence of results and the continued escalation of the violence.

What every responsible and knowledgeable observer notes, however, is that the gang membership and violent behavior of ghetto youngsters can be traced to racism and poverty.

Summer job programs set up to reduce school dropout rates, recreational facilities, counseling, and educational programs are essential features of any program intended to reduce gang membership and gang violence, but these are offered fitfully—usually in hasty response to a particular crisis—and lack planning, focus, and real commitment.

Assigning street workers basically to live with gangs also helps. The gang crises of the fifties—captured in the musical play *West Side Story* and such film dramas as *The Blackboard Jungle*—spawned the creation of street workers who lived with the gangs and channeled them, gradually, into positive activities. Working with families in trouble will help, as will social services that provide meaningful assistance to youngsters and their families. Mentoring and one-on-one relationships are critically important approaches to individuals and to problem families. The battle, in a sense, is akin to the house-to-house struggle in Stalingrad during the crisis moment of World War II.

The case studies everywhere reflect anger, frustration, hopelessness, and a corrosive lack of self-regard. Ghetto kids are being programmed for gang membership and violence by a society that simply wants to pursue its absorption with pleasure. It is easy and convenient to tag these kids "gangs" and to demand that the cops have at them. Such an approach is fated to raise the levels of violence and to increase the numbers of gangs. The existence of gangs needs, of course, to be established, and the problems must be attacked. But the presence of footloose, energetic youngsters who have no place to go and nothing to do represents a different sort of problem that requires a more constructive approach.

Crimes can be committed by individuals and by groups, and they can spring from a wide variety of social, economic, psychological, and motivational sources. Many favored myths surround crimes and criminals, and these are frequently constructed to spare us the need to look within our family or society for the causes. The various faces of crime cry out for understanding if we are to devise strategies for preventing the tragedies that result.

CURFEWS

Curfews can work, but they have to be used discreetly, against youngsters suspected of being up to no good. Curfews almost always mean targeting black males and using the approach selectively, which is certain to inspire charges of discriminatory enforcement. The fact is that urban policing in America too often involves white cops trying to control the actions of black males.

As of July 1991, more cities were adopting teenage curfews. In Dallas, kids under seventeen must be home by 11 PM on weekdays and by midnight on the weekend or risk detainment.

In Minneapolis, I had cops concentrate on trouble spots that sparked violent acts, that attracted large numbers of youngsters, or that inspired frequent complaints, like a downtown shopping mall, convenience stores and their parking lots, and some popular street corners in the inner city, as well as a cruising spot. The kids were brought into the juvenile division office and held while the parents were called. If the parents failed to come, the youngsters were taken home after some hours and a record was made of the violation. If the parents showed up and took the kids home, no records were kept of the event. This approach proved very effective in cooling the city's hot spots, but it was very selectively enforced and struck disproportionately at black teenaged males. Critics pointed to the right to travel freely and to the fallacy that lies in making us less free, without adding to our safety. The issue perfectly illustrates the dilemma facing the police in a society that stubbornly refuses to examine the real problems facing these kids or to offer the educational, employment, and recreational activities so clearly needed.

Curfews can be useful in attacks on specific, temporary problems requiring a focused approach. They are useful in riots or in possible looting situations, and in combating chronic problems at given locations. As sweeping citywide programs they are worse than useless: They are counterproductive. They are, at best, temporary palliatives that, as in Minneapolis, relieve temporary pressures and problems.

Juvenile delinquency is an individual act, by a person under a given stuatutory age. Gang violence relates to deeds by numbers of individuals acting in concert as the members of an organization. Both represent dangers to the larger society.

GRAFFITI

Graffiti, the emblems of ghetto life that are the signature of urban decay, ought to remind us that they can represent a deep and real need for expression and recognition, as well as plain vandalism and the marking of a turf boundary. Recognizing these complexities challenges us to explore the realities behind the images more humanely and more wisely. Labeling graffiti sheer defacement is another way of objectifying a human behavior in order to accommodate our prejudices.

It is not an accident that some museums have actually exhibited some of the more expressive examples of graffiti as modern urban art. Graffiti may be avant-garde art, and they may be vandalism, but simply labeling all of them as exhibitions of mischief demonizes the gang issue. Dismissing the expression of anger and the desire for identity precludes learning from the graffiti, or about their creators, and dealing with them constructively. Prejudice, here and everywhere, gets in the way of understanding.

Bringing a sophisticated insight to what might easily be seen as an offensive act of mischief would help us to grasp the dynamics of the ghetto gang culture. It would enable us to see that salvageable kids get destroyed because there are no forces offering alternatives or escape.

A RESEARCHER'S PERSPECTIVE

A Yale researcher's review of the literature led him to conclude that potential youthful offenders are not deterred by a system they perceive—in terms of the experiences of their older brothers—as flaccid. Raaj K. Sah said there had to be a solid prospect of being caught, and punished, in order for a deterrent to exist. He poohpoohed the notion of poverty as a causal factor, citing the incredibly high levels of criminality and violence in the richest country in contrast to the low levels in others that are far more poverty-stricken. He cited the general sense that the criminal justice system could be evaded or defeated, even if one is caught, and the general perception that few are caught. His viewpoint seems to center on simply making the criminal justice system more efficient and effective in order to reduce crime.

Sah's study demonstrates the difficulty of analyzing criminal behavior by the young, even for highly trained and expert observers. The allure of the simple answer continues to cast its spell over all those drawn to examine such behavior as crime. The mythology deepens and intensifies as crime more closely threatens the personal lives of the overclass.

SATANISM, PROSTITUTION, AND MYTHS

Humans frequently seek scapegoats for the problems they've brought into their own lives. By demonizing an issue, we not only absolve ourselves of blame but are able to blame a despised group for our difficulties. Thus, Jews have been held to be poisoners of wells, stealers of children, and killers of Christ by people needing someone to loathe and fear. All manner of secret evil has been ascribed to the gypsies. They have become a convenient focus for crop failures, stillbirths, and other calamities. Ghetto kids make convenient targets for racist stereotypes and for whatever goes wrong in society. Worse, their sometimes awful actions are read as confirming society's worst assumptions, without that society's ever reading its own complicity into the results. The appeal of scapegoating is so great that it remains a powerful river running agelessly through the human experience.

THE MINNESOTA CONNECTION

When I arrived in Minneapolis in early 1980 to be the city's police chief, I encountered a piece of demonology called the *Minnesota connection*. This fervently held and widely reported myth held that black pimps were snatching fifteen-year-old blond goddesses from God-fearing Lutheran homes and stuffing them into a latter-day underground railroad, from which they surfaced, corrupted, in hot pants and halter tops, in Times Square, ready for action. All of the feared and hated images were contained in this simple vision.

Cops furthered the myth with lurid stories of innocence corrupted and gullible midwestern families victimized. One wrote a book and dreamed of a movie contract. The driving passion behind the spread of this myth was a religious fundamentalism that needed a fear of demons as much as a love of God.

Much was made of the hovering pimps, their blackness implicitly understood though not explicitly described. A handier demon could not be found. The image even offered the additional comfort of sparing everyone the need to look within for the source of the problem of the teenage runaway.

By the time I arrived, the myth had taken root. As I looked deeper into the problem, I discovered that prostitution, in Minneapolis and on Times Square, was mostly a desperate resort by fifteen-year-old girls who'd finally found the strength and courage to escape abusive, alcoholic, and sexually exploitive ordeals in their own homes. They had been driven into the streets not by black pimps hovering overhead but by the demons within those homes, who would look anywhere but within for the source of the problem.

Once convinced, on the basis of our arrests and our work with groups seeking to rescue these young women from the awfulness of street life (where they were indeed exploited, by blacks and whites), I attacked the myth publicly and repeatedly, centering the blame on dysfunctional families. In a very short time, the Minnesota connection was swept into the dustbin of history as another exploded myth.

The attractions of racism were not ignored for long, however, and a new myth arose a few years afterward that enabled the good burghers once again to indulge their prejudices. In this case, the center of this myth became the gangs, their blackness once again implicitly communicated in images rather than words.

Thus, problems of excluded and defeated black youngsters were transmogrified into a gang problem, which enabled the overclass to wax indignant and demand action, without imposing any self-searching for the source of the problem. Religious fundamentalism was not an obvious ingredient in this racist mixture, but it floated with the tide of prejudice and helped to feed the flames of the community's anger and fear.

James Joyce, an ardent observer of his origins, would very likely have held that Catholicism was held together more by the fears of Satan and his kingdom than by any visions of a glorious hereafter. As he made clear in *Portrait of the Artist as a Young Man*, it is the terror of hell that binds the faithful, rather than the promise of heaven. The existence of such a thing as good becomes much clearer when it is contrasted with its opposite. The existence of Satan is essential to a belief in the existence of God, and it is a characteristic of human nature that we find ourselves somewhere between these poles.

Some concentrate on the love that is God, whereas many highlight the evil that Satan represents. Religious fundamentalists, like many Catholics, have found that terror works powerfully to keep the faithful in tow.

This propensity to channel energies through fears and superstitions can be wedded to a predilection of the police to establish an industry around a public concern. Like metal filings in the air, cops can be drawn to the magnet of an issue almost unconsciously. The wide reporting of a gang problem may prompt even a reluctant chief to create a gang unit that will attract interested cops, who will create membership lists and organizational tables that confirm the existence of gangs in the city and greatly swell the perception of danger. I confess to having created such a unit in Minneapolis, succumbing to public, official, and media pressures, and thereby initiating a cottage industry that rapidly set out to confirm the alarmists' worst fears. Many crimes could be defined—by stretching a point here and there—as being "gang-related," and kids eager to belong could be counted on to claim membership in some cool gang, to acquire status, and that supposed membership would be recorded faithfully by the cops.

CONCLUSION

Juvenile delinquency boils down to a teenage boy committing a crime, either individually or as a member of a group. As the numbers of these crimes escalate, along with their seriousness, panicky citizens and legislators reach for quick answers. The handiest has been harsher treatment. But we have also seen striking examples of a humanist approach that attempts reforms through constructive and positive steps.

The results of both the positive and the negative models have been dismaying. Both can be said mostly to have failed. Reliance on either precludes the eclectic approach that holds out the best hope of tailoring the response to the challenge represented by the individual youngster in trouble.

A search for the source of all the adult criminals stuffing our prisons and clogging our criminal justice system inevitably proceeds upstream; it must go far beyond the young delinquent because, by then, it is too late to reshape the young criminal. The trek must proceed to the origins, frequently a teenaged female who needs to be salvaged. The process has to include her life habits, prenatal care, and the birth weight and nurturing of her infant. She must be educated, employed, and supported. The absent male must be returned to the family to assume his responsibilities and to accept the consequences of his actions.

Punishments and negative sanctions have their place, too, as does the use of street workers, social welfare aides, and other intervenors.

The delinquent of today poses not so much a challenge to society as a threat to its very existence. A simpleminded reliance on any single approach is doomed to fail. Kids are too complex to sit still for any single formula, and their needs are too many and varied to be provided for by any single strategy. The enormity of the task has tempted everyone to seize the "easy" answers. The result is obvious: none of these answers, positive or negative, are working.

Juvenile delinquent is a label that conceals the most dangerous predators of our age, street criminals. We have to recognize how we shaped them and made their behavior inevitable, and we must devise programs to transform them into positive, contributing members of society and to reduce their burgeoning numbers.

None of this is going to happen until we understand our—the overclass's—complicity in the creation of delinquents and in the crimes they commit.

Chapter Four

THEORIES ON CRIME IN THE UNITED STATES

Greater than the tread of mighty armies is an idea whose time has come.

—Victor Hugo (1802–1885)

Crime is a subject about which everyone has theories and ideas but which has produced a deafening silence from its most knowing observers: America's police chiefs. Criminologists and scholars have rushed into the void with learned tomes and sweeping suggestions.

To combat crimes, conservatives counsel Draconian measures, while liberals call for improving social, educational, housing, health, employment, and economic conditions.

THE VIEW FROM A BENCH

Judge Lois G. Forer offered a seven-point plan, following her years of observations from the bench[1]:

[1] Lois G. Forer, *Criminals and Victims.* New York: Norton, 1980.

1. Gun control
2. Education
3. Restitution and heavy fines
4. Attacking intrafamily crime
5. Jobs for criminals
6. Consistency in sentencing
7. Redress for victims

Interestingly, there's not a word about more cops, more arrests, bigger jails, or tougher judges. The judge's observations are instructive for the breadth of their perspective, as well as for their recognition of the social and economic factors shaping the criminal.

ONE ATTORNEY GENERAL'S PERSPECTIVE

Former Attorney General Ramsey Clark sees the causes as plainly residing in economic inequities and racism and bids us to mount a national effort to correct these wrongs.[2]

One would seek in vain for any trace of Willie Horton in Clark's writings. His is the left's unvarnished response to the jingoism of the right.

CRIME AND AMERICA'S HISTORY

A comprehensive review of crime in America, from the Colonies to the present, shows crime to be a class struggle in which the dominant define prohibited conduct for their own fun and profit. Those in control have usually had an interest in passing laws that protect them from covetous and potentially riotous have-nots, as well as in adopting legislation that preserves and enhances their own wealth and power. America has

---

[2] Ramsey Clark, *Crime in America*. New York: Simon & Schuster, 1970.

been described as a violent and criminogenic society in which those at the top change the rules of the game to suit their purposes.[3] The writers Frank Browning and John Gerassi see America as a nation that has turned to violence and expansion from its earliest beginnings through the present. The inevitable conclusion is that the greed of capitalism has fed the flames of exploitation. Man's inhumanity to man is seen as a function of seeking economic advantage.

It is interesting that these two writers seem to be unaware—despite their encyclopedic enumerations of the sufferings inflicted on the weak by the strong over the course of our history—of the existence of Marxist criminologists who define crime in terms that perfectly mirror the observations of Browning and Gerassi. They may well be Marxist criminologists themselves, without knowing it.

MARXIST CRIMINOLOGY

In *Class, State and Crime*,[4] Richard Quinney boldly lays the issue of crime at capitalism's door and suggests that a socialist revolution may be the only way of eradicating the economic inequities and class oppression of our capitalist society.

Today, over a decade after Quinney's and Browning and Gerassi's books appeared, the bright dawn of Marxist criminology has been eclipsed by the collapse of communism. This is, to be sure, one of the minor, incidental casualties of historical disintegration, but we can now see that communism can produce crimes as well as inefficiency. The demon of capitalism, at least in the field of criminology, seems to have been partially exorcised by the revealed evils and petty corruptions of its opposite. However, we cannot, on that basis, exculpate capital-

---

[3] Frank Browning and John Gerassi, *The American Way of Crime*. New York: Putnam, 1980.

[4] Richard Quinney, *Class, State and Crime*. New York: Longman, 1977.

ism from any involvement in fueling the rise of street crime. Persuasive evidence links our freewheeling economic system with the problems we find in our cities.

The symbiotic relationship of religion and capitalism has given birth, in Latin America, to a liberation theology that flies in the teeth of the Catholic Church's message of meek acceptance of one's fate on earth in order to achieve salvation in the hereafter. The implication of this revolt is that misery is not ordained by God and inevitable, and that one must fight to achieve social and economic justice. Brought to its conclusion, the message would be clear to a ghetto dweller viewing "The Lifestyles of the Rich and Famous" on TV: He shouldn't accept his fate and ought to get out and grab some of that good life.

The disaffection of the underclass and the greed of the overclass have combined to create tensions that inevitably lead to the adoption of panic-induced solutions, mostly snatched at in desperation and with little chance of succeeding as they, at the same time, undermine democracy.

SACRIFICING THE CONSTITUTION

One of the truly remarkable developments has been the fear-triggered willingness to forgo constitutional protections in exchange for the imagined safety that this sacrifice will provide.

Under the headline "Only Emergency Measures Will Stop Crime," columnist Sydney H. Schanberg, writing in *Newsday*, suggested the declaration of an emergency and the "sacrifice [of] certain of our rights" in order to make New York's streets safer. Among these rights would be those relating to the police power to search and seize property. The specifics stop there, following a strident description of the city's carnage. The emotional column constitutes little more than a blank check for demagogues to select which constitutional provisions to suspend.

Had he studied the city's history, Schanberg would have

found litanies of disgust over prostitution, public drunkenness, riotings, and gang warfare in 1857 New York. A lawyer, George Templeton Strong, reported "most of my friends are investing in revolvers and carry them about at night." Central Park was not safe at night, and crime was rampant. New Yorkers either moved to the suburbs of Brooklyn and Hoboken or called for reform of tenements, better schools, and stronger police and courts. There was, then, room in the debate for welfare, education, jobs, and state intervention, as well as for flight and repression. There seemed to be little talk of bartering away our precious freedoms.

James A. Inciardi's vast book *Criminal Justice*[5] offers a wide variety of views on the causes and treatment of crime since our earliest origins. One of the original insights is that President Richard Nixon's ballyhooed "War on Heroin" was actually a cynical attempt to increase the power of his office through the creation of investigative agencies that could be used for political gains, such as were sought in the Watergate scandal.

Inciardi held that President Lyndon Johnson's "War on Crime," which produced what might be called this century's seminal work in the field because of the influence of its heralded report, was blunted by Nixon's agenda, which paid lip service to law and order, but which actually harbored the darker purposes of enhancing personal power and perpetuating it as long as possible. Thus did a crucial document get corrupted into "enemies lists."

A PRESIDENT'S COMMISSION ON CRIME

The Challenge of Crime in a Free Society[6] resulted from the work of President Johnson's Commission on Law Enforcement

---

[5] James A. Inciardi, *Criminal Justice*. New York: Harcourt Brace Jovanovich, 1987.
[6] *The Challenge of Crime in a Free Society*. Washington, DC: U.S. Government Printing Office, 1967.

and the Administration of Justice. It inspired the 911 phone number and a host of other innovations and reforms as it became quickly adopted by the criminal justice system generally, and by the police in particular. The Omnibus Crime Control and Safe Streets Act of 1968 created a federal agency that provided federal funds for local criminal justice agencies. The report saw the need to reform the criminal justice system in ways that would make the cops, the courts, the prisons, and the prosecutors more efficient and accountable, and it also recognized the deeper social and economic forces fueling crime.

Born out of the fear and confusion of the nascent drug culture, the current youth revolt, the urban riots, and the political assassinations of the sixties, the report and the law that flowed from it were desperate measures to stem a tide of dissolution. America was afraid and demanded action. It is instructive that, in 1991, following more than twice as many murders as 1965's total of 9,850 (there were over 24,000 in 1991), President George Bush rejected a request for the creation of a new President's Commission on Crime. He opted instead for a meaningless "summit on crime" in March 1991, which afforded a group of chiefs and their satellites a chance to spend a few days in the capital and rub shoulders with America's political movers and shakers.

The panic that produced the landmark 1967 report was prompted by a total of about 2.8 million Part I crimes (murder, rape, robbery, assault, burglary, larceny, auto theft, and arson). By 1989, this total had swelled to over 14 million, and it went up to 14.5 million in 1990, with the perennial acknowledgment that most crime continued to be unreported.

The 1967 report warned that "no single formula, no single theory, no single generalization can explain the vast range of behavior called crime." It promised a significant reduction in crime by

- Including all Americans in the benefits of American life,

strengthening law enforcement, and reducing criminal opportunities.

- Adopting broader techniques for dealing with offenders.
- Eliminating injustices from the criminal justice system.
- Adopting higher standards for criminal justice practitioners.
- Undertaking more research into crime and criminal administration.
- Allocating more money for police, courts, and corrections.
- Involving citizens, civic groups, corporations, religious bodies, and government in planning and implementing the changes needed.

The report went on to expand on these views, adopting both the liberal and the conservative approaches of help and consequences. The report contained over two hundred recommendations for specific changes and reforms, from improving education and providing jobs and recreation to having more cops, tougher judges, and more controls over offenders—and everything in between.

Some might call it a potpourri of solutions, or a wish list, but the report reflected the enormous complexity of the problem of crime. It moved and inspired the criminal justice system to the adoption of many changes and reforms over the next decade, but its influence began to wane sharply as President Jimmy Carter scaled back the federal effort by killing the Law Enforcement Assistance Administration.

That the reforms of the criminal justice system didn't work should invite us to examine the irrelevance of that system to the existence of so much crime in our society. It is possible that, a quarter century later, revisiting the issues will make the need for social and economic reforms a lot plainer if we're going to reverse this awful trend. A new look might just jostle us into launching the needed debate.

The crime and the fear that it caused appalled America in 1967. Since then, the rise in criminality has been astronomical, and the numbers of people under criminal justice control have expanded exponentially.

LOOKING BACK

John R. Howard, a black professor and a specialist on criminal appeals, made some telling points in an interview in the *New York Times* on November 25, 1990. One of Howard's observations was that such simple solutions as more cops hadn't proved to be the answer. He saw the need for cohesion, structure, consistency, and order in the criminal justice system and pointed out some egregious anomalies centering on delays and inefficiencies. He added that the death penalty wasn't a deterrent and that jailing everybody hadn't worked; yet he saw the need for a quick fix, as well as for a long-term one. People, he said, want to be safe now.

Howard cited the successes of President Johnson's Great Society and the irony of its beneficiaries reciting its flaws. The disparity in the resources going to educate middle-class whites and underclass blacks perpetuates the tensions and failures. He called crime "a problem of both class and race."

Howard called a school for black males both wrong and dangerous. It constituted, in his view, a further stigmatization of blacks who, without the needed additional resources, would be programmed for failure. This is a hard question because of the palpable need for educational programs that provide a sense of identity in many of America's uprooted blacks.

In Howard's comments, as in those of others who have taken a thoughtful look at the crime problem, there is a deep sense of gloom and resignation. He sensed that America is in no mood to debate issues of class or race and how they influence crime.

THE ADVICE OF KNOWING SCHOLARS

There is very little new under criminal justice's sun. In their wonderfully written *The Honest Politician's Guide to Crime Control*,[7] the truly eminent criminologist Norval Morris and his colleague Gordon Hawkins suggested a number of measures:

- Decriminalize public drunkenness, drug use, gambling, disorderly conduct, vagrancy, abortion, and many sexual acts between consenting adults.
- Create a legislative committee to review proposed and existing laws and weed out the proposals that don't fit social needs.
- Discover the true incidence of crime, develop strategies to cope with it, compensate victims, and do research to establish what works.
- Adopt strict gun controls.
- Adopt tough penalties for drunken driving.
- Abolish capital punishment.
- Improve police salaries, recruitment, training, and standards; establish review mechanisms; hire civilians; buy better equipment; and apply technological innovations.
- Abolish money bail; adopt community-based treatment of all offenders, adult and juvenile; establish a sentence of at least one year for a felony conviction; use alternatives to incarceration; reduce the size of the prisons; promote prison industries (e.g., manufacturing items and growing crops); establish one state correctional system for parole, probation, jail, and prison; hire more guards; and use parole and probation more.
- Use the juvenile courts to treat only crimes, not "status offenses" (truancy, running away, and other actions of the young); establish youth service bureaus; accord all

[7] Norval Morris and Gordon Hawkins, *The Honest Politician's Guide to Crime Control*. Chicago: University of Chicago Press, 1969.

legal rights to juvenile offenders; and abolish the insanity defense, and in assessing culpability, treat the mentally disturbed or dangerous as one would those with any other malady.

- Abolish units devoted to investigating organized crime, a rather shocking suggestion. (The writers devoted an entire chapter to proving that the Mafia doesn't exist.)
- Encourage research by criminal justice scholars and practitioners.

The breathtaking wit and sophistication of the prose articulates the expertness of the authors perfectly. The work was acclaimed for its intelligence and relevance. Today, more than two decades later, it looks quaint and flawed, despite the elegance of the language. The decriminalizations don't work and make cities' conditions infinitely worse. Standards of police hiring and promoting haven't changed. And the Mafia lives.

In his *Sense and Nonsense about Crime*,[8] Samuel Walker offers a much more up-to-date assessment of crime, its causes, and its possible cures. Unfortunately, because it is so knowing, this is a gloomy work devoted mostly to the exploding of such myths as locking 'em up, unleashing the cops, decriminalizing hard drugs or closing loopholes, and revamping the Constitution.

Walker's is a cautionary tale that, at its best, offers only minor, incremental hopes for progress—through banning handguns. He supports his propositions with a solid grasp of the questions and the material. Among these propositions are that most current crime control proposals, whether offered by conservatives or by liberals, are nonsense and rest on faith, not facts. Preventive detention and selective incapacitation don't work, but speedy trials might help reduce crime. Because Walker believes it isn't possible to identify future predators

---

[8] Samuel Walker, *Sense and Nonsense about Crime*. Pacific Grove, CA: Brooks/Cole, 1989.

precisely, he sees no point in trying to devise predictive formulas. He holds that mandatory sentences and the death penalty don't deter crime and that increasing the severity and certainty of punishment for drunken driving might produce short-term results, in terms of temporary deterrence, but would not really change driving habits. Weakening the Constitution (by overturning the *Miranda v. Arizona* decision or relaxing the exclusionary rule) won't reduce crime, and adding more cops or improving investigative quality won't reduce the crime rate. Walker has little faith in the ability of the police to affect crime rates, believing that these rates are affected by social and economic factors beyond the ken of cops.

Walker says that focusing on persistent predators won't increase convictions or lower crime rates; that abolishing the insanity defense and plea bargaining will have no effect on serious crime; that limiting the right to apply for a writ of habeas corpus will have no effect on crime, nor will extending the rights of victims—and that some of these actions might be counterproductive. Gun control is needed to reduce the violence. Diversion of offenders out of the criminal justice system doesn't work; probation works and should be kept and used; prison industries and parole will not reduce crime; the decriminalization of private behavior (except, possibly, heroin use) is irrelevant to burglary or robbery; the elimination of injustices in the criminal justice system won't reduce serious crimes, but adopting carefully drafted due process and equal protection rules may enhance the quality of justice.

Walker's view, profoundly skeptical and pessimistic, contrasts sharply with the confidence expressed in the works of earlier writers and attests to the darkness settling over the minds of intelligent observers. A murder toll of over twenty-four thousand—which far exceeds the Vietnam war's annual body counts—will temper the most sanguine spirits. Walker illustrates the hubris of the cloistered scholars who prompted the development of what might be called the "Nothing-Works School of Criminology."

A seminal piece by James Q. Wilson and George L. Kelling[9] stressed the importance of attacking blight and neglect in a community by way of maintaining standards relative to the orderliness of the neighborhood. Broken windows (the actual title of the piece) were to be repaired, graffiti were to be washed out, and other social sores, physical and personal, were to be addressed. This article served as a foundation for the community-oriented policing that followed, which concentrated on a sort of house-to-house, block-to-block, and family-to-family approach to attacking neighborhood problems.

The only commentaries that have stood the test of time have been those that have brought humility and doubt to the process as they examined various causation theories. It is hard to believe the optimism reflected in some of these works, but anyone thinking or writing about crime, riots, and violence today is bound to temper her or his observations with reservations and cavils. Those whose works have stood the test of time have included racial, sociological, and economic factors in their equations.[10]

Although crime is decidedly the province of the police, it is instructive that none of the foregoing theories, with the exception of the contributions made to some of the President's Commission's task forces, is the work of a cop. The texts on criminology, the criminal justice system, and corrections are the work of scholars. Even such innovations as community-oriented policing—as well as other research and theories emanating from the police world—have been furnished by criminologists or academic experimenters and scholars.

The anti-intellectual traditions of the police world have not kept its practitioners from sounding off. Police chiefs are quick to offer social theories when crime rises and to accept credit

[9] James Q. Wilson and George L. Kelling, "Broken Windows," *The Atlantic*, 1980.

[10] Edwin H. Sutherland and Donald R. Cressey, *Principles of Criminology.* Lippincott Co. 1955; Sue Titus Reid, *Crime and Criminology.* New York: Holt, Rinehart & Winston, 1976.

when it goes down, but their absence from the arenas of research, experimentation, and meaningful discourse has resulted in the adoption of approaches whose only guide is a seat-of-the-pants feeling that this or that should, or might, work. We can see from this brief review of the literature that the thinking about causes, effects, and cures is all over the lot. A unified vision—one that encompassed the long- and short-term complexities involved in the solutions offered—is desperately needed.

What even a cursory review of the literature, or an examination of the policies and practices being used to combat street crime in America, reveals is a paucity of wit and planning and a plethora of action programs that have little relation to the complex factors at work. The few studies and commentaries reviewed here amply demonstrate the need for debating, refining, and, finally, distilling all this discussion into a coherent vision.

Quick fixes and reflexive responses have resulted in a crazy-quilt pattern of programs that don't work or that lack any logical basis for adoption. This latter-day Tower of Babel demands the creation of a vehicle that will furnish a unified plan and program.

The creation of a President's Commission on Crime would bring scholars, experimenters, and practitioners together to review all that is known, to point the way for future research, to weld a national program to combat street crime, and, finally, to furnish us with a strategy that we can all follow and that has some hope of success.

Chapter Five

THE POLITICIANS' RESPONSE

A good one [politician] is quite as unthinkable as an honest burglar.
                                    —H. L. Mencken (1880–1956)

Given the often contradictory signals emitted by the criminologists, the scholars, and the few experimenters in the field, our rulers have been forced to adopt programs that have at least allayed the public's growing fears. They opted for action and gave us a steady diet of harshness to fill the void occasioned by our not having a national forum or program since the President's Crime Commission's Report of 1967.

Politicians sink or swim on their ability to read the public's palm. Better than anyone else in our society, they understand that a misreading of the public's mood means professional extinction. In the 1980s and 1990s, calls for additional taxes—however much they might be needed, or whatever the logic of the proposal—meant losses at the polls. Invoking an image that

101

spoke to subliminal racism, without becoming too coarse or obvious, could be a big winner—witness the Bush campaign's success with the Willie Horton commercials in 1988.

It is a mistake to think, as so many of us do, that politicians are stupid. They are frequently intelligent, experienced, capable men and women whose character is all too often not strong enough to enable them to resist the temptation to pander to our worst instincts. Their desire to win is too great; the easy return on the quick fix and the facile answer is hard to resist; the ephemeral promise of painful, long-term solutions is too easy to sacrifice; and the advice of cautious advisors is too persuasive to resist. Thus, we get stampedes to see who will come up with the easiest answer first.

The political career ladder in America goes from the local to the state to the federal. Presumably, and probably accurately, the most serious, thoughtful, responsible, and intelligent acts of government take place at the national level. It would be too easy to expose the farcical posturings of city councils (as we will see when we consider the fate of our cities) and even the antics of our state legislatures as they regularly toughen the penalties, but we expect the greatest sophistication from Washington.

Analyzing the principal anticrime proposals proffered by Democrats and Republicans alike, on the national level, in 1991 and 1992, offers an insight into how the public's concerns and fears about crime are handled by our representatives. Rather than offering the sort of encompassing view that a long and thorough study would provide, the parties came up with ad hoc, stop-gap, sporadic measures that would stamp their adherents as being indisputably tough on crime.

A Democratic bill expanded the death penalty to include drug offenders who kill as well as cop killers, while paying obeisance to the party's liberal roots by barring executions of the mentally retarded and those who were under eighteen at the time of the crime.

The president's bill created new categories of federal capital crimes, including attempted murder of a president and murder for hire. Drug kingpins would also become eligible for capital punishment for certain drug-related crimes (e.g., attempting to kill officials investigating drug crimes). This bill also barred the execution of those under eighteen.

HABEAS CORPUS

Habeas corpus (literally, "you should have the body") is a little-understood term that is crucial to any concept of justice. It precludes secret detentions by requiring that the accused be brought before a magistrate and charged. It also serves as a vehicle for reviewing the legality of a detention or an incarceration. Habeas corpus is the very heart of legal accountability because it requires an open and defined process in every case where a citizen is deprived of freedom by law enforcers.

However, in practice, the right has been rather mangled through a proliferation of appeals to the federal courts to review processes already concluded in the state courts, appeals prepared mostly by inmates with time on their hands and research opportunities such as to turn them into "jailhouse lawyers."

The following are problems that have arisen:

- A process that has already, presumably, been closed at the state level may be reopened.
- Uncertainty may arise about the final disposition of a case.
- Time lags may affect the availability of witnesses or discourage their participation.
- Many cases are frivolous.
- Changes may influence inmate behavior because of frustrations over rejections or jealousies over different outcomes in similar cases.
- The sheer volume may become too burdensome for the system.

- Limitations may lessen the constitutional rights of inmates.
- Review may exacerbate state–federal relations as federal courts overturn state prosecutions.
- The uniform application of legal rules ensures central oversight that the Constitution is being observed. Threat of review ensures the integrity of the process at the lower levels. The habeas corpus appeals have, however, mostly depended on individual initiatives.
- The possibility of review may encourage lax measures in the lower courts. If the state courts resign themselves to the inevitability of tough oversight by appeals courts, they may just shift the responsibilities upward and give up taking pains to ensure the integrity of the process of the lower levels.

A study for the U.S. Department of Justice[1] revealed that the acceptance rate of inmates' petitions of appeal is probably less than 2 percent, not including the rejection of some petitions as faulty.

The Republicans would place a time limit on the right of appeal and would limit death-row inmates to only one appeal. There would be no review of cases held to have been "fully and fairly" considered by the state courts.

The Democrats would limit death-row inmates to only one appeal.

Successive and multiple filings by inmates, and the raising of issues that have to be reviewed and decided by two or more courts (district and appellate courts), further complicate a process that cries out not so much for a diminution of the right of appeal but for the streamlining of the process. The creation of review bodies that would inspect the writs quickly and would then prepare an advisory for the court could greatly increase the volume handled. Rather than restricting the right, the sys-

---

[1] Paul H. Robinson, *An Empirical Study of Habeas Corpus Review of State Court Judgements.* U.S. Department of Justice Project JADAG-79-C-002.

tem ought to be providing mechanisms for speedier resolutions through faster screening processes. Appellate court decisions were found to take an average of 10.4 months to be rendered. This suggests, once again, the need to bring management reforms to such operations, rather than legislative relief that diminishes the right.

And ignoring the useful reality that every single inmate on death row has been convicted of murder, both political parties have currently leaped onto the toughness bandwagon by proposing capital punishment for a host of additional crimes, thereby greatly diluting the argument for deterrence. If we revert to anything approaching the ancient and discredited British practice of hanging people for a great many different crimes, the deterrent effect is totally vitiated and the process is deprived of all credibility.

EXCLUSIONARY RULE

During Congress's deliberations, it often looked as if the lawmakers could have used a look at the Fourth Amendment, which says:

> The right of the people to be secure in their persons, houses, papers and effects, against unreasonable searches and seizures, shall not be violated, and no Warrants shall issue, but upon probable cause (evidence of wrongdoing), supported by Oath or affirmation, and particularly describing the place to be searched, and the persons or things to be seized.

The courts have generally held that, except in exigent circumstances (danger to an officer, a reasonable basis of suspicion, and consent), a warrant is required for a search. The search warrant forces the police to act after reflection and on the basis of solid reasons; preserves a record to justify the intrusion; and secures the permission of a disinterested, experienced observer: the magistrate.

Protection against unreasonable searches and seizures is one of the central concerns in criminology—right up there with the voluntariness of confessions and the right to face one's accuser. The test of a democracy lies in its insistence that the right of its citizens to move about freely will not be unlawfully impeded. Dictatorships are characterized by midnight raids, disappeared citizens, torture, and death—all without accountability or concern about process.

For most of this century, local cops could not be asked, by a judge, whether they had legally come upon the evidence being offered against the accused. Although the Feds had had, since 1914, to prove they'd secured their evidence by legal means (a search warrant or a consent to a search), the locals were, until the 1961 *Mapp v. Ohio* case, free to introduce evidence whether it had been legally or illegally seized. Indeed, under what came to be called the *silver platter doctrine*, the Feds, when they had secured evidence in a tainted fashion between 1914 and 1961, simply turned it over to the locals, who wouldn't, and couldn't, be asked whether it had been seized in accordance with the law.

All of this changed with what is called the *exclusionary rule*, which simply holds that judges need to establish that any evidence has been seized legally and that they will exclude evidence that has not. The adoption of this rule—the first of the sweeping reforms associated with the Earl Warren Supreme Court—brought the majesty of American justice into courtrooms where it had formerly been quite a stranger.

Law-and-order toughies have railed against the exclusionary rule as one of those "technicalities" that allow hardened criminals to get off. The temptation to tinker with *Mapp v. Ohio* has proved irresistible, even though the prison population has more than tripled since the decision.

The Republicans basically eviscerated the Fourth Amendment by allowing the use of evidence that has been seized "in good faith." By this, they meant that the officers must simply testify that they had good reasons to initiate a warrantless search. This piece of idiocy ignores almost half a century of police abuses of the Fourth Amendment, during which the Feds had been held to much higher standards. It was probably the first constitutional right subjected to the rigorous test of asking the violator if he or she meant to breach it, by way of establishing whether the right had been abridged or not.

The Democrats, caught in a spitting contest, resorted to a reasonable reiteration of a court decision that held that cops executing a legally obtained search warrant could introduce evidence even if it turned out later that the warrant had been faulty. The reasoning was that the cops had at least taken the trouble to appear in court to secure a warrant, even if the document later turned out to have been improperly issued.

Each political party was trying to outdo the other in pandering to the public's panic, while trying to preserve some historical distinctions between the approaches of Republicans and Democrats.

POLITICS AND THE CRIME BILL

Recognizing the concern over the gun issue, yet unwilling to offend the National Rifle Association (NRA), the Republicans offered to increase mandatory sentences for the possession of firearms by felons, or for the use of semiautomatic firearms in drug and other violent crimes.

The Democrats, not as worried about the NRA, wanted to ban the manufacture of fourteen types of domestic assault weapons, toughen the penalties for the use of a firearm during a violent or drug crime, mandate a five-day waiting period for handgun purchases, and provide funds to facilitate a records search. These provisions were a slight variation of the "Brady Bill" because they offered localities money to upgrade their record systems and required a record search for all gun applicants.

Terrorists—nonexistent but convenient flogging subjects in the United States—would be executed, bipartisanly, for fatal bombings, assassinations, and such. There were 449 bomb threats at airports in 1975, and 4 bombs exploded. In 1989, there were 489 threats and no explosions.

President Bush wanted to require drug testing for all parolees, and the Democrats wanted to create boot camps for young drug offenders, to provide $300 million for cities hard-hit by the drug crisis, and also to authorize the testing of parolees.

President Bush's drug program—a separate bill—requested $9.5 billion for fiscal 1990, to be spent mostly on drug enforcement by various federal departments, with only $1.5 billion for treatment, education, and prevention services. The bulk of the money would go to police overtime, the hiring of more judges and prosecutors, and the building of more prisons. President Bush increased this proposed sum to over $12 billion for fiscal 1993, with the same emphasis on enforcement and the continued neglect of prevention, education, and treatment.

These, then, are the answers being provided by the national leaders of both parties as America faces epidemics of crime and drug use and a proliferation of weaponry that result in a horrifying carnage. President Bill Clinton would be well-advised to discard the Democrats' bill and start over. The confused scene is repeated in every state house and governor's suite. Yet the criminal justice system offers only the differing views of articulate professors.

As if this were not enough, Senator Alfonse D'Amato, Republican of New York, offered his own series of amendments that would, if adopted, threaten to turn the federal–state approach to criminal justice on its head by greatly increasing the involvement of the federal courts in the prosecution of crimes normally handled by the states. Historically, the states have handled about 90 percent of the prosecutions for street crimes, leaving the federal jurisdiction free to handle the more complicated transgressions, like heavy-duty drug dealing, organized crime, white-collar crime, and the occasional terrorism, which require higher sophistication, more time, and greater resources.

Senator D'Amato, facing a tough reelection campaign in

1992, and having emerged slightly scathed but legally exonerated by an ethics investigation of his conduct by the Senate, made the toughest possible noises as he asked that the Feds take over most investigations of murder with guns and allow death as the punishment. Sixty-five U.S. senators, many of whom seemed to be well aware of the dangers of this bill, voted yes. D'Amato also proposed mandatory minimum federal sentences of ten to thirty years for the use of guns in violent or drug-trafficking crimes. A whopping eighty-eight senators went along with this idiotic proposal. That this latter provision flouts the tortuously wrought federal sentencing guidelines apparently gave the senator no great pause. The sentencing guidelines were fashioned, after much study, discussion, and debate, to bring uniformity and consistency to a process that D'Amato's proposal would have rendered a nullity. The likely overwhelming of the federal courts, if they assumed the jurisdiction he recommended, similarly failed to stay his hand. No provision was offered for additional resources. A *New York Times* editorial accused him of "grandstanding." It was a charge that could have been leveled at many of the colleagues who slavishly followed his lead.

Even a putative ally of Senator D'Amato's, Chief Justice William H. Rehnquist, acting in his role of presiding officer of the Judicial Conference, pleaded with the Congress, in September 1991, to oppose the senator's proposal.

By tying all of these provisions to a sensible gun-control law, the lawmakers created such a conundrum that the NRA, despite its calls for mandatory sentences and tough treatment of criminals, had to oppose the bill, and handgun control advocates with a fondness for the Constitution have also had to oppose it. And President Bush, who opposed the Brady Bill, promised to sign that bill into law if it came to him as part of either his or Democratic Senator Joe Biden's broad anticrime bill. Politics, in 1991, continued to make strange bedfellows.

President Bush's bill was defeated in the Senate, 56 to 40, on June 20, 1991, clearing the way for a discussion of the

Democrats' proposals. The debate centered on which version was "tougher," and senators who plainly knew better saw it as in their interests to jump on the bandwagon.

The Senate, in a 71-to-26 vote, sent a bill to the House, where it faced certain alterations. The Senate's bill included the waiting period on gun purchases; increased the death penalty to include fifty-one crimes (even in states that had no capital punishment); reduced habeas corpus appeals; sustained the reasonable requirement on the exclusionary rule; provided $3.3 billion to help state and local law enforcers; provided money to hire more federal agents and attorneys and to build ten regional prisons for drug offenders; offered financial aid to cities with drug problems; included money to expand boot-camp detention centers and efforts to combat gangs, control drugs in rural areas, and conduct antiterrorist activities (there was no guarantee that the money, for any of this, would be available). The bill also increased mandatory sentences for gun crimes; created a police corps program patterned after the Peace Corps, requiring four years of police service by college graduates whose tuition had been paid; required the states to provide "bill of rights" legislation to protect cops' rights in internal investigations; required drug testing of probationers and parolees; and designated truck stops and public areas of housing projects as drug-free zones.

The House Democrats seemed intent on passing legislation that addressed the subtler questions of prevention, education, and treatment.

The D'Amato proposals were the true litmus tests of senatorial integrity because their demagogic appeal was as obvious as their lack of any hope of success. It would have been a torpid senator indeed who could not see that the proposals would not only fail to work but might really injure a federal system that seemed to be working effectively, if on a limited scale. Adoption would flood the system with street criminals, who, until then, had been processed in the state courts.

This limit on federal involvement in street crime was, of

course, precisely what the Founding Fathers had sought. That no funds were allocated in the D'Amato bill not only ensured failure but revealed the cynicism behind the proposals. All of the proposals were offered in a spastic bidding war that ignored any attempt at a long, serious study of the issue or any hope of preparing a comprehensive program.

The common threads of guns, drugs, poverty, and racism lace together many of the commentaries of the observers and the leaders cited in this chapter but in an uneven mode that clearly shows the absence of a consensus. The temptation to posture is seen not only in Senator D'Amato's proposals but in the unseemly haste of his colleagues to be seen as being equally tough on crime. As long as this thinking continues to dominate the actions of our leaders, any hope of even such modest reforms as more rational sentencing policies or the adoption of uniform and informed policies to combat drugs or crime must be deferred. D'Amato's re-election, in 1992, following a tough campaign, signaled the readiness of Americans to embrace demagogic programs.

All of this nervous "me-tooism" by the Democrats had its roots in the scorchings they'd been receiving for twenty years from their opponents.

It might be argued that the capture of the Democratic Party by its left wing in the Presidential Convention of 1972 dumped the spectrum of right to left-of-center entirely in the hands of the Republicans, who, with Ronald Reagan, were, eight years later, quick and skillful in retaining the reins. Reagan's foreign policy mostly featured a jingoist bellicosity that felicitously and fortuitously inherited the precious fruit of Russia's collapse. The domestic policy meant convincing America that lower taxes for the rich meant prosperity for all the deserving. Retribution would be reserved for poverty pimps and welfare cheats—and we all knew who "they" were. "The War on Poverty has been fought," Reagan said, "and poverty won." No need for a reprise of that discredited struggle.

The perfect symbol for the approach—with its barely latent

racism and pitiless treatment of the excluded—arrived in the person of a black killer who'd been treated gently by a woolly-headed system run by liberals and had been freed to rape and atrociously assault white womanhood. Not to belabor the point, Willie Horton became the embodiment of the conservatives' contempt for softness, and the issue—and the fate of the Democrats—was sealed.

The mistake, of course, lay in succumbing to the blandishments of the far ends of the poles. In the Democrats' case, it was the left pole. The Republicans, similarly tempted, but by the right, resisted and maintained the charade of holding the middle with men like Nixon, Reagan, and Bush, all the while repudiating the extreme right, as represented by such as David Duke in 1991. The Republican Party's repudiation of Duke demonstrated that it would not be lured into the same trap that the Democrats had sunk into at the fateful convention of 1972. Of course, in the fateful convention of 1992, the Republican party did just that—by giving its heart to its most fervid rightists and, like the Democrats of 1972, suffering defeat.

Despite the endorsement of the *New York Times,* the crime bill passed by the Democratic Senate foundered on the shoals of a threatened veto by President Bush, ironically heartening civil libertarians and civil rights groups that had seen it as an assault on constitutional freedoms. Crime politics had, again, joined unlikely forces. The bill just wasn't "tough" enough, and both sides were posturing and making ready for the presidential election of 1992. With this crime bill went the "Brady Bill." Chances are that the crime bill was aptly named, as it would more than likely have produced more crime. The much heralded assault on crime promised by both Democrats and Republicans would again be deferred—and the latter's had been a doomed and unthinking program in any case.

᠂ All of this showed the disastrous consequences of the lack of a national plan such as might have flowed from a presidential commission on crime.

The vacuum created by the lack of a unified policy was

filled by politicians with hysterical cries for blood. The conspic-
uous lack of success, over the past twenty years, did not
discourage these efforts at toughness. The absence of the national view needed to guide the effort ensured that the extreme
measures suggested would not be held up to the examining
light of a comprehensive plan.

The confusion offered by the writers and thinkers in the
field tempted the demagogues to posture and cowed the rest
into submission.

As the century grinds to a close, America's rulers are
concentrating on more cops, tougher laws, harsher judges, and
bigger prisons as they attempt to build us out of all this
violence.

None of it is working.

Chapter Six

RACISM

Man is born free, and everywhere he is in chains.
—Jean-Jacques Rousseau (1712–1778)

The problem of the underclass is indisputably the dirtiest little
secret of the criminal justice system, nationwide. It isn't politically correct even to refer to it, because it plays into the hands
of racists to offer such evidence of black "inferiority" as high
unemployment, early death, imprisonment, addiction, dropout
rates, infant mortality, teenage pregnancies, poverty and welfare rates, low educational achievement, disintegrated family
structures, and lack of visibility in corporate, political, and
professional organizations or in academe's halls.

In America, full and deep debate inevitably precedes any
attempt to cure a societal ill, whether it be civil rights, the
feminist cause, the Vietnam war, the environment, abortion,
consumer rights, or racism and poverty. Power is almost never

ceded voluntarily. Equality, justice, and rights must be wrested from the powerful.

⟶ A debate on the disabilities visited on blacks by the racism and poverty imposed by an unfeeling overclass will have to acknowledge, as a first step, that too many blacks, as the greatest percentage of the underclass, are experiencing massive failure in American society and that their future is bleak. This admission of guilt is the hurdle that must be surmounted if we are to recognize the failures and attack them successfully. The crime and violence that result are the consequences of the racist policies and the poverty that the white overclass has visited on the black underclass.

Do we even dare to discuss such delicate matters?

The question of politically correct discussion in the sensitive areas of racism and poverty surfaces in odd contexts. Many Bronx politicians, for example, deplore any description of the desolation of that borough. My own account of the poverty, criminality, and vast urban decay that I encountered as chief of police of that county from 1973 through 1976, as described in *Bronx Beat*, came in for fierce criticism because of its unrelenting gloomy tenor. Why hadn't I cited the positives? The fact was that the Bronx was emblematic of America's contemporary frontier, where the nation was battling for its soul—and losing.

To assert such truths was not acceptable.

When Hollywood filmed *The Bonfire of the Vanities*, which, surprisingly, concentrated on the dissolution of the Bronx for dramatic impact, the borough president and others protested stridently over the "wasteland" imagery. I felt the conditions would have a chance of being attacked only if they were acknowledged and confronted.

I wound up debating Bronx boosters on New York radio stations as the controversy bubbled. Malign neglect continued to be the country's policy toward its Bronxes.

The Bronx is neatly divided among half a million whites

and equal numbers of Hispanics and blacks. It, like Detroit, has become a metaphor for urban decay.

Failing to discuss the issue enables the overclass to continue business as usual, exhorting the underclass to pull itself out of the slough of misery by its bootstraps, and all the while removing both the straps and the boots. To sing the praises of the ghetto, by pointing to the odd flower that manages to crack through the asphalt, is to play into the hands of those who want to continue to neglect the cities in order to benefit the suburbs.

What we persistently refuse to see is the unique nature of the black experience in America.

THE AMERICAN DILEMMA

In the late thirties, the Carnegie Corporation sought an unbiased study of the Negro in American life and commissioned a distinguished young social scientist from Sweden to perform the task. Thus was born *An American Dilemma: The Negro Problem and American Democracy* by Gunnar Myrdal.[1] This massive study produced over one thousand pages of text and almost five hundred of notes. It grew to be widely regarded as the definitive work on race relations in America. It correctly saw the "Negro problem" as flowing from white prejudice, despite white society's expressions of belief in equality, justice, and opportunity.

Myrdal's analysis took several years and consisted of exhaustive reviews of documents, extensive travels throughout the country, lengthy interviews, and scores of observations. It encompassed the history of the Negroes from their arrival to the mid-twentieth century, and it included slavery, the Civil War, Reconstruction, Jim Crowism, and all other factors—

---

[1] Gunnar Myrdal, *An American Dilemma: The Negro Problem and American Democracy*. New York: Harper & Row, 1944.

social, economic, legal, and cultural—that contributed to what it called the "Negro problem."

The book's operative words are *segregation, discrimination,* and *prejudice.* It stresses that removing legal barriers and increasing educational opportunities would serve as rescue vehicles for the race. The vote would accelerate the process of gaining equality. The North seemed a paradigm for the progress sought. The author missed, however, the disabling effects of slavery and uprootedness on a people's ability to regroup and assimilate. Myrdal had focused only on the visible aspects of oppression and believed that the reversal of the oppressive mechanisms would result in rapid progress. Although incredibly observant and honest, he failed to assess the impact of the psychological and cultural factors attending slavery and Jim Crowism, or their implications for the future.

The encyclopedic analysis serves as a comprehensive accounting of the travails faced by blacks in the New World. Nothing escaped the notice of Myrdal. In the end, he came to the perfectly natural conclusion that jobs, education, the vote, and the breakdown of legal barriers would bring success, in the form of traditional assimilation and the assumption of an equal place in America's sun.

In revisiting the issue nearly twenty years later, in 1962, Arnold Rose, one of the principals in the original Myrdal study, found many grounds for optimism. He saw the intervening period, 1942 to 1962, as the time of "greatest changes" for the Negro in America, a view that the 1968 Commission on Civil Disorders would surely have described as decidedly optimistic, if not downright naive or wrongheaded. Still, Rose saw progress in jobs, education, and civil rights. The death of "King Cotton" and the birth of Detroit's assembly line were seen as great boons to the Negro. The generally full employment of the 1940–1954 period and the dramatic rise in Negro income seemed to hold the promise of eventual—perhaps even imminent—equality with whites.

The growth of awareness, education, and economic power

among some Negroes afforded them leadership opportunities that were channeled into the National Association for the Advancement of Colored People (NAACP), as well as into the work of such role models as Marcus Garvey, George Washington Carver, Frederick Douglass, and W. E. B. DuBois.

Growing internationalism made America more aware of world opinion, and the independence movement in Africa lent an impetus to a drive for equality in the United States. The current Supreme Court and such decisions as the May 17, 1954, *Brown v. Board of Education* quickened every civil rightist's dreams of equality.

A dichotomy between the South and the North was still clearly visible in 1962, with the North getting credit for more of an effort to dispense racial justice.

The advent of the Negro vote was also seen as a powerful stimulus for change. Black faces were beginning to emerge, and black votes were starting to make a difference. Although injustices remained, blacks were getting a fairer shake in the criminal justice system than they had had. The North was, again, given higher grades than the South.

Housing segregation was seen to accelerate with the moving of blacks into the cities and the fear and flight of whites to the suburbs. Housing came to be seen as the "most serious and least soluble aspect of the race problem."

Public facilities were being desegregated through sit-ins, bus boycotts, and marches. Blacks were becoming more assertive and less servile. The American caste system "had been broken everywhere." Prejudicial attitudes were still common "but racism, as a comprehensive ideology, was maintained by only a few." Rose's altruism led him to predict "the end of all formal segregation and discrimination within a decade."

How mercilessly history deals with our vanities. Learned scholars studied the black's problems, restudied them, and observed and evaluated every nuance under the aegis of patient, generous benefactors who afforded the scholars the luxury of labored examinations and patient reflections. What emerged were conclusions that, although logical and erudite, have been transmogrified by history into parodies. It is an objective example of the humiliations visited on the best of our members by the unforgiving forces that shape our destinies.

Gunnar Myrdal and his associates produced a gigantic study that captured every facet and meaning of the black experience in America. They clearly saw that the source of the "Negro problem" lay in white hearts. They bravely cited every injustice and fearlessly revealed our hypocrisies to us, but they now seem to have been wildly optimistic in their assessment of our commitment to our professed ideals and how we might employ them to dispense racial justice.

THE NATIONAL COMMISSION ON CIVIL DISORDERS

"Our nation is moving toward two societies, one black, one white—separate and unequal." Thus begins the seminal report of a distinguished group asked to examine the causes and possible cures of urban riots by blacks in America in the mid-sixties. The violence reached a crescendo in 1967.

The report contains many trenchant observations. Two worth special note are that "until the fact of white racism is admitted, it cannot conceivably be expunged," and that the rioting young blacks "were and they are, a time-bomb ticking in the heart of the richest nation in the history of the world."

The 1968 report speaks of segregated and substandard housing, but not of the homeless—a phenomenon created by policies begun with the emptying of mental institutions in the seventies and adding this mixed population to the alcoholics already on the street. The housing crisis was made infinitely worse by nonbuilding and the deeper impoverishment of the already-poor, following the fiscal policies of a series of presidents determined to make the rich wealthier at the expense of the poor.

The report speaks ominously of the future, but its gloom is

tinged with the naive optimism flowing from the unconscious assumption that "War on Poverty" programs would continue. We were on the brink of a 180-degree reversal, but the authors didn't see it.

The report listed the grievances that sparked the riots in the order of importance.

First level
1. Police practices
2. Un- or underemployment
3. Inadequate housing
Second level
4. Inadequate education
5. Poor recreational facilities and programs
6. An unresponsive political structure
Third level
7. Disrespectful white attitudes
8. Discriminatory justice
9. Inadequate federal programs
10. Inadequate municipal services
11. Discrimination in consumer and credit practices
12. Inadequate welfare programs

The list today looks like the innocent anachronism of a more hopeful, and trusting, age. The intervening quarter century has seen progress in political power—as the whites abandoned the cities in panic flight and left the empty husks to black mayors and black police chiefs—and in the demolition of legal barriers to full participation in the American Dream. Ironically, more subtle economic, social, educational, and cultural barriers between whites and blacks were, at the same time, being raised and strengthened.

The 1968 report constituted a watershed in American history in that it made a valiant effort to depict the problems. It described the past practices that had made the riots virtually inevitable and plotted a wise and knowing program for future action that could be described as promoting racial and economic justice for blacks. The report received wide coverage and respectful attention. President Lyndon B. Johnson placed the prestige and power of his office behind it.

The intervening years amply illustrate a collective turning-of-the-back on the problems of America's blacks by the overclass, producing the disaffection and alienation prophesied by the report.

THE BLACK EXPERIENCE IN AMERICA

With so much street crime produced by, and aimed at, Afro-Americans, it is essential that their history in the United States be briefly reviewed if we are to bring any understanding to the crises now being produced by the historical forces shaping our national experience.

Why has the assimilation of blacks failed?

Has the experience of blacks in America been unique or similar to that of other immigrant groups?

Slavery is the first and foremost difference. Blacks came involuntarily to America, literally in chains. They had their families broken and their culture and history erased and an ersatz culture superimposed by force. Blacks, uniquely (with the possible exception of native Americans, who have suffered near extinction and continuing oppression at our hands), experienced being wholly uprooted.

The first slave ship arrived in Jamestown in August 1619. By 1776, there were half a million Afro-Americans enslaved here. Nearly one in six Americans was a slave.

Black history, over the next 240-odd years, was uneven, but persistently bleak, as blacks faced oppression in the South and little comfort in the North. For purposes of congressional representation, blacks were counted as three fifths of a person, and much intellectual energy was spent chronicling a presumed imperfect development of mind and body. Hitler's racist theories of the *Untermensch* had a faithful forewarning in our own past, and we had the "ineradicable taint of color" as a convenient target. America had no need to have Stars of David sewn on coats.

Outraged by slavery, the abolitionists sparked a debate that had gathered steam by the middle of the nineteenth century. Like Rachel Carson's *Silent Spring*, which launched the environmentalists, *Uncle Tom's Cabin*, in 1852, became the vision around which opponents of slavery coalesced. The Civil War of 1861 and the Emancipation Proclamation of 1863, which freed the slaves, ended this "peculiar institution."

Reconstruction and civil rights legislation brought a hope that was rapidly extinguished by the growth of the Ku Klux Klan (KKK), and the passage of Jim Crow laws that segregated the races and launched another century of exclusion and second-class citizenship, this time under the guise of "freedom."

The blacks began a massive northward migration into the industrialized cities, where jobs were possible. Whereas in 1910 91 percent of the country's 9.8 million blacks lived in the South, by 1966 the total population had more than doubled, to 21.5 million, and the number in metropolitan areas had risen from 2.6 million to 14.8 million. The number outside the South was, by 1966, virtually identical to the entire population of blacks in 1910, or 9.7 million.

The struggles between the KKK and the NAACP waxed and waned for almost a century, or until 1954's Supreme Court *Brown* decision, which called for desegregating the nation's schools. This was the breakthrough that would result in demolishing the Jim Crow laws and practices that had kept blacks from participating fully in America's life, and that would put the racist rednecks to flight.

This legal process greatly accelerated in the mid-sixties, as a result of the pressure of a massive civil rights struggle and a sympathetic President Johnson, who managed the passage of a series of landmark laws in Congress that promoted equality for blacks, females, and minorities.

Still, the 1968 report of the Commission on Civil Disorders failed to pinpoint the long-term disabling effects of the uprooting that had accompanied slavery, nor did it anticipate the depth, subtlety, thrust, and wiliness of American racism. Indeed, at the peak of the War on Poverty, even the gloomy assessments in its pages, following scores of disorders, tend to be tinged with roseate optimism. That very year would see a collective national abandonment of the problems of the blacks. Richard Nixon was elected president, launching an era of conservatism that would prove a graveyard for the New and Fair Deals, the Great Society, and other social welfare schemes intended to help the underclass.

The report listed the basic causes of black disaffection as being pervasive discrimination and segregation, black migration to the cities, white flight, and the creation of black ghettos. The blacks were seen as having arrived in the cities too late to participate in the employment waves of industrialization or even in the explosive growth of World War II's armament industry. Only the low-level, menial, dead-end tasks seemed open to blacks. The cause wasn't slavery, Jim Crow laws, exclusion, racism, or a unique experience; it was just a matter of having arrived at the party too late. Poverty was seen as creating disparities, but the report could still claim that "most American Negro families are headed by men."

The problems so solemnly cited then might now actually inspire a longing to return to the relative innocence of 1968, at least in terms of the amount of mayhem, murder, and violence that so shocked that age and that looks so reassuringly low today.

And the blacks themselves were of two minds about that violence.

MALCOLM X
AND THE REVEREND MARTIN LUTHER KING, JR.

The black community sails between the nonviolent ideological pole of the Reverend Martin Luther King, Jr., and the intransigence and militance of Malcolm X.

Assassinated three years apart—Malcolm X by blacks in 1965, when he was thirty-nine, and King by a white racist in 1968, when he was just forty—the two have assumed mythic proportions, made even larger by Spike Lee's 1992 movie on Malcolm's life, which juxtaposes Malcolm's militancy against Gandhi-style passive resistance.

I knew Malcolm X when he was the leader of the New York mosque of Elijah Muhammad's Black Muslims and then, following his expulsion and fatal break with them, as a developing African-centered political-religious Muslim changeling who seemed to be undergoing a metamorphosis into a wiser and more global thinker at the time of his death.

Malcolm X's widely varied life holds something for everyone. The impatient and angry can find Malcolm's defiance and menace. Those searching for a thoughtful leader can find intellectual depth and broadening wisdom in his final days. Those seeking unblinking definitions of the black experience in America will find insights in such of his words as the call to obtain justice "by any means necessary."

On Saturday afternoons, Malcolm X held forth on 125th Street and Seventh Avenue, Manhattan—the heart and soul of black America—and would spellbind a sidewalk crowd with a message that often contained virulent references to whites and Jews. He'd describe the depredations of "Goldberg" in terms that made the later rifts between blacks and Jews understandable. As he progressed along his life's continuum, acolytes could choose the color that most appealed to them in the spectrum of his beliefs.

The life of Martin Luther King, Jr., was a seamless Gandhian model of consistent nonviolence and reliance on moral suasion and the courageous acceptance of the risk of inevitable martyrdom.

The black community has found itself pulled by the divergent magnetism of these contending messages, and the disintegrating black family has had to find ways of surviving, even in the midst of the pulls of violence. Here, as everywhere else in America, in the areas that matter, blacks have fared worst.

Statistical Reflections:
Percentages of Families of Various Types

Year	Husband–wife		Female-headed	
	White	Nonwhite	White	Nonwhite
1950	88.0	77.7	8.5	16.5
1960	88.7	73.6	8.7	22.4
1966	88.8	72.7	8.9	23.7

The number of births to teenaged mothers declined for the first time in 1973, following the legalization of abortion by the Supreme Court in its *Roe v. Wade* decision. Changing lifestyles, especially the growth in the proportion of births to single twenty-five to thirty-nine-year-old women, kept the table rising and masked the revolutionary impact of the decision on teenagers.

Since 1940, the number of out-of-wedlock black children has greatly exceeded that of whites (about 17 percent then vs. about 3 percent white) and the gap has widened dramatically over the ensuing fifty-plus years, despite changing values and lifestyles that destigmatized such births in the white community. By 1980, the white total was just over 10 percent as the black total approached 50 percent. Since 1986, both percentages have continued to increase despite the effects of the *Roe* decision.

The disintegration of the black family accelerated dramatically after 1968, with disastrous consequences for the wealth and stability of the unit, as well as for its safety and the safety of the larger society. Growing disenchantment, continuing racism, and a shifting value system that also affected white families contributed to the weakening of the family structure, which had not, in any case, been given much opportunity for growth in America.

The divorce rate in the general population shot up over a brief forty-year period.

Year	Divorces (number)	Rate per 1,000
1950	385,000	2.6
1960	393,000	2.2
1970	708,000	3.5
1980	1,189,000	5.2
1988	1,183,000	4.8

The trends point not only to the plight of blacks but also to the increasing decadence and hedonism of the larger white society and its mobility, independence, and changing attitudes toward family, marriage, and child rearing.

The number of births to single women has shifted dramatically in recent years. As recently as 1975, blacks had more out-of-wedlock births than whites (250,000 vs. 186,000) but by 1980, white "illegitimate" births had almost equalled those of blacks (320,000 vs. 325,000) and by 1985, whites had surpassed the totals of black out-of-wedlock births (433,000 vs. 365,000).

The birth rate per 1,000 for unmarried women remained hugely higher for black women but declined steadily, from 95.5 in 1970 to 84.2 in 1975, 81.4 in 1980, and 78.8 in 1985. In contrast, the birth rate per 1,000 of unmarried white women rose from 13.8 in 1970 to 17.6 in 1980 and 21.8 in 1985. Family values, lifestyles, and *Roe v. Wade* could all be seen as working on these dramatic shifts in the behavior of Americans.

In 1991, more than 61 percent of all black children were born to mothers without husbands. It was a rare black child who had a positive male role model present for any significant portion of his or her life.

From 1980 to 1990, America's population grew 9.8 percent, the white population growing 6 percent, and blacks more than doubling this rate, at 13.2 percent. The greatest growth rate (107.8 percent) occurred among the Asian population. This was a decade during which abortions were both available and widely resorted to, greatly reducing the number of teenaged childbirths, especially to poorer young women who would otherwise have been forced, by economic and other circumstances, to have the child.

An observer of the United States, Alexis de Tocqueville, wrote in 1830, "Slavery recedes, but the prejudice to which it has given birth is immovable." Over a century later, Gunnar Myrdal warned, on the issue of race hatred, that America "must do something big, and do it soon."

Writing in *Crisis in Black and White,* Charles E. Silberman reiterated the warning, in 1964, and called for "a radical reconstruction of American society" to achieve racial justice.

Today, looking back from the vantage point of three-and-three-quarter centuries of black experience, we can see not only that we have failed to dispense racial or economic justice but that we have, during the latest quarter century's cruelties, made things infinitely worse. The result has been such enormously rising levels of street crime and violence as to make us wish for a return to the halcyon days of "crises" and "disorders" that sparked the studies and programs of the sixties. The sixties, in retrospect, seem a more innocent age. They were also a period of struggle and of the hope that attends such strivings.

JEWS AND BLACKS

The history of the Jews in America has been one of a people who'd experienced the bitterest prejudice and who had grasped the importance of striking at social injustice, whomever it might be aimed at. Their collective conscience led them to fight for unionization, education, housing, jobs, social welfare, justice, and a host of causes broadly defined as liberal and invariably reflecting an activism that moved far beyond self-interest.

Jews were on the ramparts in every significant struggle for reform in the twentieth century. Their names were emblazoned on the dispatches from such battlefields as the urban ghettos, the South, slums, sweatshops, and wherever reforms were needed. It was Goodman and Schwerner who were lynched with Chaney in Mississippi. The words of a Jew adorn the Statue of Liberty and have inspired millions.

No people have so completely embodied, fought for, appreciated, or extended the blessings of America as the Jews, and as the struggle of the blacks erupted, the Jews who'd made a common cause with them took their places on the battle lines.

Gradually a subtle, barely perceptible shift developed that, by the nineties, had broadened into a wide chasm of hostility, best symbolized by the anti-Semitic comments of a black presidential candidate; the virulent anti-Semitism of some Black Muslim leaders; and such outrageous events as a prominent black professor's blatantly anti-Jewish speeches and lectures.

Malcolm X's references to "Goldberg" hadn't cooled Jewish ardor for the cause, but these later expressions of hostility were being seized as pretexts for the drift of the Jews into the comforts of mainstream American life.

Intermarriage, assimilation, and a general sense of having made it gave Jews the feeling that they could abandon their historic role of champions of justice. They were, like the rest of us, losing their sense of commitment to causes that transcended their own pleasures.

The blacks, desperately in need of all the leadership and energy that could be mustered, would prove to be the big losers in this shift, but the Jews lost something, too: their collective sense of mission.

By 1992, two distinguished white authors, Andrew Hacker and Studs Terkel, could describe, in eloquent and frightening terms, the worsening of race relations in America.[2] Hacker likened America's racism to South Africa's apartheid.

---

[2] Andrew Hacker, *Two Nations—Black and White, Separate, Hostile, Unequal.* New York: Scribner's, 1992; Studs Terkel, *Race: How Blacks and Whites Think and Feel about the American Obsession.* New York: New Press, 1992.

SELLING SELF-LOATHING

Within the context of the black experience, it is not hard to see crime, addiction, and violence as the products of conditions visited on the underclass by the dominant society. And with all this went a message of inferiority that caused psychic disabilities. "The worst crime the white man has committed has been to teach us to hate ourselves" were the words of Malcolm X. James Baldwin threatened a "fire next time" and spoke of the rage that comes with being black in America.

There is validity in the depth of this message, made clear by a survey that revealed that many blacks entertain negative views of their fellow African-Americans. This recent survey, by the Metropolitan Chicago Information Center, revealed that 14 percent of black adults in the Chicago area agreed that African-Americans have less "inborn ability to learn than whites"; only 9 percent of whites shared this view. More than a third of the blacks polled believed that their fellow African-Americans lacked the willpower to pull themselves out of poverty.

Years of "Black is beautiful" rhetoric and programs do not appear to have created much progress. The emphasis on developing high self-esteem seems at least an unconscious recognition of the need to attack this problem of self-image among America's blacks. There is the lingering suspicion that, without a full and thorough discussion of racism's origins, history, and complexities, blacks and whites are doomed to dance around the fringes of the issue, as they have been doing now for decades.

A racist society is transmitting the messages subtly and effectively. A study of five-year-olds showed that 76 percent of the black children chose a black doll as "bad" or inferior. This study, by Derek Hopson and Darlene Powell Hopson, also showed that 60 to 78 percent of these black children preferred playing with a white doll. Until about the age of five, these black children had preferred black dolls.

And if anybody retains any illusions about white sentiment, or about whether ours is or is not a racist society, a quick peek at the results of 1991's gubernatorial race in Louisiana provides an answer.

There, a former national grand wizard of the Ku Klux Klan and the founder of the National Association for the Advancement of White People, David Duke, ran off with substantially more than half the white vote in an election that drew a large voter turnout. That he lost to a lack-luster white did not conceal the power of his appeal to voters, who heard his message, loud and clear.

While George Bush's campaign had offered us Willie Horton in 1988, Pat Buchanan's campaign in 1992 was laced with references to white fundamentalist Christian hegemony and the admission, by a friend and former sympathizer, that the candidate's anti-Semitism could no longer be denied. Buchanan's boast, in the end, was that he'd knocked Louisiana's David Duke out of the race. Buchanan's message had been subtler. The Republican convention echoed these conservative strains.

Meanwhile, responding to the need for a more acceptable image, the Ku Klux Klan burnished its appearance and produced such promising new leaders as a cleancut twenty-five-year-old Shawn Slater, who was being groomed for a political future and who the Anti-Defamation League of B'nai B'rith described as the new species of KKK leader. In Idaho, white supremacists had shoot outs with the Feds in 1992 and denounced blacks and Jews.

At the University of Minnesota, a student met resistance in 1991 when he attempted to organize a White Student Cultural Center on campus. The effort seemed an echo of growing white impatience and a surrender to the self-pitying stereotypes feeding racism.

Klanwatch, a private nonprofit group that monitors racism, cited an increase in white supremacist groups in its 1992 report.

Racism, in its many virulent forms, was alive and well in America nearly twenty years after the nation had entered its third century.

BLACK POWER AND THE CITIES

"Black power" was one of the catch phrases of the sixties, but we have seen that whites have been only too glad to cede power to the blacks by abandoning such empty shells as Detroit and taking their jobs with them to the suburbs. The blacks could run the cities, but there just wouldn't be much to preside over. As the financial burdens of paying for welfare, housing, and other benefits were shifted to the municipalities, the federal government reduced its help. Thus, between fiscal 1982 and 1988, the State of New York lost $15.3 billion in aid from Washington. Most of this would have gone to the cities. "Black power" got translated into a shift of resources from cities to suburbs, from young to old, and from poor to rich. This shift was further translated into "from black to white." All was done in the names of bootstrappism, rampant capitalism, and the "good ol' American way." What had begun on the heights of the civil rights struggle foundered on the rocks of the over-class's realpolitik of the seventies and eighties.

By the late twentieth century, the shift of the blacks to America's largest cities was virtually complete. With the "tipping factor" of the surfacing of a few black faces, the panic exodus to the suburbs hit high gear.

Rank	City	Population	Black (%)	Hispanic (%)
1	New York	7,353,000	25.2	19.9
2	Los Angeles	3,353,000	17.0	27.5
3	Chicago	2,978,000	39.8	14.0
4	Houston	1,698,000	27.6	17.6
5	Philadelphia	1,647,000	37.8	3.8
6	San Francisco	1,070,000	8.9	14.9
7	Detroit	1,036,000	63.1	2.4
8	Dallas	987,000	29.4	12.3
9	San Antonio	941,000	7.3	53.7
10	Phoenix	924,000	4.8	14.8

Of the first five cities in the table, all had either a black mayor, a black police chief, or both, except for Houston, which had females in both posts in 1991; both were replaced in 1992.

The cruel irony was that, when black mayors and black police chiefs were in place in many American cities, the pent-up fury of black citizens tended to be suppressed and deflected, and the riots most police experts feared generally failed to materialize—notwithstanding the ghastly eruption in Los Angeles in May 1992. These reflections lead to a masking of the invisibly growing pressures in the ghetto. As the century draws to a close, most large-city police chiefs, white or black, go to bed with a silent prayer that the riot they fear "not take place on my watch." Meanwhile, the pressures increase beneath the surface, gaining expression in frequent, but individual, acts of violence. As if in echo, John Kenneth Galbraith, in his prescient *The Culture of Contentment* (Houghton Mifflin, 1992) writes of three great dangers—the plight of the under-class, the dangers posed by the military-industrial complex, and riots in our cities.

Riots had precipitated the creation of the 1968 Commission on Civil Disorders, and the general absence of riots in 1991—despite profound anguish and alienation in the ghetto—perpetuated neglect because no one felt the need to call for the creation of such a forum. Even the disorders in Crown Heights in 1991 and the 1992 riot in Los Angeles, as well as disorders elsewhere, failed to stir any real movement to social and economic reforms, although these were followed by handwringing and pious assurances of change that never seemed to become fleshed out, much less adopted.

THE SURPRISING VIEWS OF BLACKS

The much-abused War on Poverty did produce some progress, but this was violently arrested, and reversed, with the election of Ronald Reagan to the presidency in 1980.

Despite a 1991 Gallup Poll revealing that most blacks

believed their politicians were being investigated and prosecuted to undermine black political power, that many blacks
believed AIDS was a virus created in the laboratory to eliminate "undesirables" like blacks and gays, and that many other
blacks suspected drugs and alcohol were kept cheap and accessible to act as a form of latter-day enslavement, the humor of
the age could easily be characterized as complacent. The Jim
Crow laws had been fixed, and new initiatives in the Congress
were met with deafening indifference, even by liberals who
would normally automatically support such measures. Other
issues, such as the disabilities of racism and poverty, as well as
their impact on street crime rates, weren't even discussed. A
tough crime bill, increasing penalties and weakening constitutional safeguards, sparked a stampede in Washington to show
who could be toughest on law-and-order issues.

On July 8, 1991, the *New York Times* reported that even
senators who understood the self-defeating, anticonstitutional
character of these crime provisions supported them, to show
they were "tough on crime." Our leaders lined up to bash
the Fourth Amendment protections against the intrusions of
the state.

POVERTY

The amount of money that demarcates the poverty level is
the estimated annual income a family would require to meet its
minimal housing, food, medical, and other needs. As of 1990,
the amount was $13,359 for a family of four.

While other countries have been reducing the number of
those living below the poverty level, the numbers in the United
States have risen. The Joint Center for Political and Economic
Studies concluded, in a report released in Washington in September 1991, that, of the seven Western democracies studied,
the United States had done the least to help its poor. The
figures for 1992 showed that over thirty-four million Americans

were living in poverty—the highest number since 1964—and that the totals were increasing. The center found that other countries were reducing the number of their poor dramatically, through child support payments and other welfare programs, while America's poor increased, despite prosperity and a lower unemployment rate than that of the other nations studied.

Canada, Great Britain, France, Sweden, the Netherlands, and Germany were found to be doing far more to cure poverty than the United States.

HUNGER

The U.S. Agriculture Department reported in 1992 that 24.16 million Americans had been enrolled in the food stamp program as of October 1991, up almost 10 percent from a year earlier. The number of children receiving a free or reduced-price school lunch also continued to rise, to 12.7 million in October 1991.

Qualification for the programs required that the recipients be impoverished or from low-income families.

THE GROWING CHASM

The increasing acceptability of such terms as *overclass* and *underclass* in the American lexicon has been made possible by such statistics as that the average of incomes of the richest fifth had grown by more than 25 percent from 1977 to 1989, to $109.424. The poorest fifth had seen their incomes drop more than 10 percent, to $8,391.

The scandalous sums paid high corporate executives—especially when viewed as multiples of the salaries of the lowest paid employees in the company, and when one considers the often lack-luster performance of these economic royalists—contribute enormously to the growing disparity, as do, of course, our lavish payments to those who entertain, amuse, or otherwise distract us from the grimmer realities of contemporary life.

Lee Iacocca was paid $4.6 million as chairman of Chrysler in 1990, at the same time that the company was laying off workers and each new year brought banner headlines trumpeting baseball's new six- or seven- or eight-million-dollar man.

The popular notion of "trickle-down" economics has been transformed to the underclass's being "trickled on."

A Syracuse University researcher, Timothy M. Smeeding, cited research showing that European countries had made much greater progress in fighting poverty from 1983 to 1990, through national health care, universal cash payments to families with children, greater unemployment benefits, and better day care. He concluded that "we choose to tolerate more poverty than do other countries." The reality is that we don't even dare adopt the health plans and other benefits that even Francisco Franco brought to Spain decades ago.

Critics say our poor people won't work. This is a racist code phrase that cruelly ignores the agony of thousands of blacks waiting in bitter cold for a few hundred low-level jobs when a hotel opened in Chicago. The scene has been replicated countless times across America, but we seem to prefer to preserve our myths.

A book on America's schools reveals the educational inequalities that perpetuate and deepen the chasm between the over- and underclasses.[3] Manhasset, Long Island, a wealthy suburb, spends $15,000 on each student, while Manhattan spends about $7,300—and the disparities extend throughout the nation. The figures reflect white flight to the suburbs and the abandonment of blacks in the cities, and they also help to explain drop-out, pregnancy, welfare, and other rates that reflect fail-

---

[3] Jonathan Kozol, *Savage Inequalities*. New York: Crown, 1991.

ure. Can anyone believe that black kids don't know, or can't feel, they're being programmed for exclusion and defeat?

What more money buys is a better educational plant, more services and facilities, smaller class sizes, new textbooks, counselors, better paid teachers, special-education courses, athletic facilities, and other evidences that the community cares and that education matters.

In addition to the increased concentration of wealth among the rich, there has been a shift of wealth from young to old. The U.S. Census Bureau found that the poverty rate for the elderly rose from 11.4 percent in 1989 to 12.2 percent in 1990, but that it had been 29.5 percent in 1967. In that year, the poverty rate for children was 16.6 percent; it had risen to 20.6 percent by 1990.

A Federal Reserve Bank survey revealed the following: Home ownership, Medicare, and Social Security enhancements helped raise the asset value of households headed by those sixty-five and over to $218,000 at the same time that the asset value of those headed by someone under thirty-five declined to $38,600 from $45,700. In 1963, households headed by those over sixty-five made up 19 percent of the population and owned 26 percent of the wealth. In 1986, that group represented 21 percent of the population, but its share of the wealth had grown to 33 percent. This constitutes a global shift of wealth from the young to the old but still reflects a figurative redistribution of crumbs at the lower levels.

The top 20 percent of America's earners has not only continued to monopolize the economic pie, to the tune of about 80 percent of the gross national product, but has managed to increase its share over the past few years.

The Congressional Budget Office and other agencies have done studies illustrating the remarkable disparities created by the enrich-the-rich policies of the Reagan–Bush administrations from 1980 to 1992. Simply slicing the income tax at the higher levels and sharply increasing the Social Security tax created a transfer of wealth, from the poorer to the richer, of historic dimensions. This growing chasm made such terms as *overclass* and *underclass* routine descriptions of Americans, who once prided themselves on the egalitarianism of their society.

Such economic injustices become the swamps breeding the viruses of strife.

The breakup of the American family has meant that single parents (usually young women) with little children stand a very good chance of sliding precipitously down the economic chute. The most prosperous Americans continued to be married couples, with a poverty rate of 5.7 percent in 1990.

While other countries extend welfare, health, housing, educational, and related benefits to their poor—and help, thereby, to lift them out of poverty—we not only perpetuate inequities but increase them. Welfare, in fact, became the suicide word of American politics in the 1990s. The Census Bureau's figures reflect a growing number of Americans living below the poverty level, despite a decline from 25 million in 1970 to around 23 million in 1973 and 1974, the nadirs of the last quarter century. The number of the poor rose from just over 25 million in 1979 to over 34 million in 1992. The number of blacks in this status reached almost 10 million in 1990. Blacks have suffered poverty at about three times the rates of whites over that period.

As the 1990–1992 recession seemed to be coming to an end, there were 8.7 million unemployed, with an additional uncounted 1 to 2 million who were discouraged and no longer searching for jobs. Only 40 percent of the jobless were getting unemployment benefits, compared to 75 percent only fifteen years ago. Even the fast-food workers in the sixteen to nineteen-year-old age group (the highest contributors to street crime) were experiencing less employment than at any time since 1982. This problem, nevertheless, had been greatly reduced by the dearth of births following *Roe v. Wade* in 1973.

Poverty Levels[a]

Year	Percentage below poverty level		
	All races	White	Black
1959	18.5	15.2	48.1
1970	10.1	8.0	29.5
1975	9.7	7.7	27.1
1980	10.3	8.0	28.9
1985	11.4	9.1	28.7
1988	10.4	7.9	28.2

[a]U.S. Bureau of the Census

The unemployment rates not only reflect the historical disparity between whites and blacks but also demonstrate the worsening situation. Even these figures mask the plight of the working poor and those so discouraged they've dropped out of the hunt for a job altogether. The statistics, however, although limiting, are revealing in that they reflect the ability of policies of the government to affect the outcomes.

Unemployment Rates (Percentages)[a]

Year	Total (all)	White	Black
1970	3.3	3.1	4.7
1975	6.9	6.5	10.9
1980	5.0	4.4	9.6
1985	6.1	5.3	12.0
1988	4.7	4.0	10.0

[a]U.S. Bureau of Labor Statistics

WELFARE

With every state strapped for funds and forced to snip at budgets made even leaner by Washington's retreat from local issues, welfare became a popular target for the budget shapers.

The cruelty of the approach was exacerbated by already-existing disparities, with the result that tightfisted states exported their poor to more generous jurisdictions. While the sixteen states that pay the most and the five that pay the least all decreased their benefit rates in the period 1972–1991, such states as Alaska were granting over $13,000 in 1991, whereas Mississippi granted $4,764, according to a study by the House Ways and Means Committee.

The federal government's outlay for welfare for 1993 was estimated at $15.5 billion, or slightly more than the $12.5 billion destined for the maladroit War on Drugs. That the total for welfare was about 5 percent of the amount destined for defense didn't seem to trouble our leaders.

By 1990, the number of welfare families had reached a new record, and the individuals receiving assistance numbered over thirteen million, and growing. Even these figures, however, conceal the fact that only about two thirds of the children living beneath the poverty line are actually receiving this assistance. In 1973, four fifths of the eligible children received this aid.

Welfare was helping to drive males from the home; encouraging more births; doing nothing to foster accountability, responsibility, or self-help; nurturing a continuing dependence; and perpetuating the impoverished role of black womanhood.

Strangely, though, *Roe v. Wade* delivered the unexpected plus of reducing the average number of children in welfare families from three to two between 1972 and 1991.

As the debate heated, it became clear that a national program was needed, that it should be generous and comprehensive, and that it must include accountability from its recipients, to go to school or work, to bring order into their lives, and to strive to become independent and make contributions to society.

EDUCATION

The number of black high school graduates in college showed a sharp increase from 1960 to 1980, and a leveling off thereafter. The figures are particularly bleak in the case of black males.

High School Graduates in College[a]

Year	Total enrollment	White	Black	Black males	Hispanic
1960	2,279,000	2,138,000	141,000	68,000	n/a
1970	6,065,000	5,535,000	437,000	202,000	n/a
1980	7,475,000	6,546,000	718,000	292,000	325,000
1985	7,799,000	6,729,000	755,000	355,000	391,000
1987	7,932,000	6,677,000	855,000	390,000	463,000
1988	7,973,000	6,796,000	785,000	303,000	463,000

[a]U.S. Bureau of the Census

According to the American Council on Education, in 1976, 6.6 percent of all master's degrees went to blacks; only 4.6 percent were awarded to blacks in 1989. Only 811 doctorate degrees were conferred on blacks in 1989, compared to 1,056 earned in 1979. Slight rises in 1990 and 1991 failed to conceal the fact that blacks were being crammed into our prisons and excluded from our more desirable institutions.

According to the Census Bureau, while the percentage of sixteen- to twenty-four-year-old blacks without a high school diploma or a general equivalency degree declined steadily from 1970 (28 percent) to 14 percent in 1989 (still higher than the white rate), fewer went on to college (the numbers going to prison, however, increased so precipitously as to make the total incarcerated population substantially larger than the number in college), and their test scores have not risen as fast as those of whites. In 1992, the head of the National Urban League reported that "every indicator of economic well-being shows that African-Americans are doing far worse than whites."

THE FIRST YEARS

A twenty-three-year-old black who was a college football player and who had been featured in a documentary, titled *Survivors*, on kids who'd made it against great odds was found dead, with a bullet through his heart—a suicide, believed by his friends to have been caused by the sort of normal setbacks the rest of us, more carefully insulated against life's shocks, take as part of life's lesson.

He'd been beaten so frequently, and severely, by his mostly absent alcoholic father that he'd been orphaned into foster care, as a child, along with his brothers and sisters. He had grown up amid affection and caring from his foster mother but was moody and given to depression. Yet he worked hard and seemed focused and purposeful.

On the eve of his graduation, his girlfriend broke up with him. His hopes of a football career were dashed. He had, earlier, sought and received five months of psychiatric treatment, having been diagnosed as having suicidal-homicidal tendencies. He borrowed a handgun from a friend and shot himself in the chest. The autopsy revealed no drugs in his system. He left two notes: one for his girlfriend and the other for his foster mother.

His first few years had been hellish, but he'd spent the vast majority of his brief life in happier circumstances. However, his fate had, by then, been shaped. His life had been a futile search for a sense of belonging.

Endesha Ida Mae Holland, a forty-seven-year-old black playwright, stands in contrast to our tragic athlete because of her true survivor's instincts. Raised in a brothel run by her mother and uncertainly fathered by one of three men, she grew up in grinding poverty in Mississippi and had turned to prostitution to earn money.

Recruited by accident into the civil rights movement, she was radicalized and inspired sufficiently to motivate her to get a doctorate from the University of Minnesota and to become a tenured associate professor of American studies at the State University of New York at Buffalo. Her play *From the Mississippi Delta* was put on in the Circle-in-the-Square Theater in New York City in late 1991.

Could it be that, as in the movie *Citizen Kane*, the critical variable proved to be the affection of a natural mother in one case and the search for such love in the other?

By the early 1990s, many black males in America could look forward to rites of passage that included an absent father, living on welfare, dropping out of school, unemployment, addiction (to alcohol or drugs), going to prison, and, ultimately, dying violently.

THRASHING ABOUT FOR ANSWERS

One of the educational innovations of the nineties has been the creation of segregated all-black schools in which confidence and self-esteem are stressed.

In January 1991, Minneapolis began the Afro-Centric Educational Academy with thirty black students. They receive hugs and affection, are immersed in black culture and history, and are learning to connect with each other and take risks. The students spend the mornings in their home schools and the afternoons at the academy. The program includes grades 6, 7, and 8. Such basics as eye contact, no mumbling, and repetition of positive messages reinforce the academics.

Blacks form a third of over forty thousand public school students in Minneapolis and have lower test scores, lower grade-point averages, and higher rates of suspension, expulsion, and absenteeism than whites. The academy is a radical attempt to reverse the cycle of failure. It is still controversial. That it is being tried at all is a fitting measure of the desperation attending the issue of educating black youngsters. Other cities have adopted the approach despite the misgivings of the NAACP, which sees it as segregation's rebirth. The failures of the existing system have driven reformers to desperate measures.

Even successful programs are not guaranteed viability. They have to run the gauntlet of urban bureaucracies whose interests may be threatened, or they may get mired in local politics.

Parents and teachers created the Bronx New School in 1988 to serve a group of kindergarteners through second-graders, who would be one-third Hispanic, one-third black, and one-third white or "other," chosen by lot from among the school district's pupils. Grants were sought and additional teachers hired. The physical plant was refurbished and maintained. Children were to learn by doing, rather than by sitting in front of a blackboard. Strong parental involvement was required, and classes were conducted without textbooks. The school district's new superintendent labeled the school "rich" and "elitist" and moved to curb its growth through budget cuts. At the end of 1991, a determined band of parents and believing teachers were managing to keep the dream alive, but bureaucratic misgivings augured ill for the project's future.

Such black figures as Dick Gregory and General Colin Powell focus on the need for self-help, black community cohesion, and the working together of the black community in order to move forward. A small minority of blacks, like Supreme Court Justice Clarence Thomas, embrace conservatism and heap scorn on the very affirmative action programs that made their ascent possible. The stance might easily be labeled *bootstrappism*. Although certainly needed, this approach tends to let the government off the hook, while ignoring the very real historical disabilities that have led to the current crisis.

It must be conceded, however, that even within the Bush administration there were voices in the wilderness calling for programs to help the urban poor help themselves. These were offered under the rubric of *empowerment* and furthered by Housing and Urban Development Secretary Jack Kemp, who pushed for private ownership of public housing units by their tenants, and for entrepreneurial zones in the ghetto that would offer tax breaks to businesses that created jobs in the inner cities. Formerly a pariah in his own cabinet, Secretary Kemp's ideas were hugged, for lack of any other programs, by a reluctant Bush administration trying to answer the charges of neglect following the riots in Los Angeles.

This strategy constituted an attack on a major flank of the Democrats, who had monopolized the cause of the blacks and the poor. The appeal to the spirit of self-help, individual responsibility, and personal accountability that such programs contain is becoming increasingly attractive to such black leaders as Representative Mike Espy (Liberal Democrat of Mississippi) who see the future in terms of helping blacks help themselves out of poverty, as opposed to being granted doles.

EMPOWERMENT

The difficulty with the bootstrap, self-help theories offered under the formula of empowerment is that they provide a single, one-dimensional answer—although a useful part of a whole—to the hideously complex problems that face, most especially, the black poor in America. The superstrong salmon that successfully make it upstream, like the Colin Powells, actually serve the harmful purpose of convincing outsiders that many others could make it, too, in the current conditions. The reality is that these are the exceptions that prove the rule, rather than the paradigms for the future.

While the conservatives offer empowerment, the liberals offer doles that include housing, welfare, free education, and comprehensive medical care. This generous view ignores the need for the individual to exert himself or herself to get out of the poverty pit, and it fosters dependence.

As long as answers are provided without the discussion, tough exchanges, demonstrations, picketings, and other forms of the tortured debates that characterize the American Way of solving deep and complex problems, the nation is going to waste resources on ad hoc programs that won't work because they ignore vast reaches of the problems being attacked.

The unique nature of the black experience here suggests that the psychically disabling effects of uprootedness will require different remedies than those applied to assimilating other immigrant groups.

No doubt a broad, eclectic approach will emerge, but the debate must precede the prescription, or we will be left with the usual quick fixes favored by politicians. All of the approaches—"empowerment," "Black Power," "Afro-centered studies," "self-esteem development," welfare doles, enterprise zones, or whatever—hint at the possibility of a singularity and fragmentation that will not be resolved through the provision of clever programs or facile answers. Yet each of the answers speaks to some part of the problem and cannot be discarded without cost. The temptation to seize any one approach as the panacea will prove illusory, and worse. Dawn will bring the realization that the law of unintended effects has been set in motion as unexpected difficulties pop up elsewhere.

As the century nears its end, the once monolithic structure of black thinking is breaking up into more traditional liberal, moderate, and, surprisingly, conservative factions. Pushing "empowerment" programs gives the Republicans a vehicle for attracting conservative blacks who are suspicious of the debilitating effects of handouts and resistant to programs that tempt their people into self-loathing dependence. The appointment of Clarence Thomas, a black conservative, to the Supreme Court in 1991 melded perfectly with this strategy.

The disturbances in Crown Heights, Brooklyn, following an automobile accident in which a seven-year-old black boy was killed by an out-of-control car driven by a Hasidic Jew, illustrated the profound alienation of many blacks in the ghetto. A key quote in a *New York Times* story of September 8, 1991, was that many of the black youths interviewed said they "just didn't like white people." A passing Jewish scholar was stabbed to death hours after the tragic accident that took the boy's life, simply because he was a Jew, in the wrong place, at a tragically inopportune time.

There had been a simmering tension waiting for a focus. That the incident occurred in July of 1991 generated widespread fears of summer riots and impelled city officials and the mayor to institute a patrol of the streets and extraordinary measures to control, and precautions by the police and other agencies. The Los Angeles experience of a year later confirmed that their fears were not groundless.

Few issues so succinctly captured another of those unmentionable developments that has bedeviled the search for racial peace and progress as the double tragedy in Crown Heights. Here, the traditional role of Jews as champions of the black cause had been shelved. Forgotten were Goodman, Schwerner, and Chaney, bound together in common martyrdom and symbolizing the partnership that had attended Black–Jewish relations until both groups found it more convenient to lapse into their own self-interests and self-absorptions. They, and the rest of us, forgot that altruism would have to be a principal ingredient in any approach.

As New York approaches the Mayoral election in 1993 the Crown Heights divisions are becoming a battle for the Jewish votes as aspirants falsely accuse the really decent Mayor David Dinkins of anti-semitism.

What seems to be most needed is a latter-day Charles Dickens who can articulate the social problems in such dramatic and eloquent images as to capture society's elusive conscience. Black moviemakers and their movies, like John Singleton's *Boyz 'n the 'Hood*, Spike Lee's *Do the Right Thing* and the lesser *Jungle Fever*, Joe Vasquez's *Hangin' Out with the Homeboys*, and Matty Rich's *Straight Out of Brooklyn*, were serving as the antennae of the race as they depicted in vivid hues the problems faced by blacks in our society. Writers like Nicholas Lemann in *The Promised Land* and Alex Kotlowitz in *There Are No Children Here* also captured the dilemma facing America's underclass. Despite the eloquence and power of these messages, the giant has not stirred. It remains at dalliance with self-absorption and pleasure. The decay needs a more powerful muse to inspire the necessary action.

CRIME AND VIOLENCE IN THE
AFRICAN-AMERICAN COMMUNITY

The street crime problem in America is largely a black problem, as blacks are both perpetrators and victims. A brief sampling of recent statistics graphically paints the carnage:

- Black males have a 1-in-1,000 chance of becoming homicide victims (*New York Times*, December 7, 1990).
- Homicide is now the leading cause of death for black males aged fifteen to twenty-four (*New York Times*, December 7, 1990).
- Two thirds of homicides among blacks occur between family and friends (*American Medical News*, July 11, 1986).
- Black-on-black murder is the leading cause of death in black males aged fifteen to forty-four (*American Medical News*, July 11, 1986).
- More blacks lost their lives from black-on-black violence in 1981 than there were black men killed in the twelve years of the war in Vietnam (*American Medical News*, July 11, 1986).
- The percentage of violent crimes against blacks in which the offender had a gun (20 percent) was nearly twice the percentage of violent crimes in which whites were the victims (11 percent) (Bureau of Justice Statistics, April 1990).
- The proportion of robberies and aggravated assaults committed by an offender armed with a gun was higher for black victims than for white victims (29 percent vs. 17 percent for robberies; 36 percent vs. 29 percent for aggravated assault) (Bureau of Justice Statistics, April 1990).
- In 1986, black men were six times more likely to be homicide victims than white males, and black women were four times more likely to be homicide victims than white women (*The State of Black America*, "Preventing

Black Homicide," Carl C. Bell, M.D., National Urban League, 1989).

- 3.2 per 100,000 blacks compared to 2.3 per 100,000 whites experienced head-injury-associated deaths from firearms (*Journal of Neuropsychiatry,* "Neuropsychiatry and Gun Safety," Carl C. Bell, M.D., 1989).
- Gunshot wounds among young black men caused more than 80 percent of the deaths and accounted for 96 percent of the recent increase in homicides from 1984 to 1987 (*Wall Street Journal,* December 7, 1990).
- The American Academy of Pediatrics reported that gunshot wounds among children in urban areas increased 300 percent from 1986 to 1988 (Center to Prevent Handgun Violence, April 1989).

The slide of black males into the despondency of crime is vividly shown in the censuses of prisoners undertaken by the federal government since 1926. The black population rose from 11 million in 1926 to 29 million in 1986 (a 2.6-fold increase), while the white population went from about 100 million to 200 million. Whereas blacks were just over one fifth of the prisoners in 1926, their proportion had risen to almost half by the 1990s.

VICTIMIZATIONS

The Department of Justice's National Crime Survey revealed that, between 1979 and 1986, blacks experienced higher rates of violent and household crime victimization than whites, and that the crimes tended to be more serious against blacks.

Males, the poor, younger persons, and central-city residents (which were 56 percent black and 24 percent white) have been consistently shown to have higher victimization rates than others, and blacks, of course, fit disproportionately into most of these categories.

The violent crime rate from 1979 to 1986 was 44 victims per 1,000 for blacks and 34 victims per 1,000 for whites. Robbery rates were 18 victimized per 1,000 for black males and 7 for white males. Assailants were almost twice as likely to have a gun when attacking a black than when attacking a white (20 percent vs. 11 percent), and blacks were more likely to suffer injury.

The study did not include murder, the leading cause of death among black males in early adulthood.

Small wonder that the black community is schizophrenic about the police: fearing and hating them as an army of occupation representing their own oppressors, yet desperately needing them to provide tenuous protection against the surrounding violence. In the circumstances, the phrase "law and order" has become, despite the blacks' fervent desire for it, merely code words that mask what might be called a white plot to keep the underclass under control and out of sight.

The Federal Center for Disease Control found that the homicide rate for black men between fifteen and twenty-four rose 66 percent from 1984 to 1988. This increase was doubtless powered by the peaking of the crack epidemic. More than half the murder victims were black in 1989, the first time black victims outnumbered whites. The amazing statistic was repeated in 1990.

Just to deprive the racist of a likely refuge, it should be noted that, when last studied, the homicide rate in some sections of black Africa was about the same as the homicide rate in Western Europe and well below the rate in either white or black America. It is pretty clear that the high incidence of murder and violence among black males in the United States is related to the unique nature of their experience here.[4]

American black males are being imprisoned at the rate of 3,109 per 100,000, while the rate in South Africa is 729 per 100,000. In the United States, black males constitute 455,000 of

[4] Nikki Meredith, "The Murder Epidemic," *Science*, December 1984.

the 1 million prison and jail inmates, and 1 in 4 is under such criminal justice controls as probation, parole, community service, fine, house arrest, jail, or prison. Of those arrested in 1989 in drug roundups, 41 percent were black.

Even in areas, such as athletics, where blacks are generally held to be well off, the facts reveal the exploitation and frustration of the overwhelming majority. Society focuses on the few successes. Too many black athletes are admitted to college with inadequate preparation (Scholastic Aptitude Test scores of 700), don't graduate, and emerge illiterate. Very few make it to the pros.

Widely disparate studies in dramatically different areas have converged to confirm the growing plight of blacks.

A historic low in general Scholastic Aptitude Test scores in 1991 was found to conceal a startling dichotomy. A "disturbing pattern of educational disparity" was found between the top performing students (the white overclass) and the general student population (the rest): The students destined for success (the white elite) scored an average of nearly 100 points higher than the rest. Black students' scores declined, and some attributed the decline to less rigorous academic standards, less time spent reading at home and in schools, and too much television and too many videos.

In an August 8, 1991, *New York Times* quote, Donald T. Stewart, President of the College Board, said, "If this kind of dichotomy continues, we could evolve into a nation divided between a small class of educational elite and an underclass of students academically ill-prepared for the demands of college or the workplace."

Tennis star Arthur Ashe created the African-American Athletic Association to rescue "a generation of young Black males [that] is being totally written off." The program envisions examining the areas of government budget cuts; exploring the effects of the sponsorship of athletic events by liquor and tobacco firms; providing male models, through mentoring and counseling; and preparing youngsters for employment.

In a July publication by the National Bureau of Economic Research, John Bound of the University of Michigan and Richard Freeman of Harvard reported that the drive for economic equality had stalled in the mid-seventies. While the gap in weekly earnings between white and black men had narrowed, from 35 percent in 1963 to just 11 percent in 1975, by 1989 it had widened to 18 percent. In 1973, the black–white gap in employment rates was 9 percentage points, and by 1989, it had increased to 15 percent.

The myth of the growing black middle class took a blow with the finding that black college graduates had done especially poorly in the economic sweepstakes, as the differences widened three times faster than the gap for high school graduates and six times faster than the gap for dropouts. There were small, isolated glimmers of progress, but the overall picture was bleak.

The researchers concluded that blacks had had the misfortune of being in the wrong place, in the wrong jobs, at the wrong time. They had tended to have minimum-wage jobs when the minimum wage was eroding, and a disproportionate number were union members at a time of declining union power. Jobs in the blue-collar and manufacturing industries, where blacks tended to appear in large numbers, were being savaged by foreign competition. The researchers found that the enormous increase in the numbers of blacks in prison or on probation contributed hugely to black unemployment. Reductions in the military would make the problem much worse as the Cold War ended.

Many of the economic trends were seen to be stabilizing or reversing, sparking hope for a brighter future.

Racism did not surface as a factor in either the Harvard or the Michigan studies, but this is a logical absurdity.

A number of ironies or seeming contradictions have surfaced since the efforts of the late sixties to attack the problems of a segregated and economically bifurcated society. The first and foremost finding must be that blacks have not assimilated into American society, after over 370 years here, nor has their situation improved very markedly since slavery and Jim Crow. Since the early 1970s, their situation has grown demonstrably worse, and we have the crime, addiction, and imprisonment figures to prove it. Besides not being as rich, educated, or well housed as whites, blacks are not even as safe.

The statistics, though, tell only part of the story, although a critically important part. Decisions about blacks, by whites, across the spectrum of human activities, may be driven by hatred and fear. Many whites succumb to the temptation to feel bigger by thinking others smaller, and many whites simply fear blacks, an emotion that invariably produces harmful consequences.

Blacks want and need more law and order than any other group in our society. But they don't need it as an excuse for racist oppression. They need the police but fear police abuses. They've seen "law and order" used as the Trojan Horse of oppression.

Debating the plight of blacks will certainly provide racists with ammunition related to the appalling facts about education, jobs, family stability, crime incidence, and other indices of failure, but do the white supremacists really need any ammunition? Can't they invent what doesn't come readily to hand? And has any American problem ever given way without a full and informed debate about its origins and possible cures?

Since the early sixties, we have seen the explosive growth of the homeless; a dramatically widening disparity between the rich and the poor; worsening conditions for blacks; no abatement of racism; and rising crime levels and enormously swelling incarceration rates. The seventies and eighties have also seen the rise of black political power in the cities and the elimination of legal barriers to full participation in America's life. In general, though, the plight of the largely black underclass has worsened on all fronts.

Despite the rapidly deteriorating conditions of safety and the now routine admissions of editorialists that blacks are responsible for most street crimes, there is no move to expend such material and intellectual resources on the problem as were assigned to the Myrdal and Civil Disorder Commission studies. We simply don't want to be bothered, though we do want to be safe.

The issue is germane to our discussion because of the impact of blacks on crime, violence, urban riots, and drug trafficking in America. If we are the Dr. Frankensteins behind such monsters as Willie Horton, we are going to have to recognize that what we are looking at is really the White Problem.

Chapter Seven

GUNS

Guns don't kill people; people kill people.
    —The National Rifle Association

A well regulated militia, being necessary to the security of
a free State, the right of the people to keep and bear arms,
shall not be infringed.
    —Second Amendment of the U.S. Constitution

Most Americans believe they have an absolute, constitutionally guaranteed right to own a gun. Although the courts have long held that the right to bear arms is limited and is subject to controlling legislation, citizens overwhelmingly believe that the right to bear arms is unconditional. As a result, the National Rifle Association (NRA) has found that including the phrase "the right to bear arms" in proposed referendums virtually ensures their being approved by a majority of voters. Thus, the electorate sees no harm in passing amendments to their state constitutions that grant the absolute right to bear arms, omitting the critical reference to a "well regulated militia."

    This belief, of course, flies in the teeth of polls that consistently show a voter preference for reasonable restrictions on firearms. The anomaly places liberals in the awkward position of having to fight against placing on the ballot easily misunderstood proposals relating to the right to bear arms. When Americans are asked if they have an absolute constitutional right to bear arms they consistently—and mistakenly—say yes. This is a key flaw in the democratic process, one that has been very profitably exploited by demagogues who seek to turn a representative democracy into a direct one when it suits their purposes.

As of the mid-eighties, thirty-seven states had right-to-bear-arms provisions in their constitutions, and one other included such a provision in its laws. Although it is common practice, on state constitutional issues, to adopt the language of the federal Constitution, in this case, because of the National Rifle Association's wariness over the wording, only seven state constitutions contain any reference to a "militia." Maine's provision reads, "Every citizen has a right to keep and bear arms for the common defense, and this right shall never be questioned," but even this sweeping provision has been held to have its limits. The Maine Supreme Court held that a law preventing a convicted felon from purchasing a handgun did not violate this provision.

It is now well established in case law that the Second Amendment applies to the need for a "well regulated militia" and that the legislatures can pass laws restricting the manufacture, sale, ownership, or use of firearms (*U.S. v. Miller*, 307 U.S. 174, 178, 1939). No federal court in history has overturned a gun law on Second Amendment grounds.[1] This consensus has been affirmed twice by the U.S. Supreme Court (*Burton v. Sills*, 394 U.S. 812, 1968, and *Lewis v. U.S.*, 445 U.S. 55, 1980).

Despite the constitutional authority to restrict weaponry, we are awash in guns and the violence they cause.

---

[1] Dennis Henigan, "Exploding the N.R.A.'s Constitutional Myth," *Legal Times*, April 22, 1991, p. 22.

THE HEADLINES

We are the only nation on earth whose readers regularly awaken to such headlines as:

Stray Bullets in 3 Shootings Kill 2 Women and Wound 5
Laid-Off Employee Kills 2 at Workplace
Restaurateur Again Shoots Robber Dead
14 Year Old Fatally Shot in Head by Youth Playing with Handgun
Young Author Dies in Tragic Shooting
Suspect Bought 2 Guns 10 Days before Shootings
2 Killed and 5 Injured in Shootings at Restaurants
Houston Father Photographed, Then Killed Family, Police Say
Jersey City Policeman Shot in Face as Robbers Hold Up Jewelry Store
2 Are Slain and 2 Wounded by Gunmen in Store Hold Up
Slain Vet's Mom to Leave City That's "Out of Control"
Girl, 10, Shot in Head at Play and Man Wounded in the Bronx
Schoolyard Gunman Kills a 15 Year Old
2 Are Shot Dead and 3 Are Hurt after a Collision
Armed Man Gains Entrance to Senate Hearing Room
Navy Officer Fatally Shot at Pentagon
Bystander Killed in School Shooting
Six Dead in Gunfire at Mall

Brutal personal tragedies are concealed behind these messages.

INCIDENTS

A number of awful gun incidents, such as the killing of little children in a Stockton, California, schoolyard, have sparked a movement toward reform that gun control opponents like President George Bush deflected into meaningless, if heated, debates over assault weapons, waiting periods, reducing the number of bullets allowed in a magazine, and imposing mandatory sentences for gun crimes.

In the waxing-waning wars on guns in the United States, a predictable cycle surfaced. The first part featured an awful event, such as the 1966 Texas Tower killing of fifteen by Charles Whitman; the shooting of George Wallace in 1972, following the 1968 assassinations of Robert F. Kennedy and Martin Luther King; the California McDonald's massacre of twenty-one children and adults by James Huberty, using an Uzi semiautomatic rifle, a semiautomatic pistol, and a 12-gauge shotgun; the 1988 invasion of a Winnetka, Illinois, schoolroom by Laurie Dann, who killed one girl and injured ten others; and the Stockton, California, killing of five little schoolchildren in January 1989. (The American record was set in 1991 in Killeen, Texas, when a berserk gunman with a Glock 17 killed twenty-two people and himself. Less than three weeks later, a University of Iowa doctoral candidate shot and killed five others, before killing himself.) Such tragedies have usually been followed by a storm of demands for tighter restrictions on guns, after which the dust has settled before the next killings.

The shooting of President Ronald Reagan on March 30, 1981, produced the Joan of Arc of the gun safety movement in the form of Press Secretary James Brady's wife, Sarah. She lent a permanent presence to the struggle for sensible firearm reforms. Her husband had been severely wounded in the attack on the president. Within a decade, she became the logo, lightning rod, and the inspiration for the advocates of gun safety. The shooter, John W. Hinckley, Jr., had a history of mental illness and had bought the gun, over-the-counter, in a Texas shop that accepted his faked registration form without cavil or question.

The armaments race that Americans have conducted with each other has produced casualties across the spectrum of human experience.

ACCIDENTS

Typical of the ghastly tragedies sometimes accompanying guns in the home was the 1992 New Year's Day shooting of a four-year-old boy. He was the grandson of a Mexican immigrant who fired the gun in the air, to celebrate the New Year, and simply put it down where the toddler could find it and shoot himself in the chest.

The tragedy was compounded by the grandfather's arrest under a law that had taken effect just ten hours earlier, which makes adults who negligently store loaded weapons within reach of children criminally liable if the child is injured or killed. The penalty is three years in jail and a $10,000 fine.

Now, though her child was dead, his mother had to plead for her father's release, and he had to live with the knowledge that he was responsible for his grandson's death. The case was a latter-day Greek tragedy.

SUICIDE

Although the focus may be on outward-directed violence, which is the principal cause of fear in America, the statistics on self-directed violence—suicide—are so striking as to command a passing reference.

Of the 31,091 firearms deaths in the United States in 1984, 55 percent were suicides. Firearm suicides outnumbered firearm homicides in forty of the fifty years between 1933 and 1982. Firearms accounted for 58 percent of the 29,453 suicides in 1984![2] Handguns have been preferred, by an enormous preponderance, over rifles or shotguns.

Increases in the rate of suicide between 1962 and 1975 paralleled increases in the availability of firearms. Suicide by

---

[2] Myron Boor and Jeffrey H. Bair, "Suicide Rates, Handgun Control Laws and Socio-Demographic Variables," *Psychological Reports*, 1990.

firearms rise from 4.9 to 7.1 per 100,000 population between 1953 and 1978, while suicides by other methods remained virtually unchanged. Suicide rates are lower in states with stringent handgun control laws for purchasers and sellers; the rate is intermediate in states restricting either the buyer or the seller, but not both; and it is the highest in the states with few or no laws pertaining to either buyers or sellers of handguns. Divorce rates and crime rates are also important predictors of higher suicide rates.[3] The rates of completed suicides is, of course, much higher when guns are used.

People buy guns for self-protection and find that the weapons may be used in many unintended ways.

THE FACES BEHIND THE GUNS

The crime and violence in the ghetto are spawning tender-aged, cold-eyed killers. The *U.S. News and World Report* of April 8, 1991, described one fifteen-year-old who coolly splattered a man's brains over a drug money deal gone bad. The boy was an enforcer for a drug ring. The article cited the reasons behind the escalating violence as being the influence of Rambo images in the media, the creation by poverty and homelessness of a "nothing-to-lose" attitude, and family breakdowns and problems in school, but "by far the biggest difference ... is that the no-problem availability of guns in every nook of the nation has turned record numbers of everyday encounters into deadly ones."

A Bureau of Justice Statistics study concluded that assailants armed with handguns committed 639,000 violent crimes annually from 1979 to 1987. In each of those years, more than 9,000 of those crimes were murders. Of the 6.7 million violent crimes committed each year, 2.3 million involve the use of weapons, with handguns accounting for 27 percent of this total.

---

[3] National Center for Health Statistics.

Handguns are the most commonly used weapon in suicide, accounting for almost 13,000 such deaths in 1986. About 1,200 are killed accidentally each year with handguns.

Where do all these guns come from?

SOURCES OF GUNS

The source of all this weaponry is another matter in hot dispute, as the NRA, ignoring all the evidence other nations have amassed, continues to hold that criminals will always be able to get guns and that all that gun control laws do is to disarm honest persons. The odds against the possession of a gun by a mugger or burglar, or a rapist, in Europe or Asia are astronomically high. A victim can virtually be sure that his attacker doesn't have a deadly weapon almost anywhere but in the United States, and one is tempted to ask the NRA, "Where do all those body bags and riddled bodies come from, anyway?" Unfortunately, our weapons are now radiating to other countries in the drug chain, where they sell for fancy prices. Still, other nations have found that controlling a product like guns is much easier than dealing with others, like drugs or alcohol, for which there is an insatiable appetite. We add to other countries' problems by failing to control gun production, and thereby encouraging traffic in firearms.

A 1985 National Institute of Justice survey of 1,874 convicted felons in eleven state prisons found that 44 percent had acquired their most recent handguns from family and friends, 26 percent from fences and drug dealers, and 21 percent from legitimate retail outlets. There is a lucrative trade in buying handguns in states like Virginia, Florida, Texas, and Ohio, and selling them in states like New York and Massachusetts, which have tough gun laws. The profit ratio is usually around 300 percent to 400 percent.

A particularly cheap handgun, the Raven MP-25, costs a California manufacturer, the Jennings family, $13.00 to produce.

It is sold to wholesalers for $29.75, and a gun shop buys it for $33 to 35 and retails it for $59 to $70. Illegal traffickers purchase it and resell it on the street for as much as $300.

Ruben Floyd was a Purdue University linebacker who started buying semiautomatics at the Loading Bench and another sports store in Canton, Ohio, in April 1990. Ohio requires neither a waiting period nor a background check for handgun purchases. At first, he bought two or three handguns at a time, but he was soon wiping out the store's stock with purchases of twenty to thirty each visit.

Floyd lived in a drug-infested neighborhood in northeast Philadelphia and sold the guns to crack dealers and drug gangs. At least 86 weapons were bought by him in Ohio, and a total of 140 firearms were imported by him into Philadelphia. He trafficked in light, easily concealed pistols and Uzi look-alikes, much favored by drug dealers. The markups were from $250 for a $50 pistol, to $500 for a more powerful $200 weapon. The proliferation of weapons made the area a war zone, and there was a rash of shootings.

The Floyd investigation was stymied because Congress had barred the Bureau of Alcohol, Tobacco, and Firearms (BATF) from establishing a computerized data base of gun purchases. Such a data base would be a "precursor to confiscation" according to James Jay Baker, chief lobbyist for the NRA, and its pusillanimous congressional allies were pleased, as usual, to go along.

Testifying before the House Select Committee on Narcotics Abuse and Control on April 20, 1988, Associate Director Phillip C. McGuire of the BATF described how one suspect bought 79 firearms in the Virginia area between July 1986 and October 1987; 4 of these handguns turned up in New York City narcotics investigations. One group that included military personnel bought 150 guns for the streets of New York. Another suspect bought 84 guns during an eighteen-month period, and 6 surfaced in drug-related cases in New York, Baltimore, and the District of Columbia. These "straw-man" purchases constitute an important source of weaponry. Another source is guns stolen from private dwellings during burglaries, and a more recent popular approach has been to burglarize usually secure gun shops. This kind of burglary gets the criminals right into the original supply source.

So many bullets flying around have created a new genre of victim, the so-called mushroom, or innocent bystander, struck down by errant lead. Babies asleep in their cribs in public housing projects, where the sound of gunfire is a nightly reality, have been senselessly slaughtered. A pious woman, innocently heading for her Pentecostal church, was shot in the head and killed while riding in the van the church had purchased to protect its parishioners. A neighbor reported that his nephew had also been shot and killed at the precise location. Mrs. Antron had been helping to plan a rally against the senseless killings in the area when she became a victim on August 23, 1991. The rally, scheduled for August 24, was canceled. The newspapers delicately omitted references to anything as trivializing as "mushroom," but experienced urban dwellers could fill in the spaces without help.

SELF-PROTECTION

Americans buy handguns to protect themselves in a violent society, and it has to be admitted that there are instances in which the purchase has worked as intended. It would be both foolish and wrong to deny the episodic, if rare, efficiency of force or the occasional value of a weapon. The point is to assess the odds and make a rational choice. In the case of handguns, the evidence is overwhelming, both nationally and internationally, that purchasing a firearm for personal safety is a step taken in vain. The presence of a gun in the home is a bigger menace to its occupants than to any intruder.

Big-city residents are more than twice as likely to be victimized by guns as their suburban neighbors and more than three times as likely as people living in rural areas. A study in King County, Washington, revealed that, of 398 firearms deaths in residences, only 2 involved the shooting of an intruder. Another study of robberies in Chicago indicated that attempts to resist place the victim at much greater risk of being injured or killed. Moreover, a study in Albany, New York, of assaults and murders, found that the victims were more likely to be killed if they drew a weapon.[4]

The National Crime Survey of 1979–1985 estimated that, in 386,000 instances, victims of assault and robbery defended themselves with a gun, an annual average of 55,000. This is a tiny percentage of the millions of crimes during that period, and it ignores the dangers that the presence of a weapon poses, even to the target of the crime who is actually holding a gun. It also ignores the much larger numbers of guns that had been bought for self-protection, and that were stolen and used in crimes, as well as the suicides and accidents involving such weapons.

No reasonable person could hold, however, that the ownership of a handgun should be banned in all circumstances. The objective ought to be severe restriction of licensing to only the most imperative needs.

Any restricting legislation should be national, and it ought to include guidelines for the issuance of permits to carry guns only to those who can demonstrate an extraordinary need, who have been trained in the use of the weapon, and who have exhibited proficiency in its use. Such licensees might be persons in imminent danger who can't be afforded the needed protections by the State. One category might be the stalked woman with an order of protection from a murderous or obsessed hunter.

Our system is notably indifferent to the dangers faced by potential and likely future victims. It ought to acknowledge its

[4] Garen J. Wintemute *et al.*, "Reducing Firearm Injuries," *Issues in Science and Technology*," Spring 1991.

responsibility to provide protection or effective means of self-protection. An adamant stand against all weapons, in all circumstances, plays into the hands of the NRA apologists, who can cite the occasional use of a weapon in self-defense.

Any student of gun violence immediately recognizes the need of one uniform law for the nation, as opposed to the balkanization that has been the historical rule and that has enabled the NRA to whipsaw the various jurisdictions into accommodation.

NATIONAL LEGISLATION

The United States made two serious attempts at gun control legislation: a 1934 post-Prohibition law putting a tax on machine guns, silencers, bombs, grenades, bazookas, and rifles, and a 1968 law following the assassinations of Martin Luther King, Jr., and Robert F. Kennedy, in which gun dealers doing business across state lines were required to get a federal license and keep records, and in which sales to convicted violent felons and drug addicts were forbidden.

Otherwise, the field has been left to the states, which have created a confused mosaic of prohibitions and freedoms, unlike the regulation of autos, which is quite uniform and reciprocal, despite being state controlled. Gun buyers have, as a result, been put to the small inconvenience of traveling to adjoining jurisdictions if their state has tough gun laws.

In desperate attempts to reduce the proliferation of weapons, some jurisdictions have offered a fifty-dollar bounty for any surrendered firearm, no questions asked. That the guns aren't traced, nor the surrenderers listed, troubles many, who worry that the police may be taking in guns that have been used in crimes or stolen from others. St. Louis, New York, and Minneapolis all, however, seemed pleased with the large numbers of impressive guns taken off the streets by this amnesty program. Minneapolis collected over six thousand firearms in a well-publicized thirty-day effort in February 1992.

In the meantime, though, President Ronald Reagan, ironically the target of a shooter himself but still an NRA supporter, provided gun lovers with relief by signing, in 1986, legislation easing the provisions of the landmark Gun Control Act of 1968. His actions were of a piece with America's historical approach to firearms.

EARLY HISTORY

The passage of the Second Amendment was one of many manifestations of the colonists' suspicion of centralized authority. They wanted to ensure that the states would be able to have an armed militia, with which they could counter a central government's professional army, if necessary.

Nevertheless, the constitutional argument waxes hot, and the effectiveness of the NRA's position can be read in the American people's belief that the law of the land does indeed afford them the right to keep and bear arms, despite the myriad laws restricting gun ownership, and despite even their own belief in, and support of, reasonable restrictions.

Colonial Americans kept and used firearms to hunt, to meet real or imagined threats from the Indians, and to fight the British. Thus, the use of guns is rooted in our earliest history as well as connected to hallowed traditions and myths. Where rulers had seen fit to restrict firearms ownership in Europe, in America the gun came to be seen as the essential tool of the free citizen. It is estimated that, by 1774, the country could raise a citizen militia of half a million men, an armed force larger than any in Europe.

As gun ownership began to be seen as a threat to established order, laws were passed banning slaves and aliens from possessing firearms. The conquest of the frontier, however, came at the end of a six-shooter. In the 1830s and 1840s,

Texans fought Mexicans and Comanches and pushed for the development of a repeat-firing gun. Colt obliged with the .45 Peacemaker, the six-shooter that became the symbol of the American West.

America's love affair with its guns has continued throughout its history. The bloody mayhem of the Civil War was followed by westward expansion and the romantic myths of the Wild West. The gun became the talisman of the age, dispensing magical justice with invisible bullets. Hollywood and pulp fiction writers glamorized the scene with a series of classics on Tombstone, Abilene, and Dodge City. These were followed by the gangster genre of the Roaring Twenties. The scenes changed, but the constant was the guns. In the West, it had been the Colt .45, and in Chicago, it was the Thompson machine gun.

Television extended the mythology to the present.

The battle over the gun that Jack Ruby used to kill Lee Harvey Oswald in 1963 illustrates the iconography surrounding these weapons. The .38 Colt Cobra fetched $220,000 in a December 1991 auction in New York City. The winning bidder was an unidentified collector from New Jersey. Ruby's brother sold the gun to clear up tax debts on his brother's estate and to make a profit.

Along with the glamorizing and publicizing of the "heroics" involving guns, evidence began to trickle in that the glamorizers may have also been inspiring violence. Television, the most influential medium of our age, was found, in a 1982 National Institute of Mental Health study, to share responsibility with such other factors as poverty, drugs, and guns for the scale of violence in the country. The report concluded that "violence on television does lead to aggressive behavior by children and teenagers who watch the programs."

Follow-up studies confirmed these findings and cited the thousands of murders observed by children watching television even before they enter high school. Today, a kid can play a video arcade game that requires the killing of cops to get to the next level. A 1991 symposium of the American Psychological Association had twenty children from Washington, D.C., draw pictures depicting their daily lives. All twenty had guns in them.

Our young grow up in a milieu that extols violence and depicts it vividly through powerful media images. Rambo and Terminator movies illustrate the genre. These young people are not only the inheritors of a violent culture but the daily witnesses of its salience in the nation's life. Adding the ready availability of firearms to this equation greatly enhances the prospect of further violence.

One result is that America is an unsafe place for women. Another is that it is probably the world's most dangerous place for black males. And the kicker is that most of the violence is probably preventable through gun control, and other countries have shown the way.

AMERICA'S UNIQUE STATUS

Embarrassingly, America has emerged as unique in its toleration of firearms. Historian Richard Hofstadter wrote, "The U.S. is the only modern industrial urban nation that persists in maintaining a gun culture."[5]

Australia and Canada, both with frontier traditions much like ours, have tough gun laws and few gun deaths. Japan, with a militaristic and aggressive samurai tradition, has tight firearms restrictions, as does Israel, a nation regarded as riddled with violence. One of the occasional headlines during the Intifada, or uprising, on Israel's West Bank was "Palestinian Stabs Three Israelis." The key word, usually overlooked, was *stabs*. Even well-organized, long-standing revolutionaries find it next to impossible to secure firearms in the midst of their insurrection.

[5] Richard Hofstadter and Wallace Michael, eds., *American Violence: A Documentary History*. New York: Random House, 1971.

In 1988, handguns killed 7 in Great Britain; 19 in Sweden; 53 in Switzerland; 25 in Israel; 13 in Australia; 8 in Canada; and 8,915 in the United States. Far more Americans have been killed by handguns than have been lost in all our wars. Suicide and accident rates are also much lower in the other countries because of the unavailability of firearms there.

Switzerland, however, pursues the American mistake of local legislative approaches, which allows some cantons to permit the purchase even of submachine guns, by locals or foreigners, without a permit. One predictable result has been a small but frightening spate of multiple slayings since 1989.

For example, on March 4, 1992, a man knocked on doors and shot his neighbors with a semiautomatic rifle. At the rampage's end, the thirty-seven-year-old had killed six and wounded six before giving up. The motive was unclear, but he had known the victims. The event terrified the country and brought forth calls for national gun-control legislation.

There was a total of 4,937 murders in 1989 in West Germany, England, Wales, Italy, and France, which have a combined population equal to that of the United States. That works out to about 2 murders per 100,000 people. That same year the United States had 18,954 murders, or 8.7 per 100,000, and more than 60 percent were committed with firearms. By 1991, America's murders exceeded 24,000.

France, which, like Belgium, permits over-the-counter sales of firearms, had 5 murders per 100,000 in 1989. West Germany, with tough firearms laws and very tough penalties for their use, had less than 1 murder per 100,000 people. Firearms were used in 46 percent of the French murders, in 13 percent of those in West Germany, and in less than 7 percent of those in England and Wales.

The twelve European Community nations, excepting France and Belgium, either ban or strictly license all firearms. Frankfurt, a German city about the size of Washington, D.C., has about 20 to 30 homicides a year, compared to 489 in 1991 in our nation's capital.

The Scandinavian countries have extremely tight gun rules, and Sweden even denied gun permits to El Al Airlines' security personnel. This was believed to be the reason that the airline discontinued service to Stockholm several years ago.[6]

With only the partial exception of the two countries in Europe, the United States stands alone in its criminal tolerance of weaponry, and even in France and Belgium, guns haven't proved to be particularly serious problems. In New York City, twenty-one schools had weapons detectors in 1991, as a result of 2,170 weapons possession incidents in the 1990–1991 school year.

A front-page story in the August 16, 1991, issue of the *New York Times* announced the "Return of the Highwayman: Tourists Are Prey in Europe" and went on to describe how travelers that summer were being held up on the roads and having their train sleeping compartments burglarized, especially in France and Spain. Although the statistics were imprecise, the story reported 1,200 thefts on French trains in 1991 and more than 200 highway robberies north of Barcelona.

Among the key phrases in the article were "Violence is rarely involved," and "The assailants are usually armed with a knife, a screwdriver and, at times, with a can of Mace . . ."

Again, as in the reporting of the assaults on Israelis. by members of the Palestine Liberation Organization, the central factor was the omission of any reference to guns. The *Times* story failed to make a single reference to any firearm. Guns just weren't there, not even when serious crimes were taking place.

There are occasional stories of rising drug use abroad, accompanied by alarmed quotes from high police officials about a frightening trend toward increased firepower by traffickers.

First, we must recognize that police officials take in such phrases as "viewing with heightened alarm" with mother's milk. We should recognize these as the reflex posturings of the

---

[6] Don Moldea, "The N.R.A. Goes to War with Itself," *Regardie's*, April 1987.

profession and, while not rejecting the views out of hand, at least assume enough skepticism to look for the figures behind the assessments.

Thus, when the British police decried rising levels of armaments and violence in connection with an expanding drug trade, as reported in the *New York Times* on October 25, 1991, we need to examine the figures driving the hysteria and place them in perspective. In this case, the problem that was "now growing at an alarming rate" turned out to be that guns had been involved in "barely 3% of all serious crime in Britain."

The worldwide increase in the use of cocaine, heroin, and other hard drugs has, no doubt, led to increased levels of crime and violence. There is equally little doubt that Britain's tough handgun laws are sparing that nation untold, and uncounted (at least by police officials who like to "view with alarm") grief. No one seems to focus on the number of tragedies that have failed to take place because of gun restrictions. At the end of 1991, less than 10 percent of London's police (2,500 officers) were authorized to carry weapons.

The alarms need to be raised and considered, and they also need to be examined coldly and with an appreciation of the blessings of prevention.

GUNS AND CRIME

Ours is an extraordinarily armed society. Our armaments race with ourselves outpaces anything on the international scene. The Bureau of Alcohol, Tobacco and Firearms (BATF) estimates that private citizens possessed 200 million firearms of all types, including 66,666,000 handguns; 72,739,000 rifles; 62,432,000 shotguns; and 3 million semiautomatic assault-type weapons.

This arsenal is continually expanding through the efforts of the small arms industry.

THE U.S. FIREARMS INDUSTRY

The Bureau of the Census reported only 144 manufacturers of small arms in the United States and 13,300 people employed in the industry as of 1987, the last year for which figures are available. Two giants, DuPont's Remington Arms Corp. and Tomkins Corporation's Smith & Wesson, accounted for almost half the $1.1 billion in sales to private citizens, the military, and law enforcement.

Smith & Wesson and Sturm, Ruger & Co. produce almost two thirds of the handguns manufactured in the United States. Labor strife and organizational problems reduced the involvement of Colt Industries in the late eighties.

Because of the durability of its product, the gun industry has not experienced explosive growth. The sales and production figures clearly reflect the fears triggered by rising unrest and crime in the seventies and the purchase of handguns for self-protection. Such events as the Los Angeles riot of 1992 sparked a frenzy of gun purchases by frightened residents.

The manufacture of all firearms has grown enormously from a 1950 total of just over 2 million shotguns, rifles, and handguns to a 1975 total of over 6 million such guns. Production declined in the early eighties but resumed, rising thereafter to a 1989 peak of over 5 million. The major long-gun manufacturer in 1990 was Remington Arms, with 564,609 rifles and shotguns, and the leading producer of handguns, domestically, was Smith & Wesson, with 450,647. The leading manufacturer of both long guns and concealable firearms was Sturm, Ruger, with a total of 631,093, about evenly distributed between long and short guns.

THE TOP TEN GUN PRODUCERS

One of the ironic fallouts of the gun control debate was the passage of regulations and laws creating higher standards for imported firearms than for those locally produced. Thus have "free traders" in Washington turned the anxieties of Americans into protectionism for local gunmakers. Adding to the irony, is the absence of a separate lobbying arm by this industry, which apparently, and not without justification, feels itself well served by the National Rifle Association's efforts in the capital.

Domestic firearm production came to 1.8 million pistols and revolvers and 1.7 million rifles and shotguns in 1990. President Bush's embargo on foreign-made assault weapons that year and the fears of citizens anxious to protect themselves from rising levels of criminality and riots led to frantic purchases of these weapons. From 1985 to 1989 an additional 17,838,000 firearms were imported, a number which exceeded the total number of births during that period. The nation was well on the way to a gun census that could put a firearm in the hands of every man, woman, or child.

The NRA attributed this sudden spurt to a rising interest in shooting sports and to "people trying to protect themselves against violence." Among the weapons of choice were such murderous assault weapons as the Uzi carbine and Uzi pistol, AK-47, MAC-10, and MAC-11, and the Strike 12-Streetsweeper (aptly named).

FBI figures indicate that about 200,000 to 225,000 guns are reported stolen each year, from private owners and gun shops: these add to the arsenal in criminal hands.

As the United States became the world's leading arms supplier, a grotesque irony surfaced when cocaine-producing countries begged the U.S. government in August 1991 to curb the illegal sale of guns to their citizens. In what can only be called a deadly exchange, we were sending these countries guns in a rough barter for the drugs they were sending us. They still had a daunting challenge, however, in matching our gun mayhem statistics. Rather than adopting the sensible restrictions of other nations, it sometimes seems that we are more likely to corrupt these nations to our violent pursuits.

The Sunday *New York Times* of August 11, 1991, described

how four men were arrested in Florida as they attempted to buy $12 million in guns and missiles for use in Yugoslavia's civil war. The story also told how the state's lax gun laws enabled assassins to purchase weapons to murder three candidates in Colombia's 1989 presidential election.

Guns illegally bought in Florida have been traced to crimes in Brazil and the arming of Peru's deadly guerrillas, who are the principal protectors and extortionists of the coca farmers who produce about 70 percent of the world's crop. These guns have been connected to a coup in Trinidad and to election skirmishes in Haiti, in Jamaica, and, again, in Trinidad. The tracings have usually followed violence that led the police to recover the weapons.

The markup on guns may be 400 percent or higher, and Miami has been described as "The arms supermarket of the Americas." Los Angeles services the Orient and Texas supplies Mexico's illicit gun needs. Thus, the United States has become the world's great importer of drugs and exporter of guns.

The gun traffickers have a valuable ally in the NRA, which seeks not only to facilitate gun purchases, but which has a long history of attacking—sometimes with frightening success—the alcohol, tobacco, and firearms unit of the federal government (the BATF), which attempts to monitor and control this illegal traffic in guns. In the eighties, the NRA actually came close to having this agency abolished altogether. It was saved because of the vigorous intercession of such allies as the nation's police chiefs.

In 1980, America set a national record of 23,040 murders that would not be surpassed for a decade. In 1990, the total was 400 more, and it reached 24,020 in 1991. In 1989 and 1990, the highest per capita rate occurred in Washington, D.C., the city with the highest ratio of cops to citizens and tough restrictions on gun purchases and possession.

Until 1965, the totals had stayed under 10,000. Then a sharp upward spiral began, reaching 16,000 in 1970; 20,510 in 1975; and peaking in 1980, until the next records set in 1990 and 1991. The Senate Judiciary Committee Chairman, Senator Joseph R. Biden, Jr., held the three principal causes behind three consecutive years of rises in the murder and violence rates to be drugs, the proliferation of firearms (and their increased deadliness and sophistication, leading to serious, multiple gunshot wounds in victims), and demographics. The number of teenaged males in the population was felt to correlate strongly with street crime incidence.

The economic, social, cultural, and racial factors may drive the violence, but it is the availability of the tools that lends efficacy to the impulse. The preeminent organization ensuring the availability of all the deadly weaponry is the NRA.

THE NRA

The United States carried on an uninterrupted love affair with firearms, from Colonial times to the present, finding an ardent champion in the National Rifle Association.

Founded in 1871 in New York City, the NRA began as a teacher of marksmanship to post–Civil War riflemen. It did not move to the nation's capital until the early 1900s, when it expanded its role to include farmers, ranchers, hunters, sports shooters, and gun collectors. It then grew into a powerful lobby for permissive gun laws and had the national field to itself for most of the twentieth century.

The monolithic and unchallenged façade of the NRA began to crack with the assassination of President Kennedy in 1963, with a cheap, mail-order rifle. The murders of King and Kennedy's brother in 1968 heated the demand for some measure of gun control.

The late 1960s were a period of racial unrest, urban rioting, and escalating crime and violence rates. The nation was frightened. This fear fueled gun control initiatives as well as heightened demands for protection. There was still no national organization lobbying or otherwise fighting for gun control legislation, however, so the initiatives tended to be ad hoc and mostly relied on the proclivities of individual legislators, who had good political reasons to kowtow to the NRA and no very compelling reason, other than altruism, to fight for gun controls.

In 1980, the NRA, for the first time in its history, endorsed a presidential candidate, Ronald Reagan, despite its being a heavy player in many lesser campaigns.

The eighties and early nineties were a time of internal turmoil at NRA headquarters, as chief executives were forced to resign following charges of wrongdoing, and entire departments, like the fifteen-member public education division, were eliminated and its workers fired. This confusion came after a period of growth under the leadership of Harlon Carter, "Mister NRA," who presided over a tripling in the membership in the late eighties, from 900,000, and influenced the organization, from a distance, until his death in late 1991. The NRA's current scandals and problems are reported to have caused a loss of 335,000 members.[7]

By 1990 the NRA had about 2.8 million members, although the numbers were declining as a result of the internal wranglings. It controlled about $100 million in assets and was the fourth largest spender in political campaigns among membership-funded political action committees. Its literature announces that "Candidates are judged solely on their stand on the gun issue." And the organization means it.

Presidents as unlike as John Kennedy and Ronald Reagan were life members and champions of the gun cause, undeterred, in Reagan's case, even by a classic example of gun control gone awry, when he was almost killed by a handgun bought casually by a young man who simply lied to get it.

The NRA's first stumble with law enforcement came in 1986, when, following a bitter internecine struggle, the organization's leader, in a possible attempt to win over the NRA's

[7] Don Moldea, "The N.R.A. Goes to War with Itself," *Regardie's*, April 1987.

hard-core purists, advocated the private ownership of machine guns. The NRA had had a symbiotic relationship with cops all over the country as it conducted firearms safety and training courses and fell right in with the conservative views of most police organizations. The cops, pressured to do something about a crime rise that kept getting worse—especially in the cities—began to recognize the inevitable connection between guns and drugs and violence.

Democratic Representative Les Au Coin, from Oregon, wrote in the *Washington Post* on March 18, 1991, that he'd been "a 100 percenter" in the eyes of the National Rifle Association leadership. He wrote of the "silver bullet" waiting for defectors at the next election, but in the face of rising violence, he had decided to support the Brady Bill's call for a seven-day waiting period between the purchase of a handgun and its delivery. An op-ed piece he wrote sounds like the repentant confession of someone who has reason to fear the reach of the organization with which he's just parted company. Like many other politicians he cited the persuasiveness of police officials, who had convinced him that the NRA was wrong and that some sensible, minimal controls, at the least, were desperately needed. This was the first time in my memory that police executives had flexed their political muscles. The rank and file had been doing it, through their police unions, for years.

The NRA's toughness perfectly matches the weapons it seeks to protect. It plays hardball in the halls of Congress, on the campaign trail, against police chiefs it dislikes, and over the airwaves.

The International Association of Chiefs of Police (IACP) has a special bulletin, which has cited the NRA's efforts against police chiefs it doesn't like. Massive telephone calls and mail campaigns are launched, aimed at the chief's employers—usually elected officials—trying to pressure dismissing or not hiring the candidate. The IACP has documented attempts to keep Tarpon Springs, Florida, from hiring a chief whom the NRA despised because he'd been chief in Oak Park, Illinois, when that town had adopted the nation's toughest handgun ban and had enforced the law against a shopkeeper who chased a robber with a handgun. My own blocked appointment as Suffolk County's chief was claimed as a victory by the NRA. Other targets of its enmity have been cited, including attempts to keep a chief from appearing in a gun safety ad or testifying before a Florida House committee considering handgun legislation.

Joe Casey had a solid reputation as a conservative, law-and-order chief and acted the very paradigm of the sort of cop the NRA loved; yet he incurred its wrath when he appeared in an ad supporting the Brady Bill. The NRA called the ad "vicious" and full of "outright lies" and asked its members to write Nashville's mayor to express their outrage. The controversies played out in the pages of the NRA's *American Rifleman* and in its other literature, as well as in the police chiefs' magazine, *Police Chief.*

The NRA's tough approach belies its words of support for cops. Its ads actually convey a total lack of confidence in the police as they reflect a need for a troglodyte return to an "every-man-for-himself" philosophy that envisions a six-shooter on every hip. Its ads urge self-defense and are headlined with such questions as "Why Can't a Policeman Be There When You Need Him?" The fears thus created, and the loss of confidence in the police that they engendered, undoubtedly helped fuel the run on guns following the 1992 Los Angeles riots.

"You just have a ton of grief in your district if you don't vote with them," said Representative Terry L. Bruce, a Democrat from southeastern Illinois who opposed the waiting period. "They really really turn up the heat locally."[8] The *Times* article went on to describe the intense pressure applied by the NRA on other Congress members as they considered the Brady Bill. The NRA was described as "threatening" and "abusive" by lawmakers.

[8] "Expensive Lobbying Pays Off for Rifle Association," *New York Times*, September 22, 1988.

In another article, a newly elected sheriff in Sutter County, California, who decided to question a liberal policy of issuing gun permits, faced a possible recall that was led by irate gun owners. The effort was beaten back, 59 percent to 41 percent. Three of his own deputies threatened to run against him, to ease gun permit restrictions, if he was recalled.

NRA FRONTS

Damaged seriously by the defections of law enforcers at all levels on one issue after another, following the debacle over "cop killer bullets" in 1986, the NRA made "a very welcome contribution" to get the Law Enforcement Alliance of America (LEAA) started in February 1991.

First headed by ex–San Jose cop Leroy Pile, who'd clashed with his pro-gun-control chief over firearms issues, and later by Jim Fotis, a former police union head on Long Island, the LEAA (perhaps intended to be confused with the no longer extant, but once influential, Law Enforcement Assistance Administration, abolished in 1980) took out a full-page ad, which cost $41,065, against the Brady Bill in the *Washington Post* on May 8, 1991.

The NRA supported an insurgent in the race for the presidency of the 225,000-member Fraternal Order of Police (FOP) because of the incumbent's work on behalf of the Brady Bill and other gun-control measures. The incumbent carried 68 percent of the votes although he was outspent by a ratio of about 15 to 1. Firearms issues became the major focus in that contest.

Citing another possible NRA front, FOP President Dewey Stokes (the winner in the above race) described the Miami-based National Association of Chiefs of Police, a mostly paper organization, as another anti-gun-control group with NRA ties.

In all of these cases, formal ties are denied by the NRA, despite vague admissions that they do "help" with money and resources.

All of this is evidence, if any were needed, of the severe injuries being inflicted on the NRA by the across-the-board defection of nearly all its former allies in law enforcement.

Nevertheless, the NRA continues to wield a lot of clout in state legislatures, and it is being forced, by the opposition of cops and citizens, into subtler postures. In New Jersey, for example, for a tough law banning assault weapons, it offered a substitute that seemed to offer restrictions, while actually opening the door to such weapons by permitting the ownership and purchase of hosts of such guns (see the *New York Times* of May 26, 1991). In 1992, the state repealed the restrictions and adopted a more tolerant approach to the guns on its streets. The governor, Democrat Jim Florio, vetoed the repeal, and a newly Republican legislature, many of whose members had received NRA largess to finance their elections, had second thoughts about overturning a veto that reflected an attempt to keep minimally sensible gun restrictions in place. In the end the law they'd been elected to overturn remained in place.

NRA POSITIONS

The NRA's position has been to be tough on criminals (with mandatory sentences and tougher parole regulations) and to resist any attempt at restricting any firearm ownership or use. Its position is the "camel's-nose-under-the-tent" or "slippery-slope" argument that holds that every initiative is really just a first step toward the general confiscation of all firearms. It fights on the edges in order to protect its core interest, but in the struggle, it forgets that its middle name is *Rifle*.

The NRA's literature takes on such "myths" as that the majority of Americans favor strict new additional federal gun controls. The text conveniently ignores repeated polls showing Americans favoring reasonable gun legislation, such as the Brady Bill, by overwhelming majorities. It feeds on the belief in the right to bear arms and on the continuing reliance on the efficacy of gun ownership for self-protection.

The next "myth" attacked is the one that holds that a gun in a home is six times more likely to kill a family member than to stop a criminal and that armed citizens are not a deterrent to crime. In attempting to refute this one, the NRA cites a perennial favorite: a study by Professor James Wright that points to the armed citizen or the threat of the armed citizen as possibly the most effective deterrent to crime in the nation. The study extrapolated from a tiny sample into wildly improbable rough estimates and came up with totals that no one could either document or defend.

Another "myth" cited is that the only purpose of a handgun is to kill people.

The NRA's explanation noted Professor Wright's tired review of some sportsmen's publications and added hopefully that the FBI had reported fewer than 8,500 homicides in which handguns were used. That number, the NRA assured us, amounts to less than 0.01 percent (one hundredth of 1 percent) of the privately owned handguns. Some comfort. Some refutation. The NRA holds that handguns are used for hunting, for target shooting, for protection, and for "other legitimate and lawful purposes." There are also gun collectors. The NRA is confident that no violent intent is implied in the purchase of a handgun.

Then it takes on the "myth" that gun registration will curb crime by disarming criminals. Professor Wright again comes to the rescue with a survey of prisoners finding that 88 percent agreed that a criminal who wants to get a gun will, and that 82 percent felt that "gun laws only affect law-abiding citizens: criminals will always be able to get guns." And who, in today's America, could legitimately disagree?

Another "myth" the NRA tries to refute is that most murders are argument-related "crimes of passion" against a relative, a neighbor, a friend, or an acquaintance, committed by previously law-abiding individuals with no prior criminal records. The NRA explanation includes descriptions of the violent propensities and extensive criminal records of most murderers. It goes on to the surprising conclusion, without any cited data, that "crimes of passion" actually constitute less than 10 percent of criminal homicides. Such an assertion would require a pretty tortured and confined definition of "passion."

Professor Wright is pressed into service once again with his assertion that handguns do not play the aggressive role most often attributed to them. Then he makes an appeal to feminists by holding that denying guns to women is to guarantee in perpetuity to a woman's husband the right to beat her at will.

Another "myth" the NRA feels compelled to attack is that stiff gun-control laws work, as evidenced by the low crime rates in England and Japan. Its explanation extolls the homogeneity and stability of both those countries and their willingness to be tough on criminals. We are wimps, whereas Japan has no plea bargaining, fewer protections of the right of privacy, and more respect for law and order. The NRA cites the proliferation of weaponry in Switzerland, ignoring the often tight controls, and concludes that the availability of firearms has no relation to crime. The NRA holds that the British police have confiscated over 300,000 illegally held pistols (since World War II) and that the numbers being confiscated do not diminish by year. This assertion would lead a reader to think that an enormous weaponry is encountered in England but, when 300,000 pistols are divided by the forty-five years since the war's end, the total shrinks pretty dramatically.

Then the NRA needs to counter the calls for licensing and registration laws. A series of horror stories involving attempts at registration is recited, in which citizens' resistance to compliance is applauded as being focused on a concern for self-protection. The NRA deplores the large bureaucracy created by such restrictions, considers the additional costs of having the police enforce such a law, and decries the "invasion of privacy" that such measures represent through the data banks they create. It doesn't seem as worried about Japan's fewer protection(s) of the right to privacy, cited in another context.

And, of course, the NRA is compelled to attack the constitutional question. It holds that the Second Amendment is not limited to a well-regulated militia. All of the NRA evidence points to the right as absolute and as applying to individual citizens, not a militia. It argues that the Supreme Court has remained silent on the issue since *U.S. v. Miller.*

The stubborn, and quite shameless, adherence to this view is belied by the NRA's own efforts to change the states' constitutions to omit the militia reference and, by implication, to initiate the process by which the federal Constitution can be altered.

The NRA deplores the difficulties in transporting weapons caused by many laws and offers a series of incidents to illustrate how honest citizens have been victimized by legal constraints. Interestingly, it speaks with particular bitterness about the law's requirement of a mandated sentence for transporting guns. This, they claim, now makes gun owners criminals, subject to a severe, fixed jail sentence, while murderers, robbers, rapists, drug pushers, and white-collar or corporate thieves often go free. It concludes that mandated sentences undermine the presumption of innocence.

And to the notion that repressive gun laws would reduce crime, the NRA responds that crime keeps rising despite all the gun laws enacted in the past ten to fifteen years. One is tempted to ask what laws? Weapon control is clearly a case for national legislation, yet we've seen only feeble and rare efforts in Washington to deal with the gun issue.

Instead of a ban, the NRA suggests a mandatory penalty for using a firearm in the commission of a violent crime.

The "myths" cited do address the central issues of the gun debate in America, and the NRA's responses illustrate the tortured reasonings it uses to ensure the availability of guns to every man, woman, and child in the land. It has substituted aggressiveness for facts and has indubitably appalled many of its hunter members by some of the stands it has taken, but there is no sign of any softening in its position, despite a reported reduction in membership from over 3 million in the mid-80s to 2.3 million in 1992, according to former insider and *The Insider Gun News* editor, John D. Aquilino.

The NRA's funds come from membership dues; subscriptions to and advertisements in *The American Rifleman*, its monthly magazine; contributions from the industry, especially now that Colt has reentered as a major competitor after many months of a paralyzing strike; and the same hysterical direct-mail appeals that fuel and stoke the fires of its opponents. A typical letter from the NRA's Institute for Legislative Action Director, James Jay Baker, contains the usual assertion that those who support reasonable restrictions actually have, as their real agenda, a total prohibition of all firearms.

Because of the legitimate enthusiasms of hunters and sports folks, the NRA had center stage to itself for most of this century. It was able to forge strong links with law enforcement and politicos, while convincing its constituents of the truth of its assertions regarding the "myths" it has worked so hard to dispel. Two important developments have catapulted opposing forces onto the national scene. For the first time, the NRA has been confronted with a rival that is able to serve as the umbrella under which the fragmented factions supporting gun controls have finally been able to coalesce.

THE GATHERING OPPOSITION

Someone should try a survey on the number of causes inspired and led by people who have come to the weapons issue through some accident of fate or personal tragedy.

Gun control's symbol and heroine, Sarah Brady, was brought to the struggle, despite a conservative law-and-order background that marked her as a natural ally of the NRA, by the 1981 shooting and crippling of her husband, the president's press secretary. She has been able, through her strength and perseverance, to head an organization that promotes gun safety.

Those devastated earlier by similar tragedies had stumbled blindly about, seeking a vehicle for their grief-generated interests. Such an activist was Nelson "Pete" Shields, whose son, Nick, twenty-three, was shot three times in the back and killed on a San Francisco street, on April 16, 1974, by J. C. X. Simon and three others. The killers had engaged in a reign of terror lasting six months during 1973 and 1974, killing fourteen, severely injuring seven, and kidnapping and raping another. The group became known as the Zebra Killers, ostensibly because the police used a Z, or *Zebra*, radio band during their investigation of the racially motivated slayings. Skeptics might be forgiven if they suspected that the press was serendipitously exploiting the connection to convey subliminally the black and white contrast of the events, which so conveniently fit the Zebra's image. All of the slain were whites, and the four killers were black and associated with the Black Muslims.

In 1976, seeking relief from his anguish, Shields quit his job with DuPont and helped build up the fledgling Handgun Control Inc. The organization had been created in 1974 by Mark Borinsky, following his being held up, at gunpoint, and his decision to do something about it.

Because such nonprofits lobby the Congress for legislation favoring their cause (lobbying being the prime industry in that confusing capital), the government has made contributions supporting such efforts taxable. In order to provide contributors with a way to make tax-deductible gifts, a twin organization—devoted to educational efforts and other, nonlobbying exercises—is usually created. In this case, it was the Center to Prevent Handgun Violence. Survivors of victims and ideologically committed activists who hadn't yet been touched by gun tragedies have joined this organization to create a counterpoint to the NRA. Every day's headlines have carried stories about gun tragedies that have bolstered support for this group. The shooting of John Lennon brought Jann Wenner and his *Rolling Stone Magazine* into the fray. Other awful events have brought others.

Powered by skill, contributions, and corporate experience, gun control organizations have grown and prospered. Wenner's group, the National Alliance Against Violence, commissioned a Peter Hart poll to establish priorities for its strategic plan. This poll revealed that the people with the greatest credibility on gun issues were police chiefs.

Conservative by nature and allied by history and precedent to the NRA, only a flaky few of this blue brotherhood had engaged in combat with the gun lobby. Most chiefs felt perfectly comfortable going along and getting along with the NRA. However, the NRA's arrogance, doubtless bred by its unrivaled national supremacy, led it to a series of gaffes that lost it these critical allies: the police chiefs and, equally important, the politically minded sheriffs and rank-and-file union leaders.

A lot of this switch had to do with the NRA's misreading the times. A spiraling crime and murder rate had put the police chiefs into a state of growing anxiety. The pressures for results were tremendous, as were the cries of agony over individual tragedies. The connection among guns, drugs, and crime became too obvious to be ignored any longer, but a modest proposal for curbing the availability of machine guns was, to the chiefs' surprise, vigorously opposed by the NRA.

Then a much-decorated former police lieutenant from the New York Police Department, Representative Mario Biaggi (who was to wind up in prison as a result of the Wedtech scandal and thereby probably to confirm the suspicions of the NRA about its opponents), introduced what was generally regarded as creampuff legislation to ban Teflon-coated bullets, whose only real purpose seemed to be to penetrate the sort of body armor normally worn by cops. (How clearly I remember the gratitude I felt on learning, on October 4, 1986, that Minneapolis police officer Thomas Sawina was wearing a bullet-proof vest when he was shot in the chest with his own gun; it was the finest birthday present I ever got. A "copkiller bullet" would have penetrated his armor and probably would have killed him.)

The NRA's vitriolic campaign against banning these bullets framed the controversy perfectly. The cops were shocked. They had never dreamed the NRA would oppose such a reasonable proposal, abandon them on the first gun issue on which they'd spoken out, and be so utterly insensitive to the pressures playing on them. The chiefs felt both outraged and betrayed.

The NRA finally consented to a watered-down compromise version, one of its frequent tactics. This compromise did not mollify chiefs, who would remember the vitriol used against them personally by the Rifle Association.

The unhappiness was deepened and extended in following controversies over plastic guns that couldn't be detected by airport security, assault weapons used to gun down drug dealers and "mushrooms" with equal abandon, and the availability of Saturday night specials (cheap handguns) and other hand weapons, all of which the NRA supported. In the end, the NRA even managed to alienate such hard-core supporters as Los Angeles Police Chief Daryl Gates, who came out for a ban on military assault weapons after he'd had enough of kids and cops being shot.

Emboldened by such new allies as "Pete" Shields and Sarah Brady, both of whom symbolized respectability in its various Republican, corporate, and ideological forms, police chiefs, sheriffs, and the troops began posing for ads criticizing the NRA (most of which began with the lead "Has the N.R.A. Gone Off the Deep End?") and speaking out on gun issues. The break had become wide and visible by October 27, 1985, when a *New York Times* headline read, "Police Groups Reverse Stand and Back Controls on Pistols."

In the unfolding struggle, it became clear that the battles would be fought on many fronts and would be long-lasting and bloody. In Maryland, the NRA mounted a $6.5-million campaign to overturn a law banning Saturday night specials and lost to a coalition of police chiefs and politicians who had been able to raise a bit more than half a million dollars and who had previously avoided clashing with the powerful NRA.

Nationally, the epic struggle centered on a deliberately modest proposal to enact a seven-day waiting period between the purchase and the delivery of a handgun, in order to enable the police to undertake a background check if they chose to do so: This police action wasn't even mandated. This proposal became the battleground that pitted the NRA against Sarah Brady and her law enforcers, with Handgun Control Inc. providing the organizational muscle. In the end, even ardent NRA supporter Ronald Reagan stunned everyone, on the tenth anniversary of his shooting in 1991, by urging the enactment of the Brady Bill. It was an eloquent testament to Sarah Brady's powers of persuasion.

The Senate majority leader offered his own improvement by mandating a background check, encouraging the states to upgrade and computerize their criminal records, and accelerating the development of a central national registry of criminal archives. And this bill would provide financial resources for the effort.

By the mid-to-late eighties, the NRA had lost not only the chiefs and their organizations, but the National Sheriffs' Association and the rank-and-file cops, as represented by such large national bodies as the Fraternal Order of Police and the National Association of Police Organizations.

Notwithstanding a virtually unanimous, and nearly unprecedented, closing of the police ranks to oppose the NRA's positions, that organization still wrote in a 1984 booklet that California's law enforcement community supported its position in opposing gun control legislation and it added that the American Federation of Police (AFP), the largest police organization in the United States representing the "beat officer," had called on the Illinois Supreme Court to overturn the controversial gun ban enacted in Morton Grove, Illinois.

That no one had ever heard of the AFP didn't trouble the NRA, which was making use of a mostly paper organization with a fancy name, not for the first time in its history. The AFP has the same address and is led by the same person as the National Association of Chiefs of Police in Miami. The NRA rarely hesitates to embrace the findings of a self-created little group.

Pretty soon, the opposition was producing its own mythology and analysis booklet, through the U.S. Conference of Mayors, which listed the myths promulgated by the NRA. Among these is "Handguns don't kill people; people kill people." Another is that citizens need handguns for self-protection. The perennial chestnut that the Second Amendment guarantees the right to keep and bear arms was also dragged out. The NRA has also frequently held that handguns serve a valid sporting purpose, that the Saturday night special accounts for most of the crime with handguns and that the public will never support handgun control.

In the myths that both the NRA and the U.S. Conference of Mayors have cited, and in the responses, can be seen the battlefield over which the struggle ranges. There appears to be little likelihood that the United States will forgo its passion for guns any time soon, and the carnage seems destined to continue and to expand, pushed by the racial and economic factors behind the figures. Still, for the first time in its history, the gun lovers are faced with a credible and powerful opposition that bids fair to bloody the NRA's nose on a number of issues over the coming years.

CONCLUSION

Nonviolence does seem to work to reduce violence in some cases. Cops produced a miraculous reduction in their own deaths and injuries when, in the early seventies, they adopted strong inhibitions in their shooting practices. By enormously reducing the occasions when they could shoot others, they produced a sharp reduction in the number of times they were themselves shot, or were shot at. Over the next twenty years, the number of police line-of-duty deaths actually halved, while the nation's murder toll soared.

Controlling some forms of contraband is easier than controlling others. All cops know that, in a democracy, it is impossible to curb behavior that a large number of people want to indulge in. Drugs, alcohol, and other addictions are ready reminders of the difficulty of trying to control actions that a lot of people want to pursue.

The use of guns falls into a category that can, like the use of automobiles and other devices that require controls, be kept within reasonable bounds. Many other countries, in Europe, in Asia, and on our own continent, have found it perfectly feasible to control traffic in firearms.

Any program of control must be national. The balkanization of gun control has not worked and cannot work.

Gun legislation has been demonstrated to be constitutional, so we needn't worry excessively about the Second Amendment issues raised by the NRA.

A national program should

1. Permit the free and untrammeled ownership of rifles and shotguns but require their registration.
2. Severely restrict the licensing of concealable firearms and grant permission only in exigent circumstances.
3. Ban the ownership of machine guns, assault weapons, and other military-style firearms whose only purpose is to kill humans.
4. Allow for an eighteen-month amnesty period, during which banned weapons would be surrendered, with compensation for the owners.
5. Establish informed commissions to determine the definitions of *concealable weapons* and *assault weapons*. These commissions would follow the guidance expressed in the law. They would also determine the compensation

for confiscated weapons and rule on applications for weapons licenses.

6. Strengthen the Bureau of Alcohol, Tobacco, and Firearms to enable it to supervise and monitor the program.

7. Control, through legislation, the manufacture, sale, and possession of and traffic in firearms.

This is, obviously, a skeletal outline for a program that would be fleshed out as legislation is crafted. Such an approach wouldn't cure the underlying ills producing all the violence, but it would greatly reduce the efficacy of the violent impulses now being given free rein by the universal availability of weaponry. Controlling firearms in this way would be certain to curtail the carnage washing over our cities.

In the meantime, the body count will continue to mount.

Chapter Eight

DRUGS

In nature there are neither rewards nor punishments—
there are only consequences.
                    —Robert Green Ingersoll (1833–1899)

Our current crisis with alcohol, drugs, and other addictions is rooted in a spreading moral decay that has its parallel in Rome, with its wine, women, circuses, bread, and mobs, and that is perfectly encapsulated in the visions of Las Vegas, even down to Caesar's Palace. Can anyone observe that playground and retain the hope that altruism, selflessness, and devotion to humanity's cause remain living possibilities? Can anyone turn on a television and conclude that we're becoming anything more than consumers, hedonists, and escapists?

As the overclass takes to its diversions and pleasures, the underclass writhes in agony and strikes out. The nightly news trumpets the day's toll.

Our kids experiment with drugs and alcohol because they've

caught the message we're transmitting: Have a great time and get yours while you can. But the social dissolution of the overclass is a much longer term proposition than the daily body counts offered by the media. The problem is that, to a very great extent, the nation's value system is set by the folks having cocktails on Fifth Avenue and pool parties in Beverly Hills. Still, it is the drug-induced depredations of the underclass that trouble white America—not its self-indulgences and entertainments.

The story of crime and violence in America is a tale of citizens embedded in racism and poverty who find expression for their frustrations in riots and crime, facilitated by guns and made worse through the escapism of addiction.

Few would have, or have, worried much about booze or narcotics but for their involvement in the rising levels of criminal behavior. America seeks pleasure, and that hedonism tears at the social fabric and threatens our nation. Through flights into drugs and drink, the poor seek escape from the awfulness of a daily reality that contrasts with the images on their TV screens.

Predictably the drama has been captured on our screens by our prophets: the filmmakers. Starting with 1955's stark *Man with the Golden Arm*, which depicted the horrors of heroin addiction in the jazzy dawn of the current Druggie Age, the genre continued with *The Trip, Easy Rider, Drugstore Cowboy, Jungle Fever, Naked Lunch,* and, in 1991, *Rush.* In between came a lot of films, like *Scarface,* in which drugs played a central role.

Indeed, by the nineties, "snorting a line" had become the trendy equivalent of cigarettes or Scotch in earlier, more innocent flicks, except that there seemed to be a livelier awareness of the risks and consequences of drug use.

Documentaries like 1991's *Traffik,* on the Public Broadcasting System, graphically described the scope and risk of modern addiction, as well as the international nature of the problem—and its hideous complexity. In 1992, "Undercover Eddie" was a six-part report and "Drug Wars: The Cocaine Cartel" was a four-part TV series that attempted to capture the War on Drugs. Ironically, none of these were likely to be seen either by the target audience of addicts or by the bureaucrats assigned to fight the war.

It is just such efforts that are achieving the educational objective of convincing those who can be reached not only of the horrors of addiction and the dangers of trafficking but, perhaps more important, of the uncoolness of the drug scene. A trendy age was bound to be most impressed by the latter.

Having belatedly discovered the deep and extensive connection between drugs and crime, politicians have hastened into the breach, offering panaceas. Perhaps no war has been as fitfully prosecuted as the one on drugs, and none has been attended by so much action and so little thought.

Drug use in America has had a cyclical history that tempts many to hope that the current crisis is passing because of some trends and statistics that, on closer examination, offer scant comfort.

Addiction, a compulsive negative behavior that cannot be controlled and that produces harmful consequences, is not a new problem. What makes it dangerous in its current setting is its connection with the disaffections of the underclass and their participation in criminal acts. The toll exacted is horrific.

EARLY HISTORY

The dangers of addiction were anything but obvious to the world of the nineteenth century. Cocaine and opium were regular features of popular patent medicines that, if nothing else, produced euphoria and miraculously shunted most maladies into the background, if only for the moment. It was a sort of Golden Age of the Doctor Feelgoods, who could deliver glorious relief. The consequences would come later and wouldn't be as obvious.

Following the turn of the century came a general awareness that all that relief was exacting a toll—in addictions. A sense that something needed to be done gained momentum with scientific discoveries of the harm being produced by narcotics.

In response to such prejudices as centered on phrases like "the yellow peril," San Francisco had banned opium dens in 1875. But this ban was more a reflection of cultural bias against "dens of iniquity" than of a real awareness of the drug's dangers. Opium, morphine, heroin, cocaine, and marijuana were licit drugs in the United States until 1914.

The world's growing alarm over the effects of drugs led to the Hague Convention of 1912, which produced a treaty obligating each signatory to regulate opium traffic within its borders. In response to this mandate, the United States passed, in 1914, the Harrison Act, which became, in practice if not in its full original intent, the vehicle for enforcing restrictions on narcotics use in America.

Thereafter, the nation experienced fitful relations with euphoric substances, punctuated by more than a decade of Prohibition and growing concern over burgeoning heroin addictions. Crime rose dramatically and exploded with the crack epidemic, which peaked in the mid-eighties.

DRUGS AND CRIME

In the mid-seventies, when studies in Washington, D.C., New York, and other cities revealed the startling connection between drugs and crime, the pressure was on to prosecute a war on drugs. About three fourths of the suspects rounded up for all types of street crimes were found to have hard drugs in their systems at the time of arrest. The extensiveness of the link surprised even the most baleful observers of the criminal scene.

When the extensive involvement of alcohol in criminal behavior became clearer, the connection between addictions and violence tightened. The simple solution seemed to be to strike at the supply of drugs in order to combat crime. What never seemed to be asked was what was creating the growing demand for drugs among the underclass.

The hard drug of choice shifted—from heroin, to cocaine, to crack, to whatever the alchemists could produce next. The constant was the search for a consequence-free euphoria that blotted out the ghetto.

Officialdom's response was to ratchet punishments upward, turning drug misdemeanors into felonies and mandating ever-harsher penalties for low-level users and minor-league dealers. The penalties for the higher-ups, though rarely imposed, were already stiff enough, and there was little political capital to be garnered at those levels.

The cocaine epidemic was believed to have peaked in the mid-eighties, judging from polls of high school students. A whopping 80 percent and more, though, reported drinking alcohol within the past year, and nearly a third admitted they'd had five or more drinks in one sitting over the past two weeks. About one in five smoked cigarettes, and 12 percent reported having attempted suicide at least once. Emergency-room admissions, drug testing, and overdose deaths dipped in the late eighties but began to rise again in 1991 and 1992. The decline in use simply illustrates that the educable, reachable, malleable middle class has decided to look elsewhere for its thrills, while the poor and excluded continue to suffer.

Although binge drinking is declining, it remains a serious problem for college students, among whom the practice stubbornly persists. The broad allure of alcohol, even to the supposedly well informed, is illustrated in a 1990 study by the National Institute of Drug Abuse, which showed over 40 percent of college students admitting they'd drunk five or more alcoholic drinks in a row at least once in the past two weeks. Binge drinking by others in the nineteen to twenty-two age group had declined precipitously and had reached 33 percent in 1990.

The crime figures reflect rising levels of criminality, coupled with high incidences of addiction in the ghetto.

THE STATISTICS

Some estimate that there are about 12 million alcoholics in America. The federal government placed the number of casual cocaine users at around 8 million, including 2.2 million frequent or heavy users.

ALCOHOL

The recidivist proves as much a menace on the road as in our alleys and ghettos. The drunk driver is a repeater, who has usually been detected, stopped, and had his or her license suspended, yet continues to drive and to defy interdiction, despite contributing enormously to highway accidents and deaths.

Poor records contribute to the difficulty of detection. The misguided compassion of judges is another impediment. Lenient sentences and a growing movement toward a no-fault society—where no one is responsible for her or his actions—also contribute to the flaccid response of the system to these menaces.

Drunk drivers account for at least as many fatalities as murderers. The figures are not totally reliable because of the disparities in the quality of fatal-accident investigations from state to state. The statistics known, however, reflect that, of the about 44,000 driving fatalities each year, about half are alcohol-related. From 1988 to 1990, the total figures, in both categories, have declined slightly and would probably go to under 40,000 in 1992, for the first time in decades, mostly because of seatbelt use. Protective air bags would help as they came into wider use but the menace posed by the drinking driver was being masked by these devices.

With every action sparking a reaction, a Minnesota man who had been convicted twice of drunken driving, and who felt that a blood alcohol level of .10 was too low to impair his effectiveness as a driver, organized the Citizens Alliance for Legal Moderation (CALM) to raise the legal definition of being alcohol-impaired and to object to random roadblock inspections used by the police to detect drunk drivers. Thus far CALM has been unsuccessful.

Arrests for the sale and manufacture of illegal drugs rose from 100,000 in 1980 to 400,000 in 1989, and arrests for simple possession jumped from 368,000 in 1980 to 843,000 in 1989. It goes without saying that, at the end of at least a decade of the war on drugs, rather than the supply's drying up and drug prices skyrocketing, drugs were as cheap and plentiful as ever. The enforcement effort had focused on the small fry, and the huge profits ensured a plentiful supply of drugs and sellers. The higher-ups had hardly been touched.

The federal strategy had concentrated its resources and energies on getting the highly visible local user-dealer who has the neighborhood in an uproar. The city council members' call to the police chief always focuses on the street dealer whom the neighbors see and complain about. The Mister Bigs between the grower and the user are insulated and invisible and are frequently the benefactors or friends of the powerful.

The economics are no better on the supply side. A coca grower can expect around $350 for 500 pounds of coca leaves that will be processed into a single pound of pure cocaine that is worth $45,000 on America's streets.

America's fifteen thousand police departments follow the federal encouragement and concentrate on sweeps, roundups, and "buy-and-bust street-jump collars" that net the minnows of the trade and provide lots of time-and-a-half overtime payments to the cops.

One study estimated that, out of the 375,000 drug-affected births a year in the United States, over 100,000 are crack babies. These infants are frequently born with emotional, psychological, and physiological disabilities that make them enormously difficult to control. The long-term consequences are unknown and troubling. That the crack babies are growing up has educators, social workers, cops, jailers, and other interested observers flinching. The continuing rise in out-of-wedlock births, especially among the poor, will also fuel increases in the population most likely to seek escape in addictions.

Although the effects on humans of biological factors, versus environmental influences, have not been sorted out, there seems little doubt that ingesting drugs has consequences for the fetus, which ultimately emerges into a world that will condition her or him for failure. The comforting figures relating to reduced drug abuse hold little hope for these kids.

The director of the Office of National Drug Control Policy estimated that Americans spent a total of $40 billion on cocaine ($17.5 billion), heroin ($12.3 billion), marijuana ($8.8 billion), and other illegal drugs ($2.2 billion) in 1990, down from the almost $50 billion estimated for 1989. By comparison, Americans spent $44 billion on alcohol and $37 billion on tobacco.

Although we must be skeptical of politically driven estimates, these figures illustrate the enormous sums Americans spend on substances that only make them feel good.

MARIJUANA

Marijuana, the smokable weed known as *grass* and by many other aliases, has had, in common with all other drugs (save alcohol), a cyclical history (even alcohol consumption has had its ups and downs, but it has, historically, remained the perennial favorite of the human species).

According to the National Institute on Drug Abuse, marijuana use had been declining, after peaking in 1979, when 31.5 million Americans (17.8 percent of Americans over twelve) were estimated to have used it at least once during that year. By 1990, the estimated total was 20.5 million users, or 10.2 percent of Americans over twelve.

More than 66 million Americans have tried marijuana at least once, compared with 22.7 million who have sampled cocaine. In 1990, the National Institute of Drug Abuse estimated that 10.2 million Americans had used marijuana within the last month, compared with 1.6 million who had used cocaine.

In 1979, marijuana was an imported drug, but interdiction and defoliation efforts, as well as its bulkiness, led to domestic production. Nevertheless, its declining popularity—due, many think, to Americans' nervousness about jobs and testing and to enforcement and educational efforts—can be inferred from sharp reductions in seizures. In 1979, the U.S. Customs Service seized 3.5 million pounds of marijuana. By 1990, the confiscations had dropped to 222,274 pounds, or one fifteenth of the previous total.

The smugglers' routes across the Rio Grande saw a shift from marijuana to cocaine as interdiction pressures in Florida intensified. On December 3, 1991, a pickup truck carrying more than a ton of cocaine was seized, and a local sheriff was arrested. The interdiction was illustrative of the more lucrative nature of trafficking in cocaine.

As a consequence of the mostly successful suppression efforts, and despite declines in overall use, the price of marijuana—for which no conclusive medical evidence of harmful effects has been developed—leaped from $2,000 a pound to $6,000, in the late '80s, which is $375 an ounce, or about $25 more than gold.

Marijuana is seen as a stepping-stone drug by many, which leads to the use of harder drugs, and many users have reported paranoid feelings and a growing sense of dependency on the drug. What the reassuring statistics conceal, however, is the growing concentration of drug use among the underclass.

HEROIN

By 1992, the growing disclosures of the harm produced by cocaine and its derivative, crack, were prompting a renaissance of the formerly discredited heroin. Now the poppy was seen as producing less horrific consequences than the coca leaf, and besides, a treatment had been found in the use of methadone and naltrexone, drugs that block heroin craving.

Although statistics in the field of addiction tend to vary with the interests of those providing them, it was estimated that, at its peak, heroin addicts numbered about 750,000, whereas approximately 4.5 million were estimated as using cocaine more than casually but less than heavily. That heroin would assume a more innocent hue was the subjective, impressionist measure of how far we had slid.

The use of needles did escalate the AIDS risk, but the effects of heroin were seen as more sedentary—and hence less violent—than those of cocaine.

COCAINE

The efforts to stem the growth of coca leaves and poppies have sparked controversies about the use of defoliants that kill all plant life and endanger water sources. Latin American leaders came away from an early 1992 summit on drugs, with President Bush, disappointed that there were no additional funds to offer farmers to rotate into legal crops or for law enforcement or economic aid.

The summit produced programs to curb money laundering and to control traffic in the chemicals needed for drug production, as well as missions to other nations to enlist them in the war on drugs. Police training centers were to be established and intelligence sharing would be improved in an attempt to monitor ships and planes. Most of this, however, was seen as a cosmetic, rather than a substantive, program.

Corruption and inefficiency in the Latin nations, the power and resourcefulness of the drug barons, and enormous domestic problems, as well as poor planning and coordination—all combined to defeat the antidrug efforts in Colombia, Peru, and Bolivia. Additional global threats were seen as the drug traffickers expanded into European and Asian markets.

The political ramifications and complexity of fighting drugs could be seen from the history of Peru's insurrectionist Shining Path guerrillas, who have caused over 25 thousand deaths and over $2 billion in damage over their 12-year war with the government. Shining Path controlled and taxed the Upper Hwauaga Valley, the world's richest area of coca cultivation. Peru's president reported his country's failure to curb coca leaf production and, in response to a heightening internal crisis caused by an insurrection, suspended the constitution and assumed dictatorial powers in 1992.

The capture of Shining Path's founder, Abimael Guzman Reynoso, on September 12, 1992, was not just a brilliant coup for Peru's government but contained important possible implications for the trade in cocaine in the long run.

The plight of the strung-out ghetto dweller might well have originated in the exotic politics of the Andes.

THE STREET JUNKIE

Our prisons are crammed with street criminals. We know who they are. They are uneducated, unemployed and unemployable, and poor; many are black, addicted, and without hope or prospects.

Because the crimes they commit are so awful, and because the very foundation of our society lies in individual responsibility and accountability, we focus on the event and demand retribution. And simple justice and a commonsense grasp of human behavior require that we bring consequences to bear on negative human actions. To fail to do so would be to encourage the continuation of such dysfunctional behavior. It would be transmitting precisely the wrong message.

But to focus exclusively on the act and the actors, and to ignore the conditions that shaped the actions, is to invite the continued proliferation of these criminals. Succumbing to the temptation to strike at the predator before us blinds us to the possibility of attacking the conditions that created him. Humans behave predictably. Neglect, exclusion, and abuse will produce the monsters we love to hate.

And how do we answer the street junkie who cites a U.S. president's use of Halcion—a powerful prescription sedative dangerous enough to be banned in Britain—in order to be more comfortable on international flights. Or the injection of President Kennedy with mind-affecting amphetamine by the man who gave us the Doctor Feelgood title? Or the admission, by an Olympic athlete, of persistent drug use?

THE KIDS

I interviewed a number of fifteen- to eighteen-year-old kids who had been involuntarily sentenced to a secure treatment center in the Deaconess-Fairview Hospital in Minneapolis. Their stories contained similar threads of early experiments with alcohol, gradual evolution to drugs, peer pressures, dysfunctional families, insensitive schools, and malign influence from the central cultural artifact of their lives, TV—all reinforced by the rock lyrics and other bombardments of a thrill-seeking age.

Some of the kids, had been abused; some exploited, sexually or emotionally; and some victimized by the settings of poverty and race into which they'd been born. They had all been felled by the statistical probabilities surrounding their lives.

Sober in incarceration, they uniformly blamed themselves for their addictions and exulted in a sobriety that had restored them to a health they'd despaired of regaining, and each one candidly admitted that he or she would still be doing drugs and booze if it weren't for the awful consequences. *Consequences* is a word that flits in and out of their vocabularies. It usually translates into bugs crawling all over their bodies, horrid visions, terrible tremors, and illnesses. The drugs were producing horrid aftereffects; Mother Nature was visiting consequences on these kids for their excesses.

The young women had been routinely sexually exploited, abused, or raped. The young men had lapsed into burglaries and car thefts. They haltingly described "gross acts" at the juvenile centers they'd been sent to. All were terrified of the prospect of returning to drugs, and none could confidently assert that he or she wouldn't. Drugs had brought to these kids the rarest virtue to be found among the young: humility. It took some chastening to get them there.

The kids had come to deprecate themselves excessively. Their sense of self-worth was so low as to enable others not only to exploit them, but to get them to accept the view that exploitation was what they indeed deserved. Problems at home, at work, and in school had abounded and escalated, and most of them had wound up being expelled, fired, or thrown out of the house. Alcoholism and violence often figured prominently in their home lives. With all its dangers and problems, the street looked more nurturing and inviting than the homes these kids occupied.

Their recovery would require a forthright confronting of their past and a willingness to acknowledge their transgressions. Their stories uniformly reflected having approached death's abyss following episodes of degradation and despair. And these were the survivors.

Most had started early: some reporting being given beer or wine as early as age five. Some had been born to families in which doing drugs was the one event that brought everyone together, feeling good. The aftereffects, however, always lurked behind the temporary euphoria.

The young women had gone through miscarriages or had had babies who were "slow" or otherwise impaired, and who would remain a chore all their lives, as well as serving as living reminders of parental irresponsibility. The young men were sickened by their encounters in the institutions to which they'd been sent, confirming the findings of the "deinstitutionalists." They were clearly terrified by the prospect of returning to the ordeals behind bars and embarrassed to describe them.

The treatment—involuntarily imposed but effective, in that it sobered the kids and seemed to move them to a frank recognition of their lifelong dilemma—did not attempt to analyze the underlying causes of their addictions. Perhaps candor would lead them to the discovery of what factors had triggered their enslavement. Talking about their drug and alcohol abuse seemed to help them gain insight into their behavior, to lift their sense of personal worth, and to improve their chances of recognizing strategies for avoiding relapse.

The kids had their drug preferences, but each described experiments with enormous varieties of drugs and substances. The quest was for a high, and the drug was the vehicle that got them there. Any handy substance would have to do. Many used drugs because drugs enabled them to function more confidently and efficiently in awkward settings. Many described being influenced by an older group with which they had sought to curry favor. Acceptance by these older kids had frequently been predicated on using drugs.

MORE FACES BEHIND MORE FIGURES

The plight of these kids reminds us that data, although impressive, will never convey the realities behind the figures.

When even the chief of police of Brockton, Massachusetts, succumbs to the slavery of daily cocaine use as happened in 1990, and athletes forfeit millions because they can't pass drug tests, we can see a hint of the magnitude of addiction's pull. We can also imagine the strength of the urge when we see cops getting caught up in drug use and trade, as well as about 14 percent of nearly a million assembly-line workers tested showing positive for cocaine (21.8 percent of the users) and marijuana (39 percent). The allure of drugs and the enormous sums of cash involved create well-nigh irresistible temptations for the enforcement agencies in the struggle.

But the compulsions of addiction and the negative actions

triggered by such enslavement cannot be seen through the opaque statistics. In order to feel the degradation in its true depth, we have to study the druggie granddaughter who is taken in by a loving, doting grandmother and is sheltered and nourished for many months, together with her boyfriend. The young woman's own mother warned the grandmother (her mother) that she'd be exploited or worse, but the older woman knew that her love and faith would see them through.

The thefts, exploitations, and permanent narcotics hazes escalated until the granddaughter filched a check for $2,100, which constituted the grandmother's severance pay from a long nursing career. Threatened with arrest, as the grandmother's outrage finally overflowed, the granddaughter and her boyfriend cold-bloodedly murdered the old lady and slashed her wrists to make the murder look like a suicide.

The police blotter is dotted with stories attesting to the irresistible grasp of addiction and the willingness of addicts to undertake the unthinkable in pursuit of the next high.

IS DRUG USE A VICTIMLESS CRIME?

We are, as a people, despite puritanical attitudes toward sex and such, notably more tolerant—and increasingly so—of victimless crimes than we are of those that produce innocent casualties. There is a sense that, in a country of many freedoms, the individual is reasonably free to self-destruct. This attitude has grown more popular as the medical community has developed the means to keep the body technically alive with support systems that challenge the notion of a dignified death. The result has been the growth of "living wills" that forbid the use of artificial life-prolonging techniques beyond the point of hope of recovery. Such groups as the Hemlock Society have counseled suicide in hopeless circumstances and have even inspired an instructional book on just how to do it. The freedom to die is, increasingly, being seen as an individual's right.

Some therefore, ask: As drug use and addiction harm only the user, why not be more tolerant?

First, it must be argued that even a tolerant government has an obligation to protect its citizens from harm—even self-harm and even if it means intruding into their lives, providing the danger is serious enough. Second, the use of drugs doesn't occur in a vacuum. We've all seen how alcohol can wreak havoc on our roads, and no one wants to fly with a druggie pilot or be operated on by a stoned surgeon. A New York City transit motorman suspected of being drunk was charged with murder in connection with an August 1991 train accident in which five died. The New York Transit Authority was criticized for lax drug-testing policies. Recognizing the problem, the U.S. Supreme Court held that drug testing, in the workplace, is permitted for law enforcers and for safety-sensitive jobs.

It's clearly too late to outlaw alcohol, but educational efforts pointing to its dangers should be intensified, along with treatment and prevention approaches. The federal government ought to mandate a stern warning label for all alcohol products and tax these, and tobacco, very stiffly.

Then there are the economic dilemmas of addiction that prompt the users to commit crimes, as well as the effects of a drug that leads to child neglect and other abandonments, and the competitive battles for control of the market. The fraying of society's moral fabric occasioned by mass surrenders to decadent and dangerous pleasures is the strongest argument against decriminalizing hard drugs.

All of this points to the hideous complexities behind drug abuse, yet the federal government continues to express its faith in such bankrupt approaches as bigger prisons.

THE NATIONAL INSTITUTE OF JUSTICE
EVALUATES THE RESULTS

The report by the National Institute of Justice (NIJ), *Searching for Answers: Annual Evaluation Report on Drugs and Crime, 1990,* contains many self-congratulatory observations about the results of the hares-and-hounds chases that are today's drug interdiction efforts. The report describes low-level street operations, marrying many to that latest police fad, community involvement, while ignoring the devastating effect of narcotics on the ghetto and the fact that all this effort and money are neither diminishing the supply nor raising the price. Also safely ignored are the criminality and carnage, which continue to rise despite the scholarly assessments of NIJ and its minions, and the fact that many innovative programs are producing marvelous, but isolated, results.

Absent are any references to laborious searches for "Mr. Big," or to attempts at attacking either the supply or the demand sides of the equation, or to any significant prevention efforts. Obeisance is paid to some few, isolated treatment programs and to Drug Awareness Resistance Education (DARE), a useful program in which cops speak to school kids, in the classroom, on the horrors of addiction and how to resist peer pressures.

The assessment declares an arriving victory and congratulates those involved in developing fresh approaches. But the effort to conceal the intellectual and, indeed, moral bankruptcy at the heart of the federal program fails. The report might easily serve as the principal evidence in an indictment of the federal government for its failure to prosecute the War on Drugs with sincerity.

The agency's attitude permeates the documents it has issued on drugs. In "The Police and Drugs" (September 1989), it warns against "overestimating the significance of Mr. Big." It offers reasons why, despite the logical appeal of such an approach, it probably won't work to go after him. This viewpoint ignores the economies of scale of going after those who really control the traffic in drugs. Even if they're replaced—as they are sure to be—the price paid escalates, and the risks rise. The emphasis, though, continues to be on street-level dragnets and lots of low-level arrests. Despite occasional victories against the drug lords, all the pressures seemed to be on getting the visible dealer off the corner.

APPROACHES

President Bush's self-heralded War on Drugs is actually a farcical, cynical travesty foisted, by a quick-fix president, on a gullible and frightened public that, in its angst, has proved willing to embrace simple answers.

President Bush provided plenty of dramatic action, however. Billions have been thrown at highly visible street efforts that take that odious user-dealer off to the slammer.

The result has been a sharp increase in the percentage of prisoners in for low-level dealing and use, and for longer periods. As their numbers increase, the percentage of those incarcerated for rape, robbery, burglary, and even murder declines precipitously. This has been the most alarming trend in the rapidly growing prison population. We're caging users who ought to be coerced into treatment and releasing recidivists.

Any program that has any hope of success will have to emphasize prevention, education, and treatment as well as focusing enforcement on the big fish. These approaches will have to be informed by research and data sufficient to allow for the development of a coherent national plan. A key element would certainly be to target the international traffickers for more vigorous enforcement.

Such an approach has to recognize the hideous complexity behind drug use and addiction, and it must engage the energies of families, teachers, doctors, social workers, health providers, filmmakers, researchers, and scientists—as well as cops. Each must work, within the context of a larger strategy, to attack the problems in front of him or her.

PARENTS

Parents have a responsibility to the kids they've brought into the world. This first includes a safe, wholesome environment that must reinforce, in actions, the messages that all parents utter. Kids focus on the actions, not the words.

The point is to improve the odds of success. No formula—in dealing with either the drug problem in the home or with any of life's other problems, anywhere—will prove infallible. The purpose must be to raise the prospect of successful functioning.

Kids will ape adult behavior, whether it's drinking, pill popping, smoking, or doing drugs. Kids need to be monitored and guided in their activities, choice of friends, behavior, and so on. Communication is critical, and communication differs markedly from lecturing. It includes active, sensitive listening, for one thing.

When problems arise, professional help should be sought, as it would be for any other illness. Counseling should be obtained to ensure the avoidance of approaches that facilitate the addiction, often called *enablings*. Parents and others intimately involved frequently lapse into behavior that, because of their lack of expertness and understanding of addiction, facilitates continued use of drugs and enables the addict to remain addicted. The government has to supply the resources for treatments where the impoverished are unable to afford them.

Athletes have shown us they can function successfully, sometimes brilliantly, for brief periods, when they are using drugs. The effects aren't always obvious, visible, or immediately destructive. Still, drugs do produce a gradual deterioration in behavior, even if it is not obvious. Parents should therefore be alert to the need to observe their children's behavior very carefully. Drug use often leads to actions that are observable, such as failure in school, a choice of different friends, unexplained absences, missing money, uncharacteristic behavior, and empty bottles or missing drugs.

A typical ad run by the Partnership for a Drug-Free America urges parents to look for such telltale signs of drug use as wild mood swings or dramatic changes in behavior. Enlarged pupils, a runny or stuffy nose, or regular nose bleeds may indicate cocaine use. Some drugs, like marijuana, may produce an increase in appetite, whereas others, like crack or cocaine, may have the opposite effect. Poor concentration and poor memory, lack of sleep or unusual sleep patterns, and bloodshot eyes are other signs of drug use.

All of these effects may have other causes, but parents need to be alert and need to secure professional help if they think they have a problem.

The role of the parent is to nurture, protect, and care for the child, and this includes battling drugs. Like any other battle, it requires heavy involvement and deep understanding.

Some treatment approaches seem to be the result of serious reflection and hold some hope of producing results. Others mirror the desperation of citizens who have nowhere to turn for help, and some turn out to be the political posturings of ambitious officials who don't want to look beyond their next election or appointment. Careful evaluation is needed of the various approaches in order to replicate those that work.

USING ADDICTS AS LECTURERS

As I listened to the kids locked up in the treatment center at Deaconess-Fairview Hospital, the one thing that struck me was how profitable their experiences would have been to their peers. Using such kids as lecturers involves a risk; it may be criticized, and it has been by federal bureaucrats alarmed by the "celebrity status" conferred on such confessors, but the kids offer verisimilitude. Their accounts reek of authenticity, and the kids listening relate to the descriptions. Yet the bureaucrats seem content to rely on propaganda with an unremittingly negative message that feels, to the kids, to be untrue.

These formerly addicted kids are able to speak of the thrills and highs that drugs can bring, which are, after all, the attractions that entice so many young experimenters, and then these kids can add the horrific consequences that such bliss exacts. Their recounting the debasing, painful, dangerous, and frightening experiences then has a bite, made stronger by the balance of pleasure to pain.

Yet, in a 1988 booklet on drug prevention, the U.S. Department of Education advised, "Former addicts and pushers should not be used as speakers in prevention education settings." This statement has the hollow ring of the calls for no sex education, on the grounds that it promotes promiscuity. The extensive studies showing that our teenaged women have sex no sooner or oftener than their European counterparts, yet get pregnant and produce hugely greater numbers of children, are blithely ignored. Discouraging the use of those who have used drugs flies in the face of the experience of Alcoholics Anonymous and all the other peer counseling groups that have seemed so effective. Who, after all, has greater credibility than those who've been there and can describe the tortured journey?

When a former Minnesota Viking football star who'd been convicted of cocaine possession was given three thousand hours of community service, some of which would be spent as a speaker in schools, objections were raised in the press (see the Minneapolis *Star-Tribune* of September 15, 1991). These were that the user had escaped punishment (by not being imprisoned); that the user might achieve celebrity status or earn money as a result of the speeches, articles, and books flowing from his drug experience; that experience as a user doesn't make one a treatment expert; that the listeners might seek to imitate the speaker to achieve equal celebrity; that most of the listeners wouldn't be drug users, or likely to be, so that the speaker's experiences would be irrelevant to them; and that many approaches don't work or, at best, achieve only modest results, so why raise expectations unrealistically with such programs?

All of the objections missed the point of exposing kids to the realities of addiction and its impact on the person and those around her or him. If we can't risk exposing our kids to the truth of drug use—its highs and its lows—how can we hope to prevent their using drugs? The Department of Education's approach ignores the intelligence and curiosity of our kids and requires levels of success that other programs aren't held to. It is true that only modest gains, if any, may be made—through this or any other approach—but until the panacea is found, we will have to be content with, and use, those programs that hold out the hope of deterring kids from using.

Kids, after all, will read of the baseball player who, in 1991, was leading the league in stolen bases, batting .297, had scored 81 runs, and was headed for a career year when he twice, in July, failed drug tests to detect cocaine and was suspended. The kids can see both addiction and seemingly successful athletic functioning on the field, and they need to know what's going on behind the scenes and to understand the impact of addiction on the user's life. They need to hear about the tawdry details of hunting for a fix and about the ups and the downs and the fear of detection. They need to learn of the desperate measures taken to avoid being caught and of the increased dosages needed to function, as well as the time, energy, and money wasted. The impact on relationships with everyone, not to mention the awfulness of arrest and being jailed, needs to be graphically brought home to these kids.

How are kids to understand the seemingly successful functioning of a female speed skater who admitted the heavy use of drugs? Only she knew that the addiction had not only impaired her performance but had sealed her fate as a competitor. Yet, even as she wallowed in addiction, her coaches thought she was skating well. She knew better.

How are kids to evaluate the repeated relapses into drug use of a relief pitcher who risked a $2.3 million contract because of his enslavement?

How are kids to evaluate the drug use of one of America's most prominent mayors?

Making use of those who've been there, and who can communicate the subtle and complex horrors, becomes an essential ingredient in any educational effort.

The cultural bombardment, on the TV and movie screens, has to communicate the message, too, and risks have to be run.

Rush is a film about narcs who succumb to the temptations around them and become junkies. Such a film will probably have more of an impact than a thousand lectures.

The kids willing to listen need to get the real story behind the hoopla. The federal government stumbled badly when it made a film, *Reefer Madness*, depicting marijuana, cocaine, and opium users as violent fiends. The absurdity of the portrayals produced a boomerang effect. Instead of discouraging use, the viewers were tempted to suspect that some delicious truth was being denied them and that the government was overreacting, so they became more curious about drugs.

If a drug could be found that delivered pure pleasure and exacted no negative consequences, of any kind, only the federal bureaucrats would be likely to suspect that it wouldn't be widely used. Hedonist America is engaged in a ceaseless quest of euphoria without consequences.

TREATMENT

The central fact surrounding drug treatment is its general unavailability to addicts. The problem is exacerbated by bureaucratic inefficiencies that fail to match clients to services, leaving some treatment slots unfilled even where there is a crying need for more.

This unwillingness to service those in need or those seeking help consigns many users to dead-end lives of addiction, criminality, and self-destruction. New York City, for example, is estimated to have half a million addicts and one tenth of that number of treatment slots.

As of the fall term of 1991, Little Rock, Arkansas, made provision for treatment for drug or alcohol abuse available to all of the 26 thousand students in the city's schools. Ten local psychiatric hospitals and counseling centers agreed to provide treatment to any student referred there by any school district, and they agreed to charge reduced rates, which would be paid

by the district. Funding would come from donations raised
by a coalition of city officials and community leaders. The
program includes early intervention, drug screening, intensive
family therapy, and up to three months of hospitalization.

The police praised this program as a possible way of
preventing crime, but all such programs desperately need the
rigorous scientific evaluation that will finally provide examples
of what works and what doesn't in the treatment of addictions.

In 1992, there were about 600,000 treatment slots nationally, which were capable of serving 1.7 million addicts a year.
Just accommodating all the addicts willing to accept treatment
would require at least 300,000 more slots, at an additional cost
of $1.6 billion.

TOUGH LOVE

In July 1991, New Yorkers were horrified by the story of a
fifteen-year-old Puerto Rican girl found chained to a radiator in
her parents' Bronx apartment.

Linda Marrero had been drawn to the street, where she
found drugs and addiction. Dropping out of school, she disappeared from home repeatedly, only to return, emaciated and
battered, for protection from pushers and the mean life of the
Bronx streets. Her survival seemed a miracle, given the abuses
repeatedly visited on her and the violence surrounding her life
in the gutter.

Her parents had run the bureaucratic gauntlet of social
services, counseling, family court, and other branches but
found no help. They asked that she be taken from them and
treated, forcibly, but the court simply referred them to counseling when she clearly needed the sort of involuntary lockup
treatment that had been afforded the kids in the Deaconess-
Fairview Hospital program, described earlier. The parents
sent Linda to family in Puerto Rico, but she was returned
as incorrigible.

Finally, in desperation, her parents chained her to a radiator for two months, within reach of a bed, the bathroom, a TV, and video games and stereo.

The parents were locked up for a felony—unlawful imprisonment—but as the facts emerged and their love and concern became clear (Linda herself attested to their devotion and kindness), the charges were dropped to a misdemeanor, and the system's face softened perceptibly.

This was tough love taken to its dysfunctional extreme, out of desperation over a system that had failed to provide an escalating level of services that might have addressed the challenge. Counseling, supervision, schooling, and other approaches having failed, the system should have had lock-up medical facilities available to which Linda could have been sent.

It soon became clear that it was the system that had failed and that the parents had been driven, by desperation, to try to make up for its deficiencies. The system had failed to recognize a need to provide specific programs for the specific challenge represented by each addict. Counseling certainly has its place, but so does forced treatment.

CLEAN NEEDLES

Should the government distribute clean needles to drug addicts, in order to attack the spreading epidemic of AIDS among addicts?

New Haven, Connecticut, conducted a needle distribution experiment that was controlled and evaluated, and that showed, in 1991, that the distribution of clean needles had cut AIDS infections dramatically. The boldness of such experiments also illustrates the sort of risks always run by a government that tries to find ways to help its people.

The distribution of clean needles is typical of the hard questions embedded in the drug crisis. The only effective answers will flow from a philosophical base that is predicated on wise and ethical principles. In the case of distributing needles, for example, the issue centers on choosing the lesser evil in order to prevent a greater one. Distributing needles is tantamount to the government's tacitly approving drug use—a genuine evil. Ignoring the use of contaminated needles produces the greater harm of AIDS infection. In such hard cases, the government has to acknowledge frankly and precisely what it is doing and why.

The Netherlands, for example, appointed two scientific committees, in 1969 and 1970, to study drug use and, as a result of their reports, adopted a normalizing, pragmatic, nonmoralistic approach to drug enforcement. It focused on catching the higher-ups and tolerating the retail trade in coffee shops. Hard drug use was seen as a public health problem, which was met with easily available social service programs, methadone treatment, and needle exchanges.

By way of illustrating the illusion behind any single approach, Zurich was forced to close its experiment in drug tolerance, Platzspitz, a park where addicts and dealers congregated openly.

Started in 1987, for the use of a few hundred addicts, the park's numbers swelled to about twenty thousand users and sellers at the time of its closing in 1992. By then, drug deaths had escalated (eighty-one in 1991), and medical crises and emergencies had become frequent daily rituals. Crime and vandalism soared. Criminals and dealers were attracted from all over Europe, and the park was turned into a public toilet.

An exasperated city council closed the park and made plans to spend $1.5 million, and over a year, to refurbish and renovate the area. The addicts and dealers would, of course, now be scattered over the city.

Platzspitz is a good illustration of where decriminalization would lead.

PRISON TREATMENT

The wisdom of providing drug and alcohol treatment programs to the prison population should be too obvious to require an argument, yet the need far exceeds the available supply.

The connection between drug use and crime has been persuasively established, being one of the few areas of criminality that has been well researched.

One National Institute of Justice report, "In-Prison Programs for Drug Involved Offenders," revealed that, in 1987, only 11.1 percent of inmates were enrolled in drug treatment programs. The tremendous growth of imprisonment for narcotics offenses since, as the enforcement effort quickened and treatment resources dwindled, has undoubtedly driven this figure much lower.

Providing treatment should produce better overall conditions within the prison, but its principal value lies in preventing a return to the lifestyle that produced the crimes.

Those in treatment programs in 1987 had been heavily involved in drugs and had committed many serious crimes. They were subjected to intensive and comprehensive treatment approaches, by outside professionals, and were trained in a range of practical skills and subjected to aftercare treatment and follow-ups. Literacy and other employment skills are important components of such programs.

The chronic recidivist should be a principal target of such efforts. Being coerced into treatment should not be precluded because even those forced into treatment have been judged to have been helped by researchers evaluating such programs.

The program should be long enough to really take hold. It should include useful activities such as exercise, peer discussions, and work and literacy training. It should have sufficient resources and a good staff and should be rigorously evaluated for results.

In-prison treatment programs offer another opportunity to prevent future crimes, but the fact that the results are hard to measure diminishes their appeal to activist administrations.

THE NEED TO SEARCH

America's policy is stuck at the Draconian pole. Every legislator rushes to impose his or her tough view, pausing only to receive accolades. Mandated sentences and an upward ratcheting of the seriousness of the charge are the order of the day. The prisons overflow with low-level users and sellers who have been charged with no other crime. They take up space that might have been filled by the true menaces, who now slip between the cracks because there's no room for them in the jails. And still, we refuse even to discuss the usefulness of our approach.

In a typical excess of enthusiasm, Minnesota reacted to the crack epidemic by making the penalty for possessing 3 grams a mandatory forty-eight-month prison term. The penalty for possessing ten grams of cocaine carried a probationary disposition. It would take more than a pound of cocaine (450 grams) to warrant more than forty-eight months in prison.

The mindlessness of this approach becomes clear when we realize that crack is cocaine, cooked with baking soda, which removes the hydrochloride salt. Yes, crack is more potent, but the penalties were grossly disproportionate. The effect was to focus enforcement pressure on the street user and seller, who was usually black. An appeals court ruled the penalty an unconstitutional violation of the Equal Protection Clause of the U.S. Constitution and threw the law out.

A good example of our deafness is the issue of decriminalizing hard drugs. The few who have suggested it have been ingloriously shot down. The matter is closed. Such an action precludes our learning anything and prevents our adopting, or even discovering, new approaches.

There seems little doubt that decriminalizing hard drugs would be both wrong and foolish. We just can't have a government say it's OK to do drugs unless the evil of prohibition is demonstrably greater. But should that position stifle a debate that might detach us from the shibboleths that have mesmerized us? Might not a full discussion of decriminalization lead to discovering new strategies?

In *Drugs and Crime*, James Q. Wilson, probably the country's best known criminologist, decries the scantiness of research on drug policy and condemns the mindless activism that animates America's War on Drugs. He describes the scattering of the little information on drugs we have managed to produce and excoriates the program for lacking thought.

Wilson is totally right.

ENFORCEMENT

It's hard to imagine that an $11.6 billion program can proceed without a cogent animating vision that we would call a strategic plan, but that has been the case in the War on Drugs.

The overwhelming bulk of the funds was destined for street operations, prison construction, new prosecutors and judges, and more federal investigators.

There was an uptick in the use of cocaine and heroin in 1991, according to a national survey. This was confirmed by a sharp increase in emergency-room treatments for cocaine and heroin use during the first two quarters of 1991.

The enormous sums of cash involved in narcotics trafficking sparked the chief corruption fighter in the New York Police Department to call this area the "greatest integrity hazard and vulnerability" (see the *New York Times* of January 9, 1992). He supported his view by citing the indictments of narcotics officers in connection with drug raids. The cases illustrated the potential existence of widespread corruption in New York's drug enforcement and hinted at the likely existence of similar problems in other cities.

On another front, civil libertarians expressed concern about efforts to track prescription users of such drugs as Demerol. Some see this tracking as an intrusion and possibly as a violation of the confidential doctor–patient privilege, but law enforcers claim it is another way to monitor possible violations by users of addictive drugs like codeine or Percodan. Some addicts visit multiple doctors and receive several prescriptions. A central, computerized data bank would permit matching the information.

In a highly questionable practice, some police departments have offered crack and other forms of cocaine for sale and have arrested the would-be purchasers. Such reverse stings ignore the law that allows the police to seize and possess such contraband in strictly limited circumstances, such as arrests or confiscations of evidence. Otherwise, how could one distinguish between the cop-enforcers and the cop-junkies?

The courts have frowned on the practice, and these silly efforts have been discouraged, but they are another example of the excesses the cops will embrace to attack low-level operations.

While a lot of energy has been poured into subsidizing overtime pay and street operations by cops, the more successful programs have involved task forces of local cops and federal Drug Enforcement Agency operatives that have targeted the higher-ups, and that have used sophisticated, time-consuming, expensive approaches to net the bigger fish.

As the drug epidemic has spread globally, various nations have dealt, in their own ways, with the emerging problem.

THE INTERNATIONAL SCENE

On October 26, 1991, China killed thirty-five drug dealers by firing single bullets into their heads. The accused had been tried, paraded before a rally of about forty-thousand, and executed, all within a short period. They had been dealing in heroin believed to have been smuggled from Myanmar (formerly Burma). The authorities were sending a clear message to the small, but growing, population of addicts. The Chinese police reported uncovering 5,004 drug cases in the first half of 1991, a 50 percent increase over the first six months of 1990. As we will see later, the Chinese approach was not without its appeal to at least one American police chief.

Saudi Arabia began 1993 by beheading two Pakistanis convicted of smuggling heroin into the kingdom.

In London, the police ascribed increases in shootings and killings to a rising group of tough young heroin and crack dealers. Pressures mounted to arm London's police, but the 590 firearms incidents in 1990 indicated the still-limited level of gun violence. The debate over whether to arm Britain's police was bound to heat up with an increase in the incidences of drug dealing and of shootings related to such traffic.

In Spain, demonstrators blocked the building of a Madrid housing project for Gypsies on the basis that they would spread drug dealing in the area. Soon, twenty-thousand parents and children were marching to protest the government's tolerance of drug abuse. The anger spread to other cities as narcotics use rose and addicts were observed injecting themselves with heroin in public. The dangers to children exposed to abandoned syringes, combined with the rise in muggings and the absence of punishments, all led to the public's disaffection. Deaths due to overdoses rose steadily, from 166 in 1987 to 667 in 1990.

A United Nations survey of drug use around the world painted a bleak picture of increased heroin and cocaine use, nearly everywhere, fueled by increased marketing efforts by South American and Asian drug dealers anxious to find new outlets.

African countries formerly free of hard drugs were now even growing coca plants and opium poppies. Even Japan has seen increases in cocaine imports, although methamphetamine, a stimulant that acts much as cocaine does, remains the most widely abused hard drug there.

The international traffic constituted a series of shifts and adjustments as the hunters and their prey changed tactics and developed strategies that called for new circumstances.

As direct routes from Colombia got shortcircuited, and shipments from Mexico were increasingly intercepted, the narcotraffickers shifted to using Central America as a transshipment point and, later, as a poppy-growing region. The result was defoliations of the Guatemalan jungle. In 1991, seventeen metric tons of cocaine were seized in Guatemala, in contrast to forty-five tons in Mexico, a much larger country. Guatemala has more than a thousand private landing strips and virtually no radar. The other countries in the region are also noting increased traffic and are making larger seizures.

The dealers use private planes, small boats, cargo containers on merchant ships, tractor-trailer rigs, and other vehicles for their consignments. The United States is leading an effort to stiffen local Central American legislation on trafficking and money laundering, encouraging the use of joint maritime patrols, and establishing a regional radar network. It is also arranging for educational trips for journalists, in addition to technical assistance in programs of direct drug suppression.

The successful prosecution of Panamanian strongman General Manuel Antonio Noriega illustrated the labyrinthine complexities of international drug trafficking and the shadowy involvements of governments as their policies become entangled with the drug trade.

Noriega was charged with cocaine trafficking, money laundering, and racketeering. His defense was that he was acting at the behest of the U.S. Central Intelligence Agency and the Drug Enforcement Administration.

Carlos Lehder Rivas, a major Colombian trafficker now in a U.S. prison for life plus 135 years, testified at Noriega's trial to the corrupt involvement of many government officials in South and Central America, the United States, and even Israel and Spain. His testimony described the tangled web of foreign policies and political campaigns that intersected with the interests of drug traffickers, who use these governmental objectives to further their commerce in narcotics.

No one, in recent memory, has more graphically displayed the risks involved in going after "Mr. Big" than General Noriega, whose defense was predicated on the complicity of the U.S. government in his activities. If accepted, this accusation may implicate the highest reaches of the federal administration. At the very least, it was clear that he and the top drug dealers were operating at remarkably high levels of Inter-American officialdom.

Further suspicion of high-level U.S. government involvement in the drug trade was fed by the disclosure that millions of dollars of drug dealers' funds were withdrawn from the scandal-ridden Bank of Credit and Commerce International (BCCI) only days before a surprise 1988 arrest of five bank executives and the seizure of the bank's records. It seemed obvious that the highly secret investigation had been leaked to the drug dealers who'd been using BCCI on a daily basis to launder many millions of dollars in narcotics funds.

When the most highly placed Washington figures become connected with the activities of BCCI and its executives, what is a black street junkie to think when scores of cops, being paid time-and-a-half for overtime—from federal funds—swoop down on him and haul him off to jail?

In Peru, interdiction efforts collided with the internal insurrection led by the Shining Path guerrillas and the involvement of Peruvian security forces in collusion with the drug traffickers. The U.S. Congress froze aid to the country because of what one Representative referred to as the total and complete corruption of the Peruvian police and army (see the *New York Times* of November 11, 1991). The peasants growing the coca leaves face impoverishment without the crop, and they are often protected by the Shining Path, who collect taxes for their trouble. The government's fear of a peasant insurrection and its other grave internal problems led the president to suspend

Peru's constitution and assumed direct control of the nation in 1992.

Colombia, of course, with its Medellin Cartel and other, less publicized groups, is the focal point of cocaine trafficking on the planet. There, the War on Drugs had literally been a life-and-death struggle for control of the nation.

COLOMBIA'S AGONY AND INNOVATION

Confronted with the supply side of the dilemma, Colombia's President Cesar Gaviria Trujillo concluded that bloody suppression, which had taken the lives of thousands—including half of the Colombian supreme court's twenty-four justices, more than three hundred other judges, three presidential candidates, and scores of cops—simply hadn't worked. He opted for a radical new tack: Big-time narcotics dealers were offered a deal where they could plead guilty to one drug count and expect a reasonably short sentence, on the order of five to ten years in comfortable settings, and would be guaranteed that they'd not be extradited to the United States, a fate dreaded by the narcotraffickers.

After some negotiation and tentativeness a number of very large drug dealers, including the notorious billionaires Pablo Escobar and Jorge Luis Ochoa, submitted to justice and were jailed. Although Escobar lived in some style in the luxurious prison, built on his land and to his specifications, and although he was widely believed to be still running his cartel from behind bars, the mere fact of his incarceration strengthened the government's hand. Even his escape in 1992 might have been defined as a protest against the Colombian government's toughening stance. Despite the sometimes farcical reversals, it may be too early to dub the innovation a failure.

Seizures of cocaine increased to 46 tons for the first nine months of 1991, compared to 43 tons in all of 1990, of the total of 500 to 700 tons produced and shipped. The decline of

cocaine's popularity in the United States appeared to be leading to a shift to heroin dealing by Colombian traffickers, as
they attempted to diversify and adjust to changing market
conditions.

Violence in Colombia has abated dramatically. A country
on the verge of dissolution into chaos is slowly putting itself
back together.

It must not be forgotten that the drug issue in Colombia
plays out against a backdrop of Latin America's longest running guerrilla insurrection. The civil strife features kidnap-
pings, bombings, and murders, and it has been going on for
thirty years. The government has convinced many to lay down
their arms and integrate into the nation's life, but despite nego-
tiations, two groups, numbering about nine thousand fighters,
continue the struggle. The guerrillas also get tangled with the
drug trade and raise money by protecting coca and opium
poppy crops. The government is negotiating a truce vigorously,
but in the opinion of some observers, the demands of the
guerrillas have increased unreasonably.

Even defoliation efforts, aimed at getting coca leaf and
opium poppy growers to try alternate crops, come smack up
against American agricultural interests, which resist competition in such crops as soy beans or citrus fruits.

There seems little doubt that on all fronts, President Gaviria's initiative was daring and original. Although it is too early
to evaluate its results, the fact is that this was a wholly new
approach and, at the very least, suggested, by contrast, the
paucity of wit and the bankruptcy of ideas that has characterized America's effort.

In some respects, Gaviria's approach may be said to be informed by the debate on decriminalization. His plea-bargain approach may be the moral equivalent—and is certainly analogous
to—lowering the degree of criminalization of drug trafficking.

How might the issue play on our (demand) side of the
equation?

A debate on decriminalizing drugs might awaken us to the

folly of such mindlessly tough measures as are producing crushing prison populations of criminals who need treatment more than incarceration. Instead of raising penalties and imprisoning everyone, we might lower the sanctions and provide services and treatment, much as the Netherlands does. It is too tempting to describe such slippery approaches as successes, but their approach does seem to be working more effectively than ours, and it does have the undeniable virtue of being based on study, research, and planning.

Foreclosing the debate and assuming an intractable posture of toughness blind us to promising innovations abroad and prevent us from discovering any of our own at home. We're not even learning from such failures as Zurich's Platzspitz.

THE WAR ON DRUGS

Absurdly, Nancy Reagan's "Just Say No to Drugs" campaign has apparently had a telling effect. It became the catch phrase for an extensive effort of education that, in a variety of guises, reached a large number of kids who were ready to be influenced on drug's dangers. Madison Avenue's approach and the educational program were producing results.

The extensive and dramatic educational effort undertaken by the Partnership for a Drug Free America has had an impact. Undertaken, perhaps, in expiation for Madison Avenue's stupendously successful effort to get us to consume all kinds of nostrums, the vivid images, depicting frying brains and such, may well have influenced trends now indicating reduced drug use in the United States.

Any War on Drugs is going to require the involvement of a cross section of agencies: governmental, private, and not-for-profit. They must participate in efforts aimed at preventing drug use, educating possible users about the dangers, enforcing laws against abusers, and offering treatment to the addicted.

Such a broad effort necessarily implies participation by

health, medical, social-service, and educational bodies, as well as the members of the criminal justice system, to whom the lion's share of the burden for prosecuting the war has been unwisely assigned.

President George Bush, who'd had experience in the field through having been sent by President Reagan to Florida to lead the effort against drugs entering the United States, offered us his vision on September 5, 1989. The thrust of his approach was perfectly symbolized by his dramatic waving of a packet of drugs, bought across the street from the White House, in LaFayette Park.

It later turned out that federal agents had had to contrive the venue of the sale in order to lend dramatic force to the president's assertions. The stage-managed way in which that drug packet had been secured illustrated perfectly President Bush's approach: It would be a cynical program that would deliver action for the American people, but few results.

The plan adopted, as outlined in the National Drug Control Strategy, featured uninformed and mindless enforcement-, prosecution-, and incarceration-centered policies that fed into the fears of a spooked public.

The Inter-American Commission on Drug Policy, a high-level group that includes experts from North and South America, among them former Drug Enforcement Administration Director Peter Bensinger, issued a report in 1991 describing U.S. drug enforcement policies as either "not working" or "yield[ing] scant results in relation to their sizable costs." The commission cited abuses by South American military personnel and other problems and called for programs to reduce demand and to provide treatment, to disrupt criminal networks, and, unfortunately, to emphasize street-level enforcement.

Representative Charles Rangel, who has worked on the drug issue for years, estimated the amount spent on drugs as close to $100 billion and remained critical of federal efforts.

Despite allocating $11.6 billion to combat drugs in 1991, 70 percent of which went for enforcement, America's drug czar,

Bob Martinez, admitted stumbling over "the hard core front," which he described as inner-city residents and minorities. That Bush's general in this critical battle was the unsuccessful candidate for the governorship of Florida, and a presidential friend for whom a job had to be found, emphatically illustrates the sincerity with which Bush fought this war. That the drug czar's office was loaded with political appointees just underscored this point.

President Bush's black Secretary of Health and Human Services, Dr. Louis W. Sullivan, avoided this dangerous fact and finally admitted that "Students have heard and responded to our message to stop using drugs, but the tougher job of reaching drop-outs, the unemployed and other special populations remains" (see the *New York Times* of December 20, 1991).

A PRESIDENTIAL COMMISSION ON DRUGS

The War on Drugs has been characterized mainly by shameless political posturing by rulers intent on self-aggrandizement, from the president on down, and including Democrats as well as the GOP. A confused potpourri of approaches has featured sweeps, roundups, frozen zones, and other constitutionally suspect, and ineffective, tactics, as well as a few that have produced useful results, but that were neither recorded, disseminated, nor widely adopted. A few, isolated drug conferences have produced reports of the occasional successful programs.

Would anyone have risked voting against the Draconian drug laws that were proposed by Governor Nelson Rockefeller in the early seventies and that resulted in the flooding of New York's prisons? A sophisticated grasp of the issues would have included taking measures that provided treatment for users— perhaps under the coercive force of the threat of incarceration—and preventive and educational programs for potential users. Where was the voice of reason in New York's legislature?

Couldn't it be said that the Attica Prison Riot of September 1971, with its twenty-nine deaths and scores of injuries, flowed naturally from such official myopia?

The harvest of an exclusive reliance on toughness has been overcrowding, restiveness in the prisons, rising levels of street violence, and no abatement in either drug traffic or addiction among the underclass.

The appointment of a presidential commission on drug abuse—either standing alone or as an important arm of a larger presidential commission on crime—holds the promise of promoting the needed discussion of the manifold issues surrounding narcotics, from grower to user and everyone in between, and of developing a fixed and focused national strategy on which we can all agree. Such a commission would include the many varied disciplines involved in the drug problem and its solution and would offer a forum for informatively discussing all the issues.

Decriminalization, for example, is very likely a bad and dangerous idea, but discussing it might lead to adopting policies that emphasize deescalating the criminal penalties and to fixing our focus on approaches that attacked the problem upstream (before it takes root), in terms of prevention and education programs, or downstream, in terms of treatment.

The scholars in the field are virtually unanimous in decrying the paucity of information and the plethora of enforcement action programs. It's time to invest the program with a bit of thought and bring in such other disciplines as social services and health services to participate in the struggle.

Charlatans and experienced observers, who are usually in fields that are not related to the struggle against drugs, and who should know better than to offer panaceas in areas in which they possess no expertise, suggest the development of second currencies to reduce international money laundering and trafficking. They recommend the lightning elimination of all $100 bills (presumably under the notion that only drug traffickers use such denominations) and military interventions in drug-producing countries (a sort of "Invasion of the Month" plan for the Andes). Some favor introducing benign neglect into drug enforcement, by just ignoring the enforcement of some drug laws (a sort of decriminalization by fiat), and other silly schemes. It may be worth noting that not a single major police official has favored decriminalizing hard drugs, and the Major City Chiefs of Police have unanimously condemned the notion. Yet they did consider it and discuss this and other issues that deserve to be debated. Such forums might easily lead to other, useful discoveries, and they would, at least, promote the notion of the need to search for better answers.

The national effort has been led by a political appointee whose approach has mirrored his lackluster prospects. The drug czar's office should be abolished and the staff dismissed. Such a salutary downsizing of the government would go a long way toward allaying Americans' justified suspicions of its bureaucracy.

Elevating the Drug Enforcement Agency (DEA) to equal status with the FBI and charging it with the responsibility of overseeing the nation's war on drugs would eliminate organizational confusion. The DEA would become the distributor of federal funds, lead the enforcement effort, and coordinate programs relating to research, planning, prevention, education, and treatment. The billions now going for police overtime and the hiring of more officials and building of more prisons ought to be slashed, the programs cancelled, and the remaining funds concentrated on prevention, education, and treatment programs and on enforcement approaches that target Mister Big.

CONCLUSION

The overclass sets the tone and establishes the values that regulate our lives. It is in danger of drugging itself into oblivion, and taking the nation with it.

A brief glimpse at our Sodom and Gomorrah, Las Vegas,

will show us where we're headed, but if this isn't enough, the divorce courts, television programs, rock lyrics, movie plots, sports scene, state of our cities, and other reflections of our culture will convey the message clearly enough. The Noriega trial and the BCCI scandal conjure up the most alarming visions possible. We need a moral regeneration, and the best way to achieve it is to fight the disabling forces of racism and poverty, which produce addiction as a symptom of the underlying disease.

All sectors of society have roles to play in combating an evil as pervasive as narcotics, but our government has been particularly derelict in its failure to point the way.

The narcotics problem involves many principals along the chain of grower to user. It functions according to economic forces of supply and demand. It is a very complicated problem that is not going to give way to demagogic approaches.

Just as alcohol is related to well over half the fatalities on our roads, addictions are related to probably as much as three fourths of the crime and violence bedeviling the nation. The growing plight of the underclass holds the clear and definite promise of more to come.

Chapter Nine

FAMILY AND CITY
Society's Key Units

Except the Lord build the house, they labor in vain that build it: except the Lord keep the city, the watchman waketh but in vain.

—Psalms, 127:1

The keystones of a modern society are the family and the city. The first is the central building block of the edifice, and the second solves the need for concentrating employment, educational, recreational, and cultural resources. In the United States, both the city and the family are in trouble, and their trouble spells even greater problems for the nation.

Complex organisms that the city and the family are, the statistics will reveal fragments of a scene that, like a mosaic, must be assembled intelligently to reveal the overall vision. Although the dominant class may set a tone that is copied by all segments of society, the consequences vary, depending on the class. Divorce among the well-to-do may often be hedonistic, dissolute, or socially destructive, but it is not likely to produce muggers, robbers, or auto thieves. Among the lower classes, familial dissolution may bring more negative results.

AMERICAN FAMILIES

The divorce totals in America have precisely mirrored the murder incidence, which is itself a faithful reflection of street crime's trends. While murders went from 9,110 in 1960 to 24,020 in 1991, divorces climbed from just under 400,000 a year in 1960 to a peak of over 1.2 million in 1980.

The divorce statistics fail, of course, to reflect the casual liaisons that, among the underclass, constitute a family. The very tenuous nature of these liaisons can feed dysfunctional, and even dangerous, behavior.

A study, reported in the June 1991 issue of *Science*, of 1,700 British families and another of 1,700 American families revealed the negative impact of family conflict on youngsters' behavior and school performance. It showed that divorce spawns conflict and tension, both before and after, with negative consequences for the children. Although in this study the conflict was the focus, rather than divorce, it was the divorce that produced what could be labeled "middle-class trauma" and its resulting neuroses and psychic difficulties.

Over roughly the same period, the number of nonfamily households increased enormously. In 1960, there was a total of 52,799,000 households, of which 44,905,000 were family; 7,895,000 were nonfamily. By 1987, the household total was 89,479,000, of which 64,491,000 were families and 24,988,000 were nonfamily households. (A nonfamily household is one that consists of only one person or that contains unrelated people.)

These statistics indicate the growing fragmentation and isolation of American society.

The entrance of women into the labor force in great numbers and their increasing pursuit of higher education have resulted in increasing the number of women who have never married or have married later. Work, more education, and the rise of feminism have made women more assertive and less likely to put up with abuses in marriage. Thus, there has been a decrease in the number who are married with a spouse present. The number of women fifteen years old and over who were married, with a spouse present, declined from 62.2 percent in 1960 to 53.6 percent in 1985. The percentage divorced went from 2.6 percent in 1960 to 8.2 percent in 1985, while the percentage widowed remained stable, at 12.5 percent and 11.9 respectively. Those who were single (who had never been married) increased almost 4 percent for women and almost 5 percent for men.

A U.S. Census Bureau survey revealed that 15.8 million children, or 26 percent of those under eighteen, were living in single-parent households in 1990. Of these, 38.6 percent were living with a divorced parent, and 30.6 percent were living with a parent who had never married. Nearly 23 million Americans live alone, including about 11 percent of those thirty-five to forty-four years old. Over twenty years ago, in 1970, the percentage of this same age group living alone was 3 percent, or just about one fourth of the current total. The proportion of twenty-five- to thirty-four-year-old adults who have formed their own families declined from 83 percent in 1960 to 65 percent in 1990. The number of unmarried couples living together in 1990 had risen to 2.9 million, or 80 percent more than only a decade earlier. And the trend away from the traditional family unit accelerates, as any quick review of television programming will confirm.

The overwhelming majority of divorces were based on concerns for pleasure and convenience. To preserve the family divorce has to be made much more difficult for parents with children under fifteen. A waiting period of 1 year is needed in such circumstances.

THE FAMILY

As mentioned earlier, the crucial effect of family life was highlighted by a Bureau of Justice Statistics survey, released in 1992, that revealed that half of all juvenile delinquents imprisoned in state institutions, and more than a third of the adults in jails or prisons, have immediate family members who have also been incarcerated. The conditioning of the child, in the home, was confirmed as an important determinant of that child's future behavior. The study did not, however, rule out the effects of environment or genetics. Many of those studied had grown up not only in criminal families but among criminal friends and in criminogenic neighborhoods. Many had been born to addicted or alcoholic teenagers, so that they had been exposed to congenital problems.

Although the study focused on families, it tended to confirm the critical influences of family, environment, and genetics in shaping the violent offender. When all of the studies and analyses of street crime are brought together, however, there are two words that stand out high above all others: *poverty* and *race*.

POVERTY AND RACE

Concealed behind the figures lies a series of explosive factors concerning the growing schism between classes caused by racism and poverty. More than 60 percent of black children under eighteen live in single-parent families—double the total of twenty years ago, and growing. As a result of Medicare, Social Security benefit increases, tax changes, increasing toughness on welfare, and low wages, there has been a dramatic shift in wealth from the young to the old and from the poor and black to the rich and white. Thus, one in every five children lived in poverty in 1990, while the number of elderly poor has declined dramatically since 1970. The Reagan tax revolution drastically accelerated the separation of the haves and the have-nots, greatly increasing the wealth of America's economic royalists, at the expense of all the rest of us.

During the 1980s, a period of uninterrupted and dramatic economic growth, an additional 2.2 million children were pushed below the poverty line (then defined as $12,675 per year for a family of four). At the same time, the very rich were reaping enormous benefits, as the richest 1 percent of American families received 77 percent of the gain in pretax income from 1977 to 1989. The wealthiest 660,000 families, each of which had an annual income of at least $310,000 for a household of four, received 13 percent of all family income, up from 9 percent in the years before 1977. A study by the Children's Defense Fund found that the United States has one of the highest child poverty rates of all the industrialized nations and more than five times the rate of Switzerland or Sweden.

The absence of any plans, on the national front, to ease the plight of the poor would be scandalous in and of itself. Unfortunately for all, the reversals set in motion by the Reagan revolution—widening the disparities between rich and poor and between black and white—are certain to bring tragic consequences in the form of crime, violence, and rioting.

GOOD INTENTIONS

In a report released in June 1991, a federal panel headed by Senator John D. Rockefeller IV, called the National Commission on Children, recommended a $1,000 tax credit for each child in America, additional spending on prenatal care, greater school-choice options, increased health care for children, and expansion of the Head Start program. It joined others calling for an increase in the Job Corps program, from the 62,000 being trained per year to 93,000; time off to care for a newborn child or a sick relative; and "a comprehensive income security plan" for children. The commission emphasized the importance of moral values and decried the sex and violence on television, urging a parental boycott of such programs, as well as of offensive advertising and music.

The report, compiled by members representing a broad political spectrum, received a tepid response from the White House, whose spokesperson said, "The money's not there." The estimated cost was more than $50 billion a year, or $267 to $293 billion over the following five years. The president's spokesperson failed to state that this was less than the $300 billion spent on defense each year despite some meager, halfhearted cuts. The nation was very alive to virtually nonexistent external threats and dead to the awesome and growing internal carnage. It also ignored the huge and growing cost of maintaining all these prisoners in cages.

President Bush's own housing secretary, Jack F. Kemp, recognized the danger posed by an army of impoverished kids and in 1991 proposed measures to ameliorate the condition. The proposals were greeted by a stone wall of resistance. Later the following year, they were hurriedly, if insincerely, embraced by Bush, in the face of the Los Angeles riots and the need to frame a program—any program—in an election year.

Under the rubric of *empowerment*, Secretary Kemp's proposal depends heavily on such self-reliance programs as assisting the poor to buy their own homes, allowing them to select their children's schools, and giving tax breaks to businesses locating in poor neighborhoods. Thus, by adopting the principles of the marketplace, the fight against poverty would, or should, supposedly, appeal to the Republican conservatives who have favored "bootstrap" approaches. It didn't work that way, as the administration's resistance to domestic social and economic engineering easily carried the day.

Still, in such places as Charlotte, North Carolina, which had a small, successful program called Gateway, modest attempts were being made to get welfare dependents to go to school, to accumulate savings in a rent account, and to find jobs.

PAINFUL REMEDIES

What would a fair national system look like?

Some disparities are essential, and initiative should be encouraged and rewarded. It would be a mistake to repeal capitalism. Its rougher edges, however, need to be smoothed. The energetic and able should be paid more generously than the feckless and incompetent. The point is to modify the extremes of wealth and poverty. This can best be done through the tool historically employed to distribute wealth in America: the income tax code.

Some percentage of every dollar of income ought to be retained, but the tax bite ought to increase dramatically as annual earnings exceed $250,000 per individual. At the other end of the scale, every citizen ought to be granted an annual subsidy, from birth, which would not exceed the poverty line (e.g., $4,000 per year for every man, woman, and child) and which could be taxed as ordinary income, as Social Security benefits are taxed for the more affluent retirees.

A gadfly writing critically of inflated CEO salaries, for the *Financial World Magazine,* was dismissed in 1992 as ad revenues declined. He'd previously left *Fortune* magazine in a dispute in 1991, and he attributed his dilemma to executives who threatened to pull their advertising if he remained.

Athletes receive millions to entertain us, and even purist college sports coaches have become the economic royalists, and the celebrities, of America's campuses.

Although it is clear that the genius of capitalism must be retained, it is equally clear that the distributive justice inherent in socialism mustn't be ignored.

THE REALITIES

The federal retreat from the cities, combined with the cities' budget crises in 1991, greatly exacerbated by the 1990–

1992 recession, resulted in reduced social services for those most in need and contributed to the swelling woes of families and individuals at the margins of society.

During the Reagan years, administration officials sought to purge mentally ill, disabled people from the Social Security program in an effort to root out malingerers. The cuts were restored by the courts, but many of these people had, by then, been driven to the streets. The homeless population was further increased by the gentrification of cheap housing in some cities. The dysfunction of rent control also contributed to this problem by causing unprofitable tenements to be abandoned: thousands were chased into the streets as the buildings were boarded up or became uninhabitable. The emptying of mental hospitals made the homeless problem even worse.

ANOMIE IN THE GHETTO

The physical conditions of the ghetto are stark and depressing (many of the visitors I guided through the Bronx couldn't believe they were in America, likening the landscape to the bombed husks of cities of World War II), and the sociological condition that best describes these neighborhoods is anomie.

There is a sense of desolation, loss of control, and vulnerability. The sense is conveyed by routines of life the safety of which others take for granted: Mail has to be guarded against pilfering. A household member's trip to the local store may result in a cop at the door, with terrible news. Cobblestones are stolen from the streets and sold to suburbanites for their gardens. An empty apartment is an invitation to looters, who take pipes and fixtures; floods result.

Cockroaches and rats are the companions of ghetto residents. Tenements once bustling with the lives and hopes of working immigrants now house welfare cases who are one mail delivery removed from homelessness. Even lead poisoning becomes the affliction of the ghetto dweller.

Rubbled lots are home to forlorn figures huddled over fires in oil cans. Glass is strewn everywhere. Flowing hydrants dangerously lower water pressure, and fighting fires becomes even more dangerous.

Some movies and books play on the overclass's terror of taking a wrong turn, finding themselves in the dangerous maze of South Bronx streets. These are the enemy's lairs.

A survey taken by the Urban Institute in 1987 said that, nationwide, there were between 500,000 and 600,000 people homeless on any given night. The 1990-1992 recession unquestionably made the problem worse. Every study has revealed the complexity of the problem and the myriad mental health services and social services needed by the homeless, in addition to housing.

THE HOMELESS

Street crime has a lot to do with social cohesion and citizen involvement. The movie *High Noon* is about a society's moral bankruptcy, revealed through its cowardly reluctance to take part in ensuring a town's peace. When the hero demonstrates his contempt for the townspeople by flinging his badge to the ground, the failure of the community to provide for its own safety, in partnership with its police, earns it this stinging rebuke.

High Noon is a dramatic illustration of a commonplace fact: Our readiness to get involved—and to intervene when a socially disapproved-of act is taking place—is essential to a community's stability and safety. To avoid any confrontations, however, New York City subway riders, on any given day, will, in an effort to avoid eye contact, studiously bury their faces in newspapers.

Citizen involvement, through partnerships engineered by the cops, is what community-oriented policing should promote. It builds a sense of order and cooperation among police and citizens alike.

Criminologists have commented on the social dissolution

encouraged by the morale-deadening influences of visibly decaying conditions (such as broken windows, abandoned houses, graffiti, and disorderly behavior) about which nothing is done. Community-oriented policing insists that these issues be addressed, jointly, by neighbors and cops.

Thus, the vision of disoriented, threatening, urinating, or importuning homeless wanderers on the streets often prompts a call for housing and, as can be seen from the conditions described, services that treat the other problems. The connection between a large homeless population and street crime may seem to be quite a stretch; however, not only does their presence demoralize a community, but they frequently end up as the victims and perpetrators of crime. Any canvass and analysis of backgrounds will reveal this fact. Fully 30 percent of New York City's jail inmates are homeless men, there for crimes like petty thefts, assaults, disorderly behavior, and other actions of the drunk or disoriented. There is no Western democracy that provides adequate housing for its underclass through private sources. The government has to be, in the case of homeless, the houser of last resort.

Despite the government's blindness toward the homeless, it would appear that it is in the government's self-interest to provide public housing for its homeless. The government must serve as a houser-of-last-resort in what is, appropriately, otherwise a capitalist enterprise. Given the number of abandoned residences that have fallen into the hands of municipalities in recent years through tax defaults, one would think it would not be beyond the wit of this nation to marry the homeless, somehow, to these empty residences. Keeping the homeless in welfare hotels, at astronomical rents, is not only ruinously costly but a vivid reminder of the lack of will and imagination that we're bringing to the problem. The broken-down and abandoned edifices in our cities stand as testimony to our indifference to the homeless.

The responsibility of the government to house its municipal wanderers cannot, however, constitute the equivalent of a free lunch. There must be consequences for negative behavior, and the recipients must earn their own comfort and safety. A series of escalating housing accommodations—from least to most desirable, with movement occurring on the basis of having earned ascendancy or deserved descent—would afford the state the coercive tools that must accompany the rewards. Eviction, although not to be ruled out, probably constitutes an excessively harsh response, but deescalating into less attractive circumstances should serve as an incentive for responsible behavior. And there is always jail for the truly intractable, and there should be asylums for the uncontrollable.

Even in such cases as the plight of the homeless and the seemingly obvious solutions, however, the law of unintended consequences must be kept carefully in our planning. Every time the government gets its thumbs pressing on a problem, an unforeseen and negative reaction pops up elsewhere.

New York City discovered that often families that were doubled up with others or were otherwise housed unsuitably found ways to sneak in ahead of the truly homeless (echoing the references to the "truly needy" that were briefly popular in the Reagan years). These interlopers moved skillfully through the bureaucratic maze to qualify for new public housing. That is how those who hadn't been homeless at all somehow wound up in the public housing intended for the homeless. Some of these people were found to have given up jobs, or to have had babies, in order to qualify as welfare cases and had moved out of their residences and into public shelters to establish homelessness. The painful fact is that humans act out of rational motives, and that clever ones tend to gain advantages over the unknowing or unprepared. People will take the path of comfort and convenience if the state allows them to.

This is not to say that the effort to house the homeless ought to be abandoned. Far from it. It does, however, remind us of the complexities surrounding these simple problems and of the need to accompany reforms with accountability and controls. The incentives must be to prod families off welfare and to ensure that the deserving and needy will receive the help. The abuses not only destroy initiative but prove demoralizing to those struggling to live.

A New York City Mayor's Commission on Homelessness recommended that the city contract with nonprofit organizations for shelters for the homeless to establish a hierarchy of housing possibilities that would allow those who have demonstrated fitness to graduate into better housing. Autonomy in site selection, rent vouchers that the homeless could use in securing an apartment, and similar self-help approaches were included. The report was critical of the bureaucracy that had been created to attack homelessness. It produced lavishly expensive hotel lodgings.

THE MENTALLY DISTURBED

The release of psychiatric patients, the growing number of homeless people, cuts in federal aid, and drug addiction and alcoholism have greatly increased the population of the emotionally disturbed on the streets of our cities. The number of psychiatric beds in New York State went from 93,000 in 1955 to a 1992 total of 12,500, and further reductions were planned. The population of the homeless mentally disturbed, estimated at 20,000, poses a problem for New York City residents and the police and often results in tragedies that raise police–community tensions. The murder of Alexis Welch, described earlier, dramatically illustrates the consequences of this tragically framed policy of mindless releases or lack of interest or supervision.

Community-based programs treat some 400,000 a year, and the plan is to have 40,000 community-based beds, but as of 1992, New York State had only 29,000 completed or in process.

The shelters to which clients are sent are armories that pack seven hundred cots into one vast room and that serve three hot meals a day. These cavernous warrens house addicts, criminals, and the mentally disturbed in conditions that have frightened many enough so that they prefer to remain in the cold streets.

Typical of the persons who need to be coerced into taking their medication—through the threat of such sanctions as institutionalization—is Kevin Thorpe, a thirty-one-year-old black man whose mother called for the police when he became violent after missing a dose of medication. In the struggle with the responding cops, who sat and lay on his prone body, he died by asphyxiation. The case had been foreshadowed by the killing of Eleanor Bumpurs, years earlier in the Bronx. She was a large elderly woman who came at an officer with a knife; he shot and killed her. There were many other less-heralded, but basically identical, responses and near-misses.

The Bumpurs case was instructive for another wrinkle, the urban politics surrounding such incidents. The woman was well over sixty and black, and the cop who blew her away was white. The district attorney, under heavy pressure from the borough's black community, indicted the officer, against the conventional wisdom and, in this case, the evidence. The officer was exonerated by a jury that predictably—and, in this case, justifiably—found in his favor. The prosecutor died and was succeeded by a black district attorney. And the merry urban band played on.

Extensive training, the use of specially selected response forces, and the employment of electronic "stun guns" and other technology haven't diminished the danger posed by a growing population that comes to the authorities' attention only when it goes out of control. The anecdotes behind the statistics depict a deadened and defeated bureaucracy, mismanagement at the top, poor allocation of resources by city administrations that succumb to public fears, and a national administration that has little time for domestic policies involving inner cities and the plight of the poor and excluded.

In 1990, President Bush formed an Interdepartmental Task Force on Homelessness and Severe Mental Illness that appears to have produced nothing. The task force estimated that there were 200,000 homeless mental patients nationwide, and that programs that might help, such as outreach attempts to coax the mentally disturbed into treatment and housing, would cost around $3 billion a year. But as President Bush prepared to leave office in early 1993, the plight of the homeless had worsened and their numbers were growing as a result of the recession of 1990–1992.

THE SPECIAL PLIGHT OF THE KIDS

The problems of child neglect and abuse are reflected in the 407,000 children in foster care, nationally, in 1991. Many such children are removed from violent or abusive homes as a last resort and are bounced around the system in ways that will very likely program them for violence and failure. Many of these kids exhibit bizarre, violent, uncontrollable behavior as tiny tots and may present a danger to the families taking them in—to say nothing of the long-term risks they represent to the larger society. One five-year-old in Cincinnati shredded his clothes, ripped the soles off his shoes, tore the antenna off the TV, and set fire to the bathroom. At eleven, he strangled the family dog and had to be cast out of the home. Of course, not all foster children act in such defiant ways and some foster families are exploitative or worse. But still others exhibit behavioral and emotional problems because of congenital difficulties related to their mothers' drug use during pregnancy.

Detroit, itself a paradigm of the decaying American city, announced the opening of all-boys' schools in August 1991, to attempt to salvage 560 black youngsters who had dropped out of high school at the rate of two out of every three. About 70 percent of them were being raised by single mothers. Blacks constituted 90 percent of the Detroit school system's 170,000 students.

This plan was the most radical of a series of desperate projects seeking to reverse a deadly trend of failing inner-city youngsters who wind up dead, strung-out, or in jail. The all-boys' schools were created to offer positive male role models, instill values, and build self-esteem (the trendy theme of the time) in boys whose principal cause of death is murder and who usually join their older brothers in the lost worlds of drugs, street hustling, alcoholism, and prison. Critics pondered the prospects of success facing kids who sometimes dodge bullets on their way to school and frequently arrive cold and hungry. The supporters cited the need for structure, discipline, and interest in the lives of these boys.

There had previously been only three male employees in one of the old coed school buildings, and one had been killed in a drive-by shooting. A preschooler in the area had been shot in the back. A third-grader had had to be spirited out by security personnel because he'd held out $300 on a local drug dealer. The establishment of the boys' academies—named after black leaders Malcolm X, Marcus Garvey, and Paul Robeson—represented a last, utterly desperate attempt at reversing the cycle of failure visited on youngsters who are as much the victims of a racist, economically unjust society as their victims will later be of these boys' angry outbursts and crimes. The proposed curriculum of the school was Afrocentric, concentrating on the achievements of blacks.

One mother summed it up with "Do something for these black boys now, or you're going to be running from them later." Increasingly, these were being referred to as "The Lost Boys."

In one of those ironic twists that seem irresistible to whatever shapes human fate, a federal judge struck down the effort, as discriminating against girls, on August 15, 1991. Thus did laws against segregation—intended to secure rights for excluded black youngsters—work to prevent the adoption of measures intended to help black boys.

It should be added that the entire effort had the feel of desperation about it. The plan for an all-black boys' school was not predicated on experiments and studies that had been conducted and validated; it relied instead on the hysterical thrashings-about of administrators willing to try anything. Few things seem as futile or as preordained to fail as measures embraced in such inauspicious circumstances, when money isn't really being spent to educate these kids, and jobs aren't waiting for them. This particular effort looked cosmetic. In the end, a compromise was reached allowing for the inclusion of young women.

THE CITIES

Can America survive without its cities?

The answer is certainly no, yet the overclass continues to abandon its cities even though it is forced to rebuild and expand the downtowns so central to commerce and prosperity. The result is cities with glittering new office buildings at their core, surrounded by devastated neighborhoods. However, sanitized corridors have been cut to allow for the shuttling of the suburbanites to their homes and offices. Gary, Indiana; Detroit; East St. Louis, Illinois; Newark; the Bronx; and Camden—all are bywords for the inner rot and soul-searing devastation that our cities are experiencing. These moonscapes were once vibrant neighborhoods. All of this in the midst of the most prosperous society on earth.

POLITICAL CORRECTNESS AND THE INNER CITIES

There has often seemed to be an unholy, silent agreement between blacks and their oppressors to avoid confronting realities that, if acknowledged and discussed, might lead to the formulation of remedial programs. The syndrome has taken on the title of politically correct speech. Sensitive topics are given wide berth and are thereby ensured continued neglect.

A wonderful example occurred when the nation's top mental health official—the director of the Alcohol, Drug Abuse and Mental Health Administration—addressed the Advisory Council of the National Institutes of Mental Health on February 11, 1992. His institute was researching violence in humans and animals and attempting to identify, early in their lives, persons who may resort to violence or antisocial behavior and to find ways to treat them. He illustrated his point by commenting on the behavior of hyperaggressive primates that compensate for their shorter and more violent lives by being more sexually active and producing more offspring. His fatal transition was to compare them to humans living an unstructured, undisciplined inner-city life and to remark on the fact that these inner cities are sometimes referred to as jungles.

Despite individual factors, biological differences, or genetic variations, it is probably the loss of structure that leads to so much violence in the inner cities, he said. He immediately apologized for his remarks, following complaints. The Congressional Black Caucus and others found the apology inadequate and pressed for an inquiry. None of the reports indicated any reference to blacks, but the inference was made that he'd equated black youth with hyperactive, hyperaggressive monkeys.

On February 28, 1992, this official resigned.

Thus was research into animal and human violence encouraged by our government, and thus was the utterance of politically incorrect thought rewarded.

THE CITIES AS CENTERS OF CRIME

Crime, violence, and rioting all center in the cities, as do jobs, education, services, and opportunity.

Violent crime surged 21 percent from 1987 to 1990, with more than a quarter of the murders in 1990 occurring in just seven cities: New York (2,245 killings), Los Angeles (983), Chicago (850), Houston (568), Detroit (582), Philadelphia (503), and Washington D.C., with the highest per capita murder (472) and cops-to-citizens rates in the country. All except Detroit suffered increases over 1989. Experts cited the principal causes as drug trafficking and the availability of guns.

Derek C. Bok's final address as Harvard's president centered on "an eerie indifference" to "urban violence, the poverty, the homelessness, the hunger of children." In June 1991, he spoke at the commencement exercises of the need for "research on school reform, poverty, crime and many other social afflictions." Other prophets, such as the black moviemaker Spike Lee and his increasingly eloquent associates, warn, in wonderfully graphic images, of holocausts to come if we don't address the problems of racism, poverty, and the awful exclusions being visited on blacks in America.

But the cities' problems aren't due only to Washington's neglect and white flight. Poor management, municipal scandals, abuses relating to perquisites in office, surrenders to municipal unions and other special interests, indifference to the ghetto, and general recklessness have characterized many of the nation's city halls. One has only to scan the morning paper for egregious and frequent examples. It is a great pity that elected officials are not subjected to such rigorous pressures as caused an electrical engineering conglomerate to adopt a 30-30-30 approach, in which it reduced head office staff from 880 to 28 by laying off 30 percent, transferring 30 percent into offices selling their services to the firm on a competitive basis, and putting 30 percent into the company's operating units. Other giants have been scrambling to study the approach.

Instead, New Yorkers get accounts of lavish refurbishings of municipal offices, stolen campaign funds, a questionable transfer of property by a high official, and other peccadilloes that rain on the citizens uninterruptedly.

Mired in neglect, the ghetto residents seethe.

RIOTS

Every urban police chief's nightmare centers on the burning visions encompassed in the ominous phrase "long, hot summer." Widespread burning, looting, shooting, and killing are the specter that haunts the chiefs. *Riot* is the word that summarizes the fear.

In preparing his doctoral dissertation, *A Delphic Forecast of the Future of Law Enforcement*, FBI agent William L. Tafoya created a carefully winnowed list of experts—scholars, practitioners, and experimenters—on policing and put a series of questions about the future to the panel. High on their list of concerns was the threat of urban riots.

These urbanologists knew that every city contains a combustible mixture of anger and energy, awaiting the spark of an incident. In a very real sense, the hiring of black police chiefs may, at least partially, be attributed to the search for a way to forestall the explosion. Angry blacks may be mollified by the presence of a black face in the chief's chair, a key post in the lives of ghetto residents. Debates about controlling the police, as embodied in the controversies surrounding the establishment of civilian review boards, may also be said to contain the seeds of concern about preventing large-scale disorders.

And because riots that have failed to occur are hard to measure, who can say—despite the occasional disorders that have dotted the municipal landscape in recent years—that the policy is a failure? It is at least conceivable that the levels of anguish caused by racism and poverty might well, without the presence of a reassuring black face in a central position of power, have boiled over. Black mayors, taking to the streets in campaigns to stop widespread violence, may well have provided a credibility that has forestalled general looting, burning, and pillaging. Almost subconsciously, America seems to have been buying peace by installing blacks in high municipal posts at the same time that it has been abandoning the cities.

The incident that precipitates a riot has usually been the shooting of a black youngster by a white police officer. But this is only the most dramatic example of a host of incendiary possibilities.

Earlier I cited the incident in Crown Heights, Brooklyn, on August 19, 1991, of a car driven by a Hasidic Jew jumping the curb and killing a seven-year-old black boy. This event ignited the area into days of disorders that included clashes with the police and the Hasidim. A visiting Jewish scholar was stabbed to death. The looting had the ironic effect of costing the blacks employed in those stores their jobs. Bottle- and rock-throwing incidents even had the city's black mayor, David Dinkins, as the target. Molotov cocktails were hurled, police cars were burned, and shots were fired as marauding bands of black youths suddenly had a focus for pent-up frustrations and fury.

What the Crown Heights disorders of 1991 and the Los Angeles riot of 1992 illustrated is the permanent existence of anger, awaiting a precipitating event that will focus the diffuse hostility on a definable target. Usually, the targets become the police and the shops, but as in the Crown Heights case, they may also be neighbors. The Hasidic sect is a tightly knit and incredibly organized and politically powerful group which has been seen by neighboring blacks—as Korean grocers have been seen—as competitors for services, jobs, schooling, and housing and whose success has engendered deep hostility.

In one of those subtle and understated political signals that betokens a shift in power, and that is given so quietly as to clearly seek to prevent any discussion, the police announced they'd cease the thirteen-year-old tradition of providing an escort to Hasidim that enabled them to celebrate Hanukah, on December 6, 1991. Complaining of this new policy, a rabbi accused the police of caving in to pressure from blacks, who'd claimed the cops had been extending preferential treatment. In fact, they had done just that, and as the Hasidim and the blacks lived cheek by jowl, the favoritism proved too blatant to be ignored. The police blandly claimed that the change had occurred after a "routine review." Right. Meanwhile, the escorts of the Grand Rabbi, to and from the cemetery (one of which had triggered the fatal accident), would continue, for "security reasons."

The Hasidim are, it must be said, wonderfully religious, dedicated family people with a tradition of hard work and scorn for the pleasures driving so much of the rest of the

United States. What the cops were responding to, though, was the realpolitik of their unity, as represented on the ballot.

The central fact, as accurately depicted in Spike Lee's *Do the Right Thing* and *Jungle Fever* and in John Singleton's *Boyz 'N the 'Hood*, is that the exclusions and disabilities worked by a racist overclass on the blacks produce a profoundly alienated and hostile group of youngsters. These kids have nothing to lose, little to live for, and handy targets for their anger in the whites and in the glittering shops around them.

These are the urban dramas being played out in cities that are decaying and regenerating at the same time, causing prophets of gloom to point at the decay and the optimists to cite the development of glittering buildings. The obvious fact is that the processes of death and rebirth are occurring simultaneously, and the only relevant question is: Which is happening at the faster rate?

Newark has experienced a rebirth of its downtown, where $6 billion in new construction has occurred since 1986. Meanwhile, its surrounding neighborhoods are dying. Unemployment reached 12.6 percent in 1991, and an additional 52,000 residents fled to the suburbs between 1980 and 1990. Its riots of 1967 left 26 dead and much of the city devastated. White flight to the suburbs drove the population from 382,417 in 1970 to 275,221 in 1990. The city's school system is in shambles, and it suffers from the second worst (New York City ranks first) per capita AIDS infection rate in the nation. High-speed ribbons wind their way around the city, past and over dangerous ghettos, between suburban homes and downtown offices. Even the railroad station can be accessed through a pedestrian bridge over the street that precludes stepping on city asphalt. The city's median income is $12,000, and about one third of its residents were on welfare in 1991. Housing is a critical need, as 8,000 to 10,000 families are homeless, and countless others are doubled up or making do. The city's public housing stock is in a decrepit state, as its government has suffered paralysis on the question of new housing and finds itself unable to refurbish existing housing.

REACTIONS OF OBSERVERS

The president of New York's City Council, Andrew Stein, in an op-ed piece for the *New York Times* dated May 21, 1990, discussed the city's "combat zones" and described how everyday, routine tasks, like going to school or using public transport, have become dangerous adventures where the innocent have to run gauntlets of gangs and thugs. He cited the removal of cops from the neighborhoods as part of the cause of such violence and added some blame to "civil liberties groups and activist judges." The centerpiece of his logic was that the cops had been discouraged and hamstrung and that here had been a general retreat from discipline and punishment. He called for a return of the cops and mandatory jail time for offenders and derided "inventive readings of the Constitution [that] give endless procedural rights to a violent minority." One has to wonder when he had last visited Rikers Island or read the imprisonment statistics for his city and state. Yet Council President Stein was accurately reflecting America's zeitgeist *vis-à-vis* the homeless and the excluded underclass.

Miami abandoned its plan to shuffle several hundred homeless persons into a baseball stadium and, instead, adopted an ordinance calling for a $500 fine and a sixty-day jail sentence for those ubiquitous panhandlers who wash car windows at intersections.

Washington, D.C., closed two emergency shelters in August 1991 and made plans to reduce even more beds and to restrict the number of nights people could use the shelters. A 1984 law that required the city to shelter the homeless was repealed.

Santa Barbara confined its homeless to a public lot, out of sight of the downtown shops.

Berkeley, a notably tolerant college town, adopted a voucher system in which citizens could buy certificates for merchandise, from local shopkeepers, that they could give the homeless, who would redeem these for food and other necessities. The purpose was to prevent panhandling.

Along bus stops and elsewhere on America's streets, seats are being removed to discourage street people, and public toilets have disappeared.

As we entered the second decade of the homeless–street-people problem the nation's mood was clearly turning impatient. Politicians like Andrew Stein hoped to capture the spirit and ride it to higher office.

Writing in *U.S. News and World Report*, John Leo cited appalling statistics about the numbers on welfare, the anarchy in the subways, the "army of derelicts" on the street, the millions of not-executed warrants for offenders, the half-million drug abusers, and a monstrous educational bureaucracy. He described the awful conditions of central Harlem, where 80 percent of the children are "illegitimate" and 10,000 babies are "born toxic" (addicted to crack or other narcotics). Then he got to the familiar crime statistics, but he made a mistake when he cited the 8,757 robberies in 1952 and the 93,387 in 1989, forgetting, if he ever knew, that the New York Police Department of 1952 routinely "canned" (failed to record) a lot of crime, especially robberies, because it made the city administration look bad. Against this, of course, it could be argued that current apathies keep many New Yorkers from reporting robberies today. In a few anecdotes, Leo described how the violence was finally reaching the rich and famous: "Random, pointless violence is now everywhere and no one is safe." Later he added, "There's a feeling among hardcore New Yorkers who love the city that something resembling a total breakdown of the social order may be under way and that New York may not make it." He called for an effort to bring "the white and black middle class together to confront a largely black crime wave." He concluded with "Things are starting to spiral out of control."

In bucolic, corporate, sanitized Stamford, Connecticut, the police union ran radio ads that had shots and screams piercing the sylvan peace as it called for higher wages and the hiring of more cops. It was precisely the sort of campaign most likely to work on the overclass fears that are fed by the nightly news.

MUNICIPAL FLIGHT

Of course, Americans have learned to adapt to a life outside the cities. First, they moved out and thereby changed bedrooms. Then, they built shopping malls and found recreations in the suburbs. Next, they took their jobs, or tried to, as large enterprises moved out. The abandonment of the cities, figurative and literal, was complete. The sores were left to fester and grow.

Up the coastal highway from Stamford, Bridgeport went broke and filed for bankruptcy in June 1991, to avoid having to pay the burdensome union contracts of its cops, fire fighters, and garbage collectors. It was a municipal protest of state and federal policies that were seen as an abandonment of the economically depressed and racially isolated cities across the land. The officials blamed Washington for abandoning the core cities. They also cited selfish suburbs that refused to help. Their anguish was symbolized by their haste to point fingers and avoid being blamed, as the escalating problems intensified the pressures unbearably.[1]

In their viewpoints, the officials were echoing the Minneapolis planning director's call for metropolitan government to suck the middle class back into helping to solve core city ills.

The fabled mobility of Americans is reflected in federal Census Bureau figures which show that 18 percent of the nation's households moved in 1989 and that nearly half moved between 1985 and 1989. Over the period when murder and

[1] "Bridgeport Uses Bankruptcy Act to Avert Deficit," *New York Times*, June 8, 1991.

divorce were tripling, 1960 to 1989, over 91 percent of the nation's households had moved.

Atlanta's black mayor, Maynard H. Jackson, asked the city council to adopt a stern measure against aggressive street begging, sleeping in vacant buildings, and hanging out in parking lots. The language, using words like *accosting* or *forcing oneself* on another, or causing fear of harm or crime, was reminiscent of the discredited vagrancy and loitering statutes of prior years. It seemed an attempt to criminalize behavior that an unfeeling overclass was imposing on ghetto dwellers or on those it had made homeless.

A shoe-shiner received thirty days in jail because he couldn't make the fine. His lawyer said it was "illegal, for the moment, for poor people to do anything on the streets of Atlanta" and added, in an echo of *Gone with the Wind,* that "not many people give a damn about the poor people on the streets."

The pressure for Jackson's action apparently came from business and corporate interests anxious to sanitize downtown and to make the 1996 Olympic Games more successful. Similar measures were aimed at panhandlers and the homeless in New York, Miami, Seattle, and a number of other cities.

Such oppressions could only lead to the intensification of pressures and an increased resort to desperate measures.

CARJACKING

"Carjackers" became the newest menace in Detroit in mid-1991, as brazen and low-skilled robbers put guns to the heads of motorists stopped at traffic lights, robbing them and driving off in their vehicles. Another wrinkle was to bump others' cars and steal their vehicles when they emerged from their metal cocoons to inspect the damage. The car that did the bumping was also usually stolen.

Almost three hundred "carjackings" were recorded in Detroit and its environs in August 1991. One twenty-three-year-

old man refused to give up his car at a car wash and was shot
and killed. A woman who tried to speed away to save her new
vehicle was also murdered. The practice quickly spread to
other cities.

In New York, robbers shoplifted and stole the car keys of
mall parkers and drove off. The scenes had the unreal look of a
society out of control. Car theft rose to 1.6 million in 1990, a 50
percent increase over 1981. In New York State, carjacking carries a much greater penalty: life in prison for stealing a car at
gun point, while simple car theft carries a five-year sentence.
This suggests that the carjackers lack the skills needed to steal
cars with security protection, and it also illustrates that the
punishment lacks deterrence for people with little to lose.

The Detroit police continue to adhere to their policy of
using decoys only very sparingly, in vice and narcotic cases,
because of the mayor's antipathy for these units; he cam-
paigned, in 1973, against such practices.

In Miami, in 1991, a vacationing British couple, sixty-three
and fifty-nine, stopped to ask directions and were immediately
held up by the occupants of the other vehicle, who shot them
when they refused to turn over their valuables. The wife was
shot in the chest and the husband in the shoulder. The case
seemed a fitting paradigm for the age.

HARDENING HEARTS

Studies by the Crime Control Institute in Washington, D.C.,
the Center for Social Research at the City University of New
York, and the New York City Citizens Crime Commission cite
how New Yorkers' attitudes and behaviors have changed, over
the years, to reflect the increased level of threat. New Yorkers
fear not only crimes, but what we might call importuners or
intervenors, who aggressively ask for change, wash car windows menacingly, virtually mug us on the subway on the
pretext of religious support, or devise cunning schemes to

separate us from our money through guilt or fear. Aggressive begging, for example, where the accoster pushes hard for some change and follows the reluctant giver, hurling threats and imprecations, has even acquired a label *rough tailing*. Such exactions have become another urban tax. New Yorkers are also very threatened by the unexpected and dangerous reactions of the angry or disturbed street people.

In New York, one homeless shelter is seven hundred cots, each a yard apart, on an armory floor. It is part of a system serving twenty-four thousand homeless a day. It houses some in separate sections: homosexuals, Dominicans, Jamaicans, the mentally disturbed who can't be led to taking their medication, alcoholics, the sick and elderly, drug addicts, street criminals, the disabled, loafers, and the vaguely defeated. The shelter's director speaks sensibly of the need for structure, discipline, accountability, and bootstrappism. He doesn't mention the dearth of programs or services that might help, but they loom as discernible shadows behind his words. The shelter is run as much by the inmates as by the keepers. A Devil's Island sort of mentality pervades the place as the evil partnership—accommodation, really—plays itself out in the lives of its users. It is a two-tiered hell in which the bureaucracy oversees the externals and the tougher clients supervise the subtler aspects. Small wonder so many are terrified of such places and refuse to go to them.

THE PUBLIC'S IMPATIENCE

On October 15, 1991, police and bulldozers cleared and razed a shantytown of makeshift homes on empty lots on Manhattan's Lower East Side. An estimated two hundred squatters were displaced. Police made only one arrest. The neighbors had complained of defecations, urinations, open fires, hydrant showers, and other undeniable dislocations of urban orderliness. The squatters had been offered accommodations in the city's cavernous shelters, described by some as dangerous and unsuitable. Only a minority accepted the offer.

City Hall's reasoning centered on complaints from the neighboring residents, fights, loud music, and unsanitary conditions. Things "had just got out of control."

Many of the dispossessed had been ejected from Tompkins Square Park in a notable clash with the police in 1988 that injured 50, resulted in 31 arrests, and produced 120 complaints of police brutality—and one of the first of those home videos of cops' flailing nightsticks. Notwithstanding the evidence of another police riot, on irrefutable videotape, the few cops accused of assaults were exonerated by ever-tolerant juries. The outcome strongly reinforced the cops' well-known code of silence.

In 1992, the Minneapolis police announced they had secured the permission of building owners to question, and possibly arrest, loiterers, drinkers, and possible drug dealers on building stoops. Two thousand "No Trespassing" signs would be posted in the inner city, to enable the police to roust "outsiders" who "dealt drugs" and bothered residents. This program has been greeted enthusiastically by property owners and their association.

That city's planning director, in a book entitled *Old Problems in New Times*, suggested:

- Building subsidized housing for low-income families, two thirds in the suburbs.
- A 1 percent tax on the sale of homes to finance the housing.
- A luxury tax on homes valued at over $250,000.
- A limit on dividend and interest tax deductions of $150,000 on mortgages. Interest paid on amounts over $150,000 would lose the tax deduction.
- An effort by the Metropolitan area government to get the suburbs back into addressing the core city's problems.

The mayors and officials of the suburban ring labeled the

book socialistic and otherwise concealed their enthusiasm. The Minneapolis *Star and Tribune* praised the program in a September 25, 1991, editorial and urged it on the new state governor, who was certain to greet the proposals icily.

In Miami, several hundred of the city's approximately six thousand homeless huddled under Interstate 395 as they awaited delivery on promises of shelter. A judge later officially sanctioned the existence of this FAVELA. Santa Barbara passed a no-sleeping, no-camping ordinance, and Cincinnati gave tickets, carrying a $114 fine, for aggressive panhandling. Atlanta, Chicago, and Columbus have similarly adopted harsh measures. Signs prohibiting car window washing have sprouted.

TOILERS IN THE WILDERNESS

On the other side of the coin, New York was initiating a massive redevelopment scheme for a huge chunk of Harlem that would provide 2,200 new apartments and 300,000 square feet of commercial space, as well as a wide variety of social-service, artistic, and recreational programs.

The cost, funded publicly and privately by foundations, would be about $200 million. The area's churches were heavily involved in the planning in the summer of 1991, but even in the ghetto, some expressed reservations and fears. There was also more than a hint of concern about how the economic pie of redevelopment would be cut up. The Bradhurst Project would be a key test of Mayor Dinkin's ability to produce, and the outcome was far from obvious in 1993.

The problem has been that, faced with such needs, the federal administration's invariable answer has been that "the money's not there." Outlays for defense, Gulf Wars, the War on Drugs, and tax cuts have ensured that this would continue to be the case when it comes to domestic social-welfare programs.

New York City's budget crunch has meant reductions in programs that brought lunches to the home-bound and eliminated workers who provided prenatal services. There were cutbacks on drug treatment programs for crack addicts and addicted mothers, at the same time that the city was scraping together funds to strengthen a bloated and chronically mismanaged police agency. Programs to reduce the shockingly high infant mortality rates and to prevent the lead poisoning of children have also been cut back. School health programs and inspections of day-care centers have been slashed.

More homeless will be crammed into fewer shelters— already frequently avoided because of the dangers and indignities they house—and those in public housing will receive fewer services, repairs, and needed monitoring and controls.

Each of these abstractions contains individual human tragedies that ultimately add up to additional problems for all New Yorkers. The city's decay proceeds inexorably forward, even as huge personnel increases have been planned for the police through 1994. Even the politically powerful senior citizens have lost services, a true measure of the depth and severity of the fiscal crisis.

CIVIC AMENITIES AND CITY LIFE

New York is a city in which trash baskets cannot be kept on the sidewalks because they are stolen as outdoor barbecue grills, where shrubbery is chained securely to prevent its theft, where bicycles are routinely dismantled by their owners to preclude their being stolen, where a gang of teenaged girls stabbed passing white women with hatpins, where cars are stripped and left to lie like metal carcasses on the cityscape, and where eye contact is avoided and the promise of rescue has faded. It passed being merely uncivil a long time ago. Now it is downright dangerous, and its residents are voting with their feet and fleeing.

Corporations have banded together, taxed their members, and hired twenty-nine uniformed security guards to patrol a

150-block section of midtown Manhattan as part of a growing movement toward purchasing police services privately.

It seems increasingly clear that the nation's real problems are centered in its urban areas and that nothing is being done about them. The neglect results in homelessness, addictions, crime, social dissolution, and terror.

Can the nation make it without New York City?

Many would like to believe the answer is certainly yes, but the realities point elsewhere.

SHIFTING POLITICS AND SHIFTING RESOURCES

The abandonment of the cities by the overclass and by its administration in Washington has been accompanied by a dramatic shift in political power. As we've noted, America's ten largest cities are likely to have either a black mayor or a black police chief, or both. This political revolution has been marked by a series of anomalies, such as aggressive police tactics, to be discussed later, that have resulted in the arrest of, or the shooting of, large numbers of blacks, while decoy operations, stakeout units, sting setups, and related tactics have been largely abandoned. The mayors, however, have mostly succumbed to overclass pressures to keep the underclass moving and out of sight, without providing the services needed to help solve the crisis. Resistance to additional taxes and the drying up of federal money make any additional expenditures prohibitively costly, politically.

The crises of our cities have many origins.

The cities, in my experience, have been woefully mismanaged by politicians who have never faced making a payroll or addressing a stockholder's meeting. The closing of mental hospitals, the spreading crack epidemic and other addictions, the growing plight of the underclass, and the problems caused by a recession all add to the preexisting street population, formerly made up mostly of alcoholics. The urban centers have also been abandoned by whites and by their surrogates in the nation's capital. Republicans were rewarded with an unprecedented string of victories in presidential elections.

As if to echo the racist siren call of the 1988 Willie Horton song, the vice president, in a February 1992 speech, derided New York's failure as a "welfare state," thereby making it, and the following hollow roar for family values, that election year's themes. The winner, Bill Clinton, also sought his votes mostly in the suburbs. The overclass votes; the underclass doesn't.

Certainly, there must be jails, punishments, and accountability, but there must also be services. The government has to furnish housing, educational, welfare, health, and social services sufficient to sustain a decent level of life. There must be sanctions for transgressions, such as reductions in assistance, downgrading in housing accommodations, and other penalties.

Every city should have a detoxification center to which public drunks can be taken involuntarily and held for up to seventy-two hours in a hospital–prison-like setting, to sober them up, clean them up, evaluate them medically, and refer them to longer term treatment before releasing them.

Every city should have a psychiatric center to which the mentally and emotionally disturbed can be taken for brief treatment, evaluation, and possible institutionalization through court order. Those who refuse to take medication or who cannot be helped through medication or outpatient treatment will have to be returned to secure hospitals. The number of psychiatric hospital beds must be increased if only to provide a threat (an expensive one) to coerce those out there to take their medicine. The mentally disturbed who pose a danger to the community are mirror images—in terms of the risks—of the prison recidivists who prey on society.

The mixture has to be both tough and tender. There is no inconsistency between democracy and order, although there is both danger and inconsistency in giving the cops implicit instructions to keep the underclass under control, without providing the legal tools or explicit policies for doing so. Evidence of police brutality and other wrongdoing is largely due to the informal messages being conveyed to the police that every cop senses are awry with the explicit legal mandate. Democracies can't afford such hypocrisies. A society can't order cops to keep order in the streets and clean up messy conditions if it fails to provide the detox, mental, and other facilities needed to cope with the street people. Yet this society does.

The government has an obligation to provide safety as well as the services that make voluntary compliance at least possible.

As matters now stand, the United States is much more likely to perish because of what is happening to its families and its cities than because of any external threat.

If the overclass rolls up its sleeves and takes on the city problems of racism and poverty, it may rediscover the altruism that energized it for two centuries and may buy, for the nation, another lease on democratic life.

Chapter Ten

THE CRIMINAL
JUSTICE SYSTEM
The Cops

Justice, sir, is the great interest of man on earth.
—Daniel Webster (1782–1852)

The challenge of street crime is supposed to be met by what is
known as the criminal justice system (CJS), which is assigned
to prevent, deter, detect, rehabilitate, incapacitate, and otherwise deal with crime and criminals. The system's mission is
plain: to make society safe, or at least safer.

Criminal justice in America is principally a local affair. Federal laws probably cover less than 10 percent of what we can call
street crimes, and the federal prisons hold less than 10 percent of
the over one million persons incarcerated. A case could be made
for the proposition that the CJS has been remarkably successful in
providing America with the world's highest incarceration rate:
One of every four adult black males is under some form of
control, and the prison population has tripled in fifteen years.

A low and slipping clearance rate (the number of crimes solved through arrests) serves as a sobering reminder of the danger of such an assertion. Although the CJS has improved in recent years, the fact is that the overwhelming majority of crimes go unsolved. The system is saved by the fact that criminals are inveterate repeaters and finally trip up and get caught.

No one person is paid to think for, or oversee, the system. Each component fights for its turf and its share of resources. And then, the CJS enters the picture only after the criminal has been shaped and the crime committed.

The CJS is composed of cops, judges, corrections officers, prosecutors, defenders, parole and probation officers, and ad hoc players like sheriffs, legislators, and federal, state, and local functionaries of all sorts.

ELASTICITY

The CJS possesses the unexpected quality of elasticity. Despite a crushing volume of cases, it adjusts and adapts and somehow avoids crashing. When overburdened, the system widens the holes in its nets, to allow a greater number of the arrested to swim free. It is undiscriminating but flexible. Mandated actions that threaten its functioning (like Massachusetts's insistence on jail time for gun crimes) are massaged into manageable practices that more or less observe the letter of the requirements, while mangling the spirit. The system has a powerful survival instinct that, in keeping with the law of unintended effects, never seems to respond straightforwardly, as it lunges and lurches toward the mirage of perfect justice that it professes to be chasing.

COORDINATION AND COOPERATION

The various parts of the CJS interact as they are forced to do, vigorously, but they coordinate fitfully and cooperate jealously. Separate fiefdoms are forced to battle for scarce and dwindling resources (except for the cops, who get the lion's share of everything), exacerbating tensions and heightening imbalances, as the various parts compete in the budgetary marketplace. Turf battles are fierce and continuous. The CJS is an arena in which the cops have an unvarying and growing edge, as frightened citizens grasp at the visible and reassuring relief that comes with a blue uniform on the street. Mayors understand the political value of hiring more cops.

Everyone seems to agree that preventing crime requires an efficient system that provides apprehension and swift and certain justice, combined with a fair and speedy trial. The importance of providing consequences for human actions is never clearer than in the field of crime.

The frustration of cops, today, comes from the dissonance that accompanies implicit assignments to control the underclass, without the necessary legal tools to accomplish the task.

When constabulary duty's to be done,
The policeman's lot is not a happy one.
                        —*Pirates of Penzance* (1879),
                        W. S. Gilbert and Sir Arthur Sullivan

THE WORLD OF THE COPS

Organization of Police Departments

Police agencies are usually organized into three segments: patrol, investigative, and support services. The mission is to protect life and property, preserve the peace, detect and arrest offenders, enforce the law, and prevent crime. Local cops address this mission by concentrating on street crime, responding to 911 calls, and enforcing the traffic laws.

Although police agencies hire civilians to perform ancillary functions, the cops' world is ruled by cops. It is a secretive world of rules—both explicitly and covertly conveyed—and of permanence. Employees usually stay at least twenty years, kept in by such factors as that it's the best job they've ever had or are likely to get, and the promise of a pension after a relatively short stay. It is also fun work because they get to see a lot of life in the raw and, despite the development of cynicism and a sense of hardness and isolation, obtain insights into human nature and help people in distress. It is also an outdoor job, done under minimal supervision.

Chiefs and other key executives come not only from the ranks but from the ranks of the departments in which they've spent their careers. Outsiders are rarely hired, and national searches are few and frequently mask charades in which the process has been wired for an insider.

The outward pressures—to make the streets safe and to respond to emergencies and provide order—are tough enough, but they are straightforward and legitimate. Although cops don't like to be pressed to do better when they feel they're trying hard, they can understand and accept the public's fear and anxiety.

The subtler pressure to keep "undesirables" under control and out of sight is a more difficult business because cops don't have either the tools or the authority to make the black, the poor, the homeless, the addicts, the mentally disturbed, and the alcoholics disappear from America's downtowns, no matter how hard the chamber of commerce presses the mayor and the city council.

The Culture

Entering cops, who have been carefully screened through a lengthy and elaborate background investigation, quickly adopt the organizational vision being conveyed by their peers, their union leaders, and the administration. This vision centers on such values as "We're the good guys and they're (the "assholes" and criminals) the bad guys, and whatever we do is OK and whatever they suffer is deserved."

The world doesn't understand their complex and largely unmentionable mission, so cops don't discuss it with "civilians." Cops wind up talking to other cops, and few relationships are as deep or intense as the platonic love of a cop for his partner. That the partner may be a she really complicates the dynamics, as Plato gets removed from the equation. The insularity and isolation are precisely mirrored in the Mafia's culture, which is usually described as exclusive and hostile to outsiders. Like cops, Mafiosi mostly talk only to each other.

In such tightly sealed societies, codes inevitably intrude. *Omerta*—the Mafia's code of silence—is more rigorously observed by cops than by Sicilians, especially in these halcyon days of high-level defections and betrayals within the Mafia. Organizational loyalty turns informers into pariahs. Adherence to the value system—whether legal or moral or not—is the cop's first requirement. Not only is it hard to get cops to testify against cops (the *sine qua non* of any cop prosecution that is to entertain the faintest hope of succeeding), but it is hard, as many prosecutors know but few will admit, to get cops to testify truthfully on matters they consider important, if a lie will achieve the objective sought.

That juries (grand, petit, or civil) continue to believe in and support cops, who are "putting our lives on the line, every night, to protect you," comes as no great surprise to America's reluctant district attorneys, who have little appetite for pursuing even criminal cops. Convicting cops of crimes, whatever the weight of the evidence, is just about the hardest task a prosecutor can undertake. Even a videotaped depiction of cop pushing a citizen's head through a plate-glass window for no good reason wasn't enough to convict a Long Beach, California police officer, and the Los Angeles cops were mostly acquitted of beating Rodney King, Jr., despite a videotape of that assault.

Of the 152 officers interviewed in the 1988 police melee in Tompkins Square Park in New York City, not a single cop testified to any wrongdoing by any other officer, despite scores of complaints of brutality and videotapes showing indiscriminately flying nightsticks. Of the eight thousand complaints investigated by the New York City Civilian Complaint Review Board between 1987 and 1988, not a single one featured a cop voluntarily incriminating another. Keeping the cops as servants of the law, rather than as its masters, is the most daunting difficulty facing any police chief.

Most cops enter as altruistic civilians, eager to help others, and then they become acculturated to the real values of a pressurized organizational environment. They finally leave, weary of the human beast and profoundly skeptical about its real nature. In between, they have a ringside seat at a show of such dark complexity and fascination as to turn many of them into overweight alcoholics with ulcers, poor marriage risks, and people with a higher than average temptation to commit suicide. Suicide, in fact, is such a taboo subject that national figures on police suicides are not kept. From 1986 through 1990, the New York Police Department did report thirty-four in its ranks, almost twice the rate of the general population's suicides.

Policing's reward are tremendous: membership in a tightly knit club with national connections, professional courtesies, and a common language, and having real power and becoming repositories of society's secrets. The job also serves as a vehicle to the middle-class suburban life with its one-family homes and other accoutrements. It is a world in which all the members receive at least the benefit of every doubt. I know that I was feared and condemned by my colleagues in three police agencies, despite never wavering from the principle of giving cops the benefit of the doubt. Cops want more: they want to be protected against such charges as followed the Rodney King, Jr., incident, whatever the evidence. They feel resentful and abandoned when it doesn't work out that way.

Whistle blowers are rejected and expelled—in the very rare instances where they surface at all. Forcing cops to testify against other cops takes tremendous leverage. The Knapp Commission investigation of the New York Police Department (NYPD) in 1972 usually required the real prospect of a jail sentence—and the threat of being placed among prisoners who would be certain to harbor a true animus against ex-cops— before there was any hope of "turning" a cop against fellow officers. Police lore is full of examples of cops being driven from the ranks by otherwise uninvolved colleagues because they'd blown the whistle on Dirty Harrys.

Organizational messages are transmitted in actions, not words. All of the words are ideal. Any inquiry about any police agency would reveal all of the orders in place, calling for civility, justice, truth, and a firm commitment to America's values. The real message is conveyed in how a chief responds to allegations of brutality or corruption, in such personnel actions as hirings and promotions, in the chief executive's attitudes and statements on a wide variety of issues, and in the image that he or she conveys in daily responses to crises and challenges and when there are other opportunities to communicate beliefs.

The Los Angeles Police Department was never told to go out and beat up blacks, but an uncompromisingly aggressive posture toward "the enemy" is easily translated into roughness on the street.

The power of the police culture and its creation of an "us versus them" view of the world can be seen in the firing of two cops from the Tampa police department in early 1991 for uttering racial epithets in separate incidents. That both cases involved the use of the term *nigger* was, in itself, unremarkable, but that in both cases the officers uttering the phrase were black demonstrates dramatically how powerful police acculturation may become.

A task force investigating the awful tragedy surrounding Philadelphia's 1985 attempt to evict MOVE, a then obscure urban cult whose name implied a return to Africa, found that the burning and killing flowed from the internal decay of a badly mismanaged police agency. Sooner or later, the internal problems and deficiencies surface as urban tragedies. Sooner or later, the organizational culture and its real messages are translated into behavior that results in such monstrous failures. Yet the connection between cause and effect and the disparity between real messages and ritualized boilerplate never seem to be made.

The learned studies undertaken after some fearful urban tragedy, like the Christopher Report on the Los Angeles Police Department (LAPD), mostly go unread and gather dust.

Despite all that has been written, filmed, and spoken about the police, most citizens haven't a clue to the true inner workings of their local agency. A Dallas reporter joined that city's police department after having done scores of police stories. His summary of the experience was "You can't understand what it's like unless you do it."

Dangers, the Recruiting Pool, and Power

Police work is not as dangerous as most would believe, and the rate of cops being killed has actually dropped dramatically since the early 1970s.

Police work attracts the children of the blue-collar class, who work and save and pay their bills, but who don't send their kids to college or overprize education. They are often the class in closest competition with blacks for jobs and housing. Recently, there has been a fierce struggle for these job slots, and blacks now constitute 13.5 percent of the nation's cops, with women comprising 8 percent of the total in 1992.

The entrants who develop into "thumpers and takers" (the more energetic and enterprising "meat eaters," as opposed to the passive majority of "grass eaters") rarely constitute more than 1 or 2 percent of the total, but they are often the leaders and set the norms for acceptable behavior.

Cops have enormous power and the temptation to use it when they confront "assholes" on the street. They also know the system is sympathetic to them and will help them all it can. Cops see any truculence or resistance as a direct challenge to their authority, which must be put down immediately. Blacks, frequently angry and anxious to assert themselves against an oppressive system, almost reflexively react in precisely the most dangerous way with cops and reap predictable consequences. A paradigm was Don Jackson, whose perfectly legitimate, but seemingly defiant, questioning of police authority resulted in his getting his head bashed through a plate-glass window in Long Beach, California.

A sociological study of New York's cops found that they'd been psychologically brutalized by the street conditions they faced daily. Breaking the siege mentality created by institutional forces proved a daunting task. Many police executives, of course, actually—consciously or unconsciously—reinforce the nightstick mentality.

Experts tend to believe that it is easier to change police behavior on the street, through monitoring, supervision, and tough investigations of police wrongdoing, than it is to change police attitudes, and that the emphasis should be on controlling actions more than thoughts.

Even the elite FBI has not been spared complaints of racism, as internal polls, lawsuits, and threats of legal action have revealed grievances over discriminatory recruitment, hiring, and promotion policies. As of 1991, about 88 percent of the FBI's ten thousand agents were white. About 10 percent were female, almost 5 percent were black, and 5.5 percent Hispanic.

Police Recruiting

The way to build an effective and efficient police agency precisely matches the way good ball teams and other successful organizations are put together. It begins with establishing high standards that still keep the agency in the marketplace as a viable work force. It will almost certainly mean breaking the blue-collar class's possessive grip over the hiring pool.

For starters, requiring a clean and responsible history in work, personal life, military service, and other activities can be combined with insisting on a college degree. In 1970, less than 4 percent of the nation's cops had college degrees. In 1990, the figure had risen to 23 percent, despite the general absence of any raising of the requirements.

Hiring ought to proceed on an orderly, scheduled basis that allows the police agency to investigate the background of applicants and to hire and train them on an assimilable basis. Too many agencies hire large numbers, all at one time, because of public panic and political ambitions.

The next step in winnowing out the unsuitable should be a year's probation, during which the rookie works under the tutelage of experienced, carefully selected senior field training officers, who regularly evaluate, in writing, the neophyte's performance and prospects for future success.

Maintaining health, weight, and conditioning standards should meld with continuous training throughout the cop's career.

All of these steps, and more, are easily attainable in today's labor market, especially given the opportunities for psychic reward inherent in police work, the very respectable salaries offered, and the urge to serve that lies just beneath the surface of so many of our young. Nationwide, less than 10 percent of the applicants are accepted. In Chicago, in 1990, thirty thousand applied for six hundred police jobs.

Why, then, do so few police agencies even begin to use the choices afforded them by a buyer's market, which would clearly allow them a dramatic increase in entrance standards? Political pressures produce a fits-and-starts strategy that has the mayor hiring a huge class to accommodate a current crisis, while providing a photo opportunity. Such initiatives are frequently followed by layoffs. Internal pressures, by incumbents and their unions, also work to perpetuate the status quo.

Police departments have bought decades of problems by succumbing to the temptations to hire an unexpectedly large number of cops, given them by politicians responding to blaring headlines, without considering filtration and assimilation factors. Years later, the people are treated to statements by high police officials that "Yeah, that bunch of crooked cops came from the notorious class of '85, when we hired hundreds, indiscriminately."

Economically, "the job" belongs to a social level that is at least a cut below the logical market. Civil service jobs mostly belong to families who protect that property right assiduously. These have been traditionally the preserves of the blue-collar class.

And many hold that raising standards is another barrier to minority recruitment. This view ignores the fact that the biggest obstacles to hiring blacks is their lack of connections in the police world, to the hostility of the same black leaders who decry raising educational requirements as "heightening the barriers" while still denouncing the police institution, and to the racism that pervades every aspect of employment, everywhere, for blacks. It is no secret that, for good and bad reasons, the police are not in good odor in the ghetto.

The police organization is society's principal instrument of justice and its key tool in the struggle against street crime. It has to reflect the society it serves and strive to attract the best and the brightest.

Police agencies are going to have to learn that the abuse of power inevitably leads to that power's being curbed, and often, therefore, to impeding activities that are essential to the public's safety. The LAPD had to give up using a legal, and often more humane, choke hold because of publicity attendant on abuse of that tactic. The NYPD entered into a legal agreement curbing its intelligence-gathering operations because of its nervousness over contesting a lawsuit accusing it of spying.

The murder of Puerto Rican independence activists in a police ambush on July 25, 1978, following the infiltration of a group planning to sabotage a television transmitter, proved another example of a totally legitimate intelligence operation being twisted into criminal behavior by overzealous cops.

The Missouri State Highway Patrol undertook illegal internal wiretaps in an effort to secure personal information on its employees between 1981 and 1987. The agency was wracked by the disclosures, which were followed by the suicide of a high-ranking member and charges against several officers.

If a police agency is to be aggressive and effective, it must earn the confidence and support of the people it serves, and it can do this only by functioning absolutely legally and pursuing legitimate interests involving the public's need to be served. The police must be guided by the Ciceronian ideal that "The good of the people is the chief law."

In the final analysis, most outsiders would be surprised at the issues that insiders think germane to heightening police effectiveness.

Inside the Police Agency

The largest and most important part of the CJS are the cops, who start the entire process by arresting the suspect and propelling him or her into its workings.

Conservatives speak of unleashing the cops and of ceasing to handcuff them with court decisions that circumscribe police power. Liberals call for the expansion of individual rights and limiting police discretion.

Cops have a huge cornucopia of laws to choose from, or to ignore (they can't enforce them all), and they frequently exercise this discretion on the basis of their assessment of the target. An "asshole" is certain to receive tough treatment. The decision to arrest may be driven by factors such as attitude, overtime pay possibilities, or the cop's prejudices, none of them having much to do with objective circumstances.

LITERATURE ON THE POLICE

A review of the police literature—of which there has been an explosion in recent years—is instructive for the concerns that repeatedly surface:

- The difference between the public profession of the agency and the on-the-street behavior of its cops.[1]
- The secretiveness of the police world and the ignorance of the public about its workings; the police code of silence and the powerful forces of acculturation and peer pressure working on its members; and the wrongness of TV and movie images of cops. All of these are closely interrelated.
- Police cynicism and isolation.
- The twin bugbears of brutality and corruption.
- The dichotomy between the explicit mission of controlling crime and the implicit charge of keeping the underclass under control.
- The rise of police unions and the power they wield over the agencies.
- The transformation of the reform of civil service into a paralyzing force that prevents needed changes.
- The problems relating to the selection of police chiefs and the effect these have on management initiative and efficiency.
- Police resistance to the elevation of easily achieved entrance standards and to the adoption of such innovations as a police corps of college graduates, whose

[1] Jonathan Rubinstein, *City Police*. New York: Farrar, Straus & Giroux, 1973.

education would be subsidized in exchange for four years of service in the police ranks.

- The reflexive attacks on court decisions such as those flowing from the Earl Warren Supreme Court, and the tendency of the police to deflect public pressure and criticism onto such other elements of the CJS as prosecutors, judges, or jailers.[2]
- The constant demand for more cops, without regard to systemic impact or real needs.
- The predilection for numbers, in terms of low-level drug arrests and other products of sweeps and round-ups, at the expense of concentrating on higher-ups and chronic recidivists.
- Resistance to recruiting women, blacks, gays, and other "minorities."
- The abuses that creep into such police operations as handling demonstrations; developing intelligence on dangerous groups; aggressive tactics such as using a special-weapons assault team (SWAT), stakeout units, decoys, undercover assignments, and other controversial approaches.
- Reluctance to enter such sensitive areas as family crime, that is, incest, child abuse, woman battering, and so on.
- Resistance to such citizen volunteers as police auxiliaries, Guardian Angels, and community patrol groups.
- Police hostility to the press.
- Police resistance to police review boards and other intrusions.
- Police attitudes toward the public.
- Likening a domestic dispute among blacks to *Gorillas in the Mist*, following the beating of Rodney King, Jr., which illustrates the flagrant stereotyping in police agencies.
- The fragmentation of police agencies and the problems of coordination and cooperation within the CJS.

---

[2] Richard A. Staufenberger (ed.), *Progress in Policing*. Washington, DC: Police Foundation, 1980.

- The slippery nature of crime statistics and the need to upgrade a central, national criminal file.
- The lack of career mobility in policing that leads to stagnations and inbreeding.
- Concern over large-scale urban riots as a result of a police incident.[3]
- Vocal acceptance of the importance of community support in any crime fighting effort, but silent resistance to any hint of powersharing.
- The shocking involvement of drugs with crime and the increasing incidence of gun violence.
- A continued reluctance to connect racism and poverty with street crime because of the unpopularity of such liberal notions.
- A continued commitment to increasingly repressive measures, coupled with a stubborn belief in their efficacy.

The problems cling stubbornly to life despite the urgent need for reforms and the problems' growing every day.

What once seemed an awful crime crisis now pales into innocent mischief when compared with an urban holocaust that took over 23,000 lives in 1990 and over 24,000 in 1991.

The issues raised in the literature don't address the one emerging truth: The police and the rest of the CJS are fundamentally irrelevant to the levels of crime, which is not to say they can't be made more effective within their very limited roles.

THE BEATING OF RODNEY KING, JR.

Events such as the videotaped beating of Rodney King, Jr., by the LAPD on March 3, 1991, greatly strengthen the hand of those calling for control over police abuse of power. It was,

---

[3] William L. Tafoya, *A Delphic Forecast of the Future of Law Enforcement*. Doctoral Dissertation, University of Maryland, 1986.

contrary to the vision of George Orwell, a case of Little Brother watching, through the camera's eye, the actions of Big Brother.

The police beating of Rodney King can be understood only within the context of a secretive and powerful police culture that has been given the task of controlling the underclass in a racist society. The police, unable to protest because of complex reasons relating to their power and their desire to keep it secret and whole, bridle at the task and complete it according to their churlish norms. Thus does keeping "undesirables" out of sight and under control become transmogrified, on the street, into thumpings, third-degree methods, and other illegal responses.

It was shocking for the viewer to observe the end result of policies of toughness that had been demanded for so long.

SHAPING THEIR OWN RESPONSES

The police, keepers of society's darker secrets and privy to the knowledge of the human capacity for evil, find isolation convenient, inescapable, and, finally, irresistible. No one understands. And no one particularly wants to talk about it, given the tacit edict to keep the underclass under wraps.

And yet, police work is helping and rescuing and facing dangerous situations boldly. It is important work, and cops derive deep satisfaction from its pursuit. They love being cops. Basically, no one quits, even though they may become alcoholics, divorced, suicides, or overweight candidates for early death. Their frustration comes when the assignment isn't straightforward and explicit.

So the police have adapted and have learned to make arrests within constitutional strictures and have managed to flood the system and cram the prisons and jails until they burst. The problem is that it has all been done reactively, in response to public and political pressures, and has not been based on any coherent plan or carefully wrought strategy. Thus sweeps, roundups, and low-level collars have become the order of the day. Everybody has been arrested and the cops have done their jobs, haven't they? Look elsewhere for any blame about rising crime rates. The cops have become adept at shifting the blame to liberal judges, plea bargains, and "country club" jails, even as they have come to recognize the danger of guns and have divorced themselves from the National Rifle Association.

Yet incidents like the Rodney King beating and the videotaped slamming of Don Jackson's head[4] at least hint at the existence of hidden dysfunctions that police executives seem to be papering over.

These events, like My Lai in Vietnam, convey the uneasy impression that perhaps our servants aren't really doing our bidding. Nevertheless, we continue to cave in to chiefs' cries for "more" even as other services are slashed and the city teeters on bankruptcy.

MORE COPS

When President Richard Nixon came to the White House in 1969, he decided to make the capital a showcase for the nation. With characteristic hubris, he'd make Washington a model of safety. He very quickly more than doubled the police force, following the wisdom, prevailing to this very day, that the invariable answer is more cops.

The traditional measure is the number of cops per 1,000 population, with the norm being around 2. The capital went to more than triple this ratio, in a city already overloaded with special-purpose police agencies guarding everything from parks to federal sites to tourist attractions.

---

[4] Don Jackson is a black male and a police officer who sought to prove the racism in the ranks by having an NBC news crew secretly film his encounters with cops. The acquittal of the cops who assaulted him, despite the film, demonstrates still another of the hidden realities of policing: the difficulty of convicting cops of wrongdoing.

The folly of relying on hiring more cops to make us safer is plainly illustrated by data that seem to create almost the opposite proposition, that the more cops you have the less safe you are.

Thus, Washington, D.C., with a cop-to-population ratio of 6.2 per 1,000 citizens—the nation's highest—also had the highest number of murders per capita in 1991. The second highest cops-to-population city, Detroit, with 4.7 per 1,000, has a notoriously high rate of street crime. Chicago, with 4.1 per 1,000, also has a high crime rate. The nation's cities are the incubators of street crime, and increasing the number of cops has no impact on crime.

Twenty years later, Nixon's dream of making the capital a national showcase turned into the nightmare of becoming the murder capital of America, despite the existence of very tough gun laws and a carpet of blue over the city.

A group of experts polled in 1990 on the question of New York City's hiring of five thousand more cops basically refuted the notion as wasteful and misplaced and called for management reforms that would strengthen the agency without additional hirings and recommended diverting the funds set aside for the additional officers to other areas of the system or to social welfare programs aimed at prevention.

The attraction of "more cops" has not, however, lost its allure—for chiefs, mayors, or citizens. The alternative option would be to manage more efficiently, and that thought is anathema to the caretakers of our municipalities.

THE NEED TO MANAGE

Brutality and corruption exist, but so do waste and mismanagement. The socialists have discovered that, without capitalism's merciless competition and struggles for profit, foggy theories of distribution and flaccid approaches to production don't work. It would not be too great an exaggeration to hold that the economic miracles of Germany, Japan, and the United States were based on the management theories imposed by the demands of capitalism. The pitiless marketplace forces everyone to run harder, and it consumes those who falter. Government, however, is socialism, not capitalism. No one has to meet a payroll or the challenge of a competitor or to face an angry stockholder's meeting. And unfortunately, management, waste, and inefficiency are not subjects that our very vigorous overseers, the press, tend to find very interesting. This lack of interest plays into the hands of our rulers, the politicians, who have neither an interest in nor an appetite for management innovations and reforms.

I can recall the abuse heaped on me by the Minneapolis City Council for returning budget surpluses in eight of the nine years I was there, as a result of economies in overtime costs, reductions in the bloated bureaucracy, modernization of the physical plant and equipment, and a green-shade, beady-eyed examination of every expenditure.

They'd "given [me] the money to spend." It wasn't my business to economize. I was shortchanging the citizens. Never mind that arrests rose, that responses to emergencies were uniformly made within six minutes, or that traffic enforcement more than tripled. I was a "bean counter." The police union encouraged the council members in their opposition to economies. The other department heads got the message very clearly and scrambled to spend any left over funds at year's end. And there was nothing unique in their approach. In New York I outraged a committee searching for a new chief by suggesting that the NYPD could be sharply reduced and made to operate more effectively and efficiently. (In contrast, in Washington, D.C., the police chief called for the hiring of more cops and put those on the rolls on overtime), although that city had more cops per capita than any other.

New York's cops, for example, work two to a patrol car and don't work eight-hour shifts or forty-hour weeks. Deficiencies are made up with costly overtime. Sickness and disability retirement abuses abound. There is a bloated officer corps, a sprawling and decaying physical plant, too many precincts, inadequate equipment, and low entrance standards, as well as poor training for the personnel. The 911 system needs to be modernized, performance and productivity need to be emphasized, and volunteers need to be used more fully. Outdated units need to be revamped or abolished, and such aggressive tactics as stings, decoys, and stakeout units need to be revived. Overlaying community-oriented policing on this mess is to lay a rug over litter and debris. What New York, and every other major city in the nation, needs is not more cops but a management audit and tough leadership.

Substantial economies of scale are easily possible through centralizing and combining such functions as 911 dispatching (which can also be civilianized with lower paid replacements for cops) or training, but these suggestions frequently bump up against political considerations, executive egos, union ambitions, or civil service impediments.

In a very real sense, the citizens are right to resist additional taxes. They can feel the government's indifference to the kind of tough management they themselves encounter on their jobs every day. I've never seen an agency of government that couldn't be managed better. Waste and inefficiency abound in a bureaucracy. One of the results is that the loss of faith in government leads to failures to provide essential services, in health, education, housing, welfare, employment, and so on. As the need for such services as policing and corrections is perceived to rise (correctly or, mostly, incorrectly), the temptation is not to reform and manage better, but to throw additional dollars at the problem. This approach insures continued starvation for other, needed—but less sexy—programs. The resultant failures undermine the citizens' faith that government can do anything right.

In this management-indifferent environment, an agency that produces cops, not managers, will present chiefs who have no managerial perspective or training and who won't be penalized for these deficiencies.

The crisis in policing is a matter of leadership and management, not of a scarcity of resources. Mayors, the most important figures in law enforcement because they select the chief and furnish his or her marching orders by issuing policy directives and assigning priorities, have to take the selection of the chief and the monitoring of the agency's performance more seriously. One easy method of monitoring performance is to insist on an annual report, styled on the corporate model, and to pay attention to its contents.

Most of the more prominent recent studies of the police were inspired by negative situations that hinted at broad systemic failures that needed to be attacked.

The Knapp Commission's investigation revealed widespread corruption and bribery in the NYPD of the sixties and early seventies. A task force studying the Philadelphia Police Department in the mid-eighties and following the disastrous police action against MOVE reported problems in personnel selection and training, the physical plant, equipment, and other areas, all of which indicated management failures.

The Christopher Commission provided a devastatingly critical analysis of the LAPD's culture, policies and practices, following the beating of a black citizen in early 1991.

And a report on Boston's police might best be described by quoting the *Boston Globe*'s headline of January 15, 1992: "St. Clair Panel Blasts Police Failings, Urges Roache's Ouster, Other Changes."

Management and the chief are clearly inseparable, yet the connection is rarely made, and mayors continue to appoint the chief as if they were selecting the city's premier cop rather than hiring a CEO for a major agency.

NEW TECHNIQUES

Sometimes the police have embraced new ideas simply because of expediency, rather than because of some deep conviction concerning their efficacy.

We saw earlier how the law enforcement literature is monopolized by tomes by researchers, experimenters, and scholars, rather than by police practitioners. The innovative ideas sweeping across the police landscape tend to be introduced mostly by outsiders. The anti-intellectualism of the police, which inspires them to scorn poetry, music, ballet, or painting as being the provinces of effete snobs, cuts them off from the realm of ideas that inspire wise action. Cops and their chiefs believe, with the rest of the nation, in the practical efficacy of vocational training—even in college—but they find it hard to see a purpose in philosophy, literature, language, history, or any of the other disciplines that might invest their actions with thought.

COMMUNITY-ORIENTED POLICING

Community-oriented policing (COP) is the brainchild of Herman Goldstein, a professor at the University of Wisconsin's Law School in Madison. Like most of the notions that periodically influence police policies, this one is deceptively simple. It posits that the community has a large stake in its own safety, that it has a real sense of the problems it faces locally, and that it ought to participate in the solutions in partnership with the police. The police would cooperate permanently and closely with the neighborhood, working on the problems identified by the residents—whether they involve police matters or not—and prescribing solutions following a diagnosis. For example, this approach might involve the police as advocates for the community with other levels of the bureaucracy.

The idea flows naturally from James Q. Wilson and George L. Kelling's "Broken Windows" article in *The Atlantic*, in which they held that conditions of decay—graffiti, abandoned car hulks, unrepaired broken windows, and other evidences of neglect—communicate a breakdown in controls that invites further depredations and lowers a community's morale and will to maintain standards. The police, being the only permanently present arm of government and the one agency that can't say no to any citizen's request for service, would serve as the connecting link between the people and the services they require.

Still in its nascent stages in 1993, the reform promised to change and greatly expand the role of the police, with consequences that could not always be foreseen. Much is made, by advocates of this reform, of the "tyranny of 911," which tethers cops to their radios and forces them to speed from call to call, thereby precluding the sort of intimate connection with the community envisioned in COP. What is lost is the enormous service provided by 911, which itself is less than a quarter century old, and the needs of the individuals calling for that help.

COP, however, plugs into the public clamor for "the cop on the beat"—the security blanket of policing. It ignores the technological march that has made us a much more efficient nation by dehumanizing processes, replacing people with machines and insisting that the people we do employ use more and more technology. Thus, the police world has become more efficient by putting cops in cars, adopting 911, using radios and computers in those cars, and strengthening the support system of the responders.

COP rightly centers on building a partnership with the people—a long overdue reform—but the enthusiasm for the idea threatens to sweep away the central priorities of fighting street crime by making higher quality arrests; responding faster to illnesses, injuries, accidents, and other true emergencies; and providing tough traffic enforcement. These three priorities, in a very real sense, work against the notion of such time- and energy-consuming partnerships as would result from cops getting out of their cars to work with the people.

COP is sweeping all before it in the nineties. It is seen as the panacea. But the law of unintended effects lurks offstage, ready to chasten hasty improvisers.

The adoption of such innovations rests with police executives, often opaque, distant figures who have come to office through processes that have little to do with how they'll perform in place.

COP, with its invitation to cut across bureaucratic turf lines, as other agencies are impressed to solve a community's problems, has an immediate and almost irresistible appeal. The police are always present in the ghetto. They are instantly accessible. They have clout with the bureaucracy. They have a deep interest in forging real bonds with an alienated community and need vehicles for such links. The police have always needed citizen help, and a surprising—and usually unmentioned—number of crimes are solved only because of the information provided by citizens, who have their own reasons, noble and ignoble, for providing such help.

The police have a serious concern about the dangers posed by an angry and frustrated population that sees them as the agents of the unseen oppressor and as little more than an army of occupation. Police leaders are particularly worried about ghetto uprisings, yet the insular, secretive police culture works against including outsiders in the agency's internal deliberations and operations.

COP holds the promise of diverting scarce municipal resources to the areas that need them most, through the advocacy of the police. Rubble-strewn lots can be imagined as community gardens, ballfields, or playgrounds, given police interest in bringing them about. Ghetto kids can be taught to swim, by cops, in pools in local schools. Summer jobs and recreation and education programs can be pursued by the police, who, as their experience and expertness widen, will learn how to secure grants and otherwise tap into enabling opportunities.

Graffiti might be removed, unsightly conditions corrected, broken windows mended, troubled families helped, and other sources of community tensions addressed through joint police–neighborhood efforts. Clearly, a much broader mandate than crime fighting, responding to emergencies, and traffic control is envisioned by COP.

Houston, an early adopter of COP, was criticized by its

auditors for producing few results with the innovation. The evaluation cited diminished energy in the categories of arrests and responses to emergencies. The auditors called for a more balanced approach. Faced with rising crime, Houston's police department responded with additional patrols that promoted visibility but did little to make arrests or respond to emergencies faster. The result of both initiatives was to confuse and demoralize the cops and to highlight, once again, the central problem of management facing America's police. In this case, it appeared that the administrative compass had been set awry by the tensions of a tough, and ultimately unsuccessful (for the incumbent and her female police chief), mayoral race.

Nevertheless the *New York Times* described the program favorably and editorialized on the merits of foot patrol strategies used by the NYPD, crediting them with reducing crime in some areas.

An expansion of role equates with an expansion of power, and few have remarked on the potential for police power's growth, and abuse, in the euphoria surrounding COP.

There is also the conflict inherent in serving as the tools of the overclass in attempting to control the underclass, while pursuing COP objectives that necessarily involve close working relations with the underclass. The ghetto is, not surprisingly, the site that holds the greatest promise for the widest use of COP, and it is surely the site where the resistance will be greatest.

Ironically, the force working most stubbornly against COP is the resistance to intrusiveness by police agencies. The success of COP is most seriously threatened by the insularity of the police and their reflexive resistance to outsiders.

Is COP police work? Not in the definition of the Mustache Petes who ruled the police world for eons, but perhaps so in the view of visionaries who seek to take the industry into the future.

COP may well be a more complicated idea than its progenitors realize. There are no doubts as to its potential for accomplishing a lot of social good, but such possibilities often include great risks.

COP may envision a totally new form of cop, and we haven't really learned to guide and control the old one very well yet.

CONTROLLING THE POLICE

If the police are to be effective in dealing with street crime, they have to be open to scrutiny. This means a real review, but not necessarily control, of the internal disciplinary process. A tough and determined chief is the best assurance of a clean and effective department.

The methods used to control police wrongdoing should be as vigorous and inventive as those used against criminals.

Internally these controls should include:

- Replication of the circumstances of patterned police wrongdoing to test for abuses.
- An energetic and proactive internal affairs division that investigates charges.
- Polling and testing techniques that determine organizational actions, as well as audits and inspections.
- The use of early-warning tracking methods to detect those with numerous charges of brutality or corruption. A review of internal records following the beating of Rodney King, Jr., by the LAPD revealed forty-four officers who had been the subjects of an average of 7.6 accusations of excessive force or other improper tactics, compared with an average of 0.6 for all officers reported to have used force.
- The use of decoys, internal spies, self-initiated integrity tests, surveillances, and other aggressive techniques.
- Monitorings of all sorts, such as taping of incoming

calls in cases where rudeness or inaction are alleged; 911 calls are now generally taped.

- A requirement that officers report all uses of force and that interrogations and confessions be videotaped.
- An open, responsive organizational environment and culture.
- Administrative restraints and controls on when an officer may shoot, on how to conduct police chases, and on how to handle stops, frisks, searches, and interrogations.

Externally the controls should include:

- A review and comment process that reports internal conditions to the people.
- The involvement of CJS agencies in monitoring police behavior.
- The full participation of the FBI in investigating police wrongdoing.
- The use of civil suits to obtain redress.
- A menu of accessible possibilities for the use of aggrieved citizens.
- The use of investigative commissions or task forces to recommend reforms.
- A vigorous press that doesn't hesitate to undertake investigative reporting of the police.

Having over twelve thousand police agencies report to the Uniform Crime Reports results in a fragmentation that produces appalling records. The disarray of these records taint any attempt to create a central data bank that might be used to apprehend fleeing felons or might make any meaningful contribution to the recovery of stolen property, the identification of chronic recidivists, or the execution of outstanding warrants.

Centralization, although indisputably providing opportunities for enhanced efficiency, is not a panacea either. The

French police proved this in the summer of 1991, as they attempted to track the assassins of an Iranian dissident. The police had the benefit of a centralized and computerized record system into which hotel clerks entered the names and passport or identification card numbers of all guests, yet the police consistently discovered the whereabouts of the suspects only after they'd checked out of the hotels. They had, however, a tool whose potential is totally unavailable to envious American cops.

Reducing the total number of police departments through the adoption of county government would probably greatly enhance the cohesiveness of the police and produce economies of scale without creating the frightening monster of a national police. County government, which frequently includes the central city and its surrounding suburbs, can also provide an opportunity to suck the fleeing whites, who have gone to suburbia, back into struggling with municipal problems that need their resources, energies, and talents.

Insistence by the FBI on higher quality record maintenance and input, as well as the adoption of a national identity card, would enable the police to identify currently slippery criminals and greatly improve police operations. In a sense, the Social Security number has evolved into our national identity number, but it is not usable by the CJS. We seem to be backing into the adoption of a national identity card, avoiding explicit references to it and thereby stifling awkward debates. Instead of creating an Orwellian omnipresent state, our data banks grow to be of service to commerce and to verify credit status.

But the greatest potential for the improvement of police operations unquestionably lies in better management. The police establishment is an Atlantis in our midst that must be known, controlled, and directed. The real meaning of the LAPD incident is how important it is to understand and control agencies that exercise so much power in the name of the people.

CHIEFS: TENURE AND SELECTION

The Los Angeles police chief, for example, had basically been appointed for life. This remarkable tenure was granted to protect the chief from politics, as if the post were anything but a political pulpit. The reforms of civil service came to be twisted into subversions of the democratic process. The genius of a democracy is the dynamic of change. Even the best considered and most desperately needed reforms will atrophy into corruptions if left unquestioned and unchanged. We elect politicians to run our cities. These officials then appoint department heads. The whole idea is that, if the municipal service delivery is inadequate (fire, police, education, sanitation, social services, etc.), the mayor's head will roll. The spoils system of appointing friends, relatives, and cronies, without regard to qualifications, inspired reformers to create civil service, which has now, itself, evolved into an instrument of abuse as municipal unions learned how to use it to take control of their agencies.

Representative democracy—in which we choose our leaders to represent our interests and serve our needs—is undermined when the people lose the power of removal. One of the cardinal principles of management is to give enough authority to carry out the responsibilities assigned. The functionary has to have the power and resources to carry out the mission. Sending a general with inadequate resources would not have produced the expected results in 1991's Gulf War.

To make matters worse, we equate "politics" with partisanship. The first connotes the acts of government, and the second implies catering to special interests—usually at the expense of the broad interests of the people. Such intellectual confusion exacts a real price as we act on our misconceptions and produce such anomalies as freezing incompetents or tyrants in place.

When the people of Los Angeles succumbed to a powerful chief's plea for insulation, they were protecting him from any hope of being controlled through the mayor's appointment powers.

REMOVING THE POLICE FROM POLITICS

By cleverly playing on public outrage over corruption in the ranks, and by deftly using his credibility with the public, William Parker, the Los Angeles police chief who shaped this agency, was able to convince Angelenos that their best interests lay in appointing a chief even the people couldn't remove, except in the extremely rare circumstances of illegal actions against him. Simple fecklessness, obduracy, truculence, or unwillingness to bend to the people's will—the hallmark of any democracy—wouldn't do it. Thus, Parker would "remove the police from politics."

And can anyone seriously entertain the suspicion that the police chief's job is apolitical? It may, and should, be nonpartisan, but it can't be nonpolitical. Every act of government is political.[5] A chief serving at the mayor's pleasure must be granted powers of appointment that enable him to control his agency. Civil service has evolved from reform to a straitjacket in which functionaries have no loyalty to police chiefs or their policies, nor any need to fear reprisals for resistance or failure. Tenured chiefs are locked in place and are inviolable, but they are themselves paralyzed when they lack power over their staffs.

Another reform—police unionism—has, through the political muscle and financial resources made possible by dues checkoffs, become a major player in city politics. Police unions are now frequently cited as the principal obstacles to police

[5] Edward K. Hamilton, *Police Productivity: The View from City Hall*. Washington, DC: Police Foundation, 1975.

reforms. They often play a role in the selection of the chief and run a lot of police departments.[6]

A tough and determined chief will manage sternly; will develop mechanisms for rooting out brutality, corruption, inefficiency, and waste; and will maintain an aggressive posture toward crime, while providing better, faster service. In order to secure such a paragon, mayors will have to treat the search and selection process as seriously as colleges treat their searches for their presidents.

The LAPD incident should have illustrated just how ignorant the American people are of police operations, even while fatuously assuming they understand them perfectly. The people take their information from TV and movie depictions that have been jazzed up beyond any practitioner's recognition. These depictions are not documentaries. The needs of fiction have no connection with the grim, but frequently boring, realities of the street. What the LAPD incident most clearly illustrated was the need for an informed debate on what the police mission really should be. We can't just ask the cops to make "undesirables" disappear.

And while we talk of a single, unified police world, we have to acknowledge that the police universe contains cultural poles created by the separate histories of the individual agencies.

THE POLICE WINGS

The police, despite their *sui generis* nature and broad similarities, entertain the usual divisions of liberal and conservative philosophies within the ranks. Every agency has its Rambos and its bleeding hearts, and everything in between. And every agency has its own bent, shaped by the political rulers of the city.

[6] Anthony V. Bouza, *Police Unions: Paper Tigers or Roaring Lions? Police Leadership in America.* New York: Praeger, 1985.

As the power in the cities has shifted from white to black rule, the political direction has been distinctly, although not uninterruptedly, leftward. The city's power centers still know what buttons to push to get even liberal black mayors to pursue law-and-order policies especially in the areas of drug enforcement and cleaning up the glittering downtowns. Nevertheless, police departments led by black chiefs tend to be more sympathetic to the plight of ghetto residents than those led by whites.

We might hold that, in the eighties and early nineties, Los Angeles represented the right wing of police conservatism, while Detroit stood for the left. Such polarities result in policies that translate into actions, by the cops on the street, that surface as aggressive police patrols versus passive operations that eschew such tactics as stakeout, decoy, sting, and SWAT approaches.

As the blacks gained power in the municipalities, the whites abandoned the cities. From 1980 to 1992, the national administration supported that trend, enriching the overclass through tax and other policies and starving the cities of the resources needed for education, health, housing, welfare, jobs, and related services.

The Republicans gave their hearts to their right wing in 1964, with the nomination of Barry Goldwater, but took it back in 1968 with the election of the more centrist Richard Nixon. In the process, they espoused policies that enabled them to hold the center even while quietly advancing the interests of their conservative constituents. This process proved a scam that produced virtually unprecedented political prosperity in presidential elections. The Republicans adopted tax-cut and defense-spending programs that precluded the Democrats' even timidly suggesting any domestic welfare program that might cost a nickel.

The Democrats gave their hearts to their left wing in 1972, with the nomination of George McGovern and the turning over of their convention to the minority fragments they'd formerly embraced, but that they'd never allowed to rule the party.

McGovern's stunning defeat proved a final repudiation of the left, but the Democrats never managed to regroup, and they remained a soulless, programless band that had forgotten its origins and mission. As such, they had been doomed to wander the political wilderness—presidentially—for all but four years since 1968. While their secret hearts may be in the cities, they know the votes are in the suburbs. By centering his appeal on the suburbs Bill Clinton seemed, in 1992, to have formally shed the McGovern legacy. The question would be whether he'll ever remember the cities and their plight.

These distant developments may well appear unrelated to such commonplaces as police policies and programs but we will see that in this phase, as in all others in American life, when Washington sneezes the rest of us catch pneumonia.

The right and left wings of policing simply mirror the political realities flowing from our nation's capital.

The abandonment of the cities led to the neglect of the black and the poor, centered in the municipal ghettos, with predictable consequences for their lives and ours.

While neither President Bush nor you, the reader, will ever see ourselves as the creators of the criminals who commit the awful depredations we see on the nightly news, the fact is that, until we do, we are fated to see their repeated emergence, from the swamps we've created, to launch another assault on us. In this gigantic mosaic, crime and violence become symptoms, and cops become the treaters of external symptoms. Yet the cops do have a role in all this, and if we are to hope for their reform, cops must first be understood. The veil of secrecy has to be pulled back. Americans will have to confront their own delusions and fashion sensible and realistic policies for the police. At this moment, the cops are getting subliminal messages, in the form of codes about "making the streets safe," that will translate into the beating of more Rodney Kings.

What is it that we want cops to do?

If we could answer this question—or even face it—we might fashion the cops into responsive and effective instruments of justice.

The LAPD incident was a defining moment in American policing that, for better or for worse, will change the institution. It became a mirror flashing in our faces, revealing the frightening visage of a people who'd sent their cops out to control an underclass of blacks, the homeless, the mentally disturbed, beggars, public drunks, and other undesirables. If this vision is not confronted, then the training curriculum will be revamped, the chief replaced, and other cosmetics applied, but the slide into the abyss will accelerate. The police will have seen us come to the crossroads and apply the blinders. The message will be reinforced that they're an army of occupation doing our secret bidding. It will be as if we condoned the My Lai incident. This will not be business as usual, but a radical and explicit affirmation of what used to be implicitly and subtly conveyed. We will have lost our innocence.

WHAT WORKS?

In 1982, the National Institute of Justice asked the Police Foundation to find out if there was anything the police could do to alleviate the public's paralyzing fear of crime. The resulting report appeared in 1986.[7]

In the years following the President's Commission on Crime (1967), studies had revealed a number of factors that were felt to be compelling:

1. Increasing the number of police doesn't necessarily reduce the crime rate or raise the proportion of crimes solved.

   Comment: I agree completely with that finding and with the additional attribution of crime rates to social and economic factors.

[7] Jerome H. Skolnick and David H. Bayley, *The New Blue Line: Police Innovations in Six Cities.* New York: Free Press, 1986.

2. Random motorized patrol neither reduces crime nor improves the chances of catching suspects.

   Comment: I generally agree with this but offer the caveat that some cops are better than others at spotting suspects and making on-the-street arrests. I also believe faster response increases the chances of apprehension in the act. Mostly, though, visible patrol displaces crime.

3. Two-person patrol cars are no more effective than one-person cars in reducing crime or catching criminals.

   Comments: I'd go further and suggest that two-officer cars are less effective. The partners distract each other. Single cops tend to be more fearful, cautious, and alert, and the backup is generally more than sufficient to furnish needed protection.

4. Saturation patrolling does reduce crime, but only temporarily, largely displacing it to other areas.

   Comment: This was the classic error behind the NYPD's Operation Pressure Point, which sought to rid the Lower East Side of Manhattan of illegal drug traffic. It served to clean up the area for gentrifiers, but the volume of crime and drug trafficking in the city was not affected. The criminals and dealers just moved their operations.

5. Cops on patrol rarely encounter muggings, rapes, robberies, burglaries, or murders.

   Comment: The notion of uniformed cops as crime fighters is one of the more durable of the police myths. The fact is that uniformed cops don't make important felony arrests. Mostly these are effected by detective and plainclothes units.

   There is a political bombshell concealed in all this as well, in that the police know very well how to catch burglars, robbers, and other criminals, but the tactics used, although perfectly legal, are frequently politically unpalatable.

The police can predict, from an analysis of frequency and location tables, about when a liquor store will be held up and can assign trained units to counter such assaults. These are called stakeout units, and they were too successful in the sixties, as they repeatedly blasted holdup men into oblivion.

Detroit, one of the cities studied in this report, once had a Stop the Robberies and Enjoy Safe Streets (STRESS) unit that shot so many blacks that it was disbanded as a result of community pressures, including the charge that the cops had become juries, judges, and executioners. A mayoral aspirant's promise to disband the unit swept the promiser into office.

Similarly, stings and decoy operations have lapsed into disuse simply because of the political ramifications of making too many arrests of black street criminals.

Fear of summer riots, the increasing militancy of urban blacks, and their growing political power have made these approaches too volatile to be widely embraced, even by embattled chiefs. Many police agencies have quietly shifted to other forms of fighting crime and have directed such undercover approaches to more popular efforts, such as the one against drugs. The ironic result is that even greater percentages of blacks are swept up, as they are the ones most heavily involved in low-level street use and dealing.

6. Improving response time to emergency calls has no effect on the likelihood of arresting criminals or even on satisfying involved citizens.

Comment: This has become the prevailing wisdom, but I don't agree with the studies in this area. Response time is a nebulous concept. The biggest chunk occurs between the time the citizen recognizes the need for a cop and the call's entrance into the delivery system. Nine-one-one went a long way toward cutting that time, and other innovations, such as not needing a coin to make the call over a public phone, have also helped.

A real reduction in response time—defined as the time a citizen realizes the need for a cop and the arrival of that cop—will result in more arrests, interdictions of crime, and rescues. Faster response will also boost citizens' confidence, causing them to call oftener and earlier, and will inhibit wrongdoers who, knowing the cops will arrive quickly, have to tailor their actions accordingly.

7. Crimes are not solved through criminal investigations conducted by the police departments.

Comment: This problem has always illustrated, to me, the folly of studying detectives whose chiefs don't know how to use them in the first place. Detectives have mostly become "soft-soap artists" and report takers for the police administration and are sent on cases only to mollify the victims.

Using detectives sparingly and appropriately—concentrating on cases having the promise of solvability (through evidence gathered, the testimony of witnesses, fingerprints at the scene, etc.) will produce more arrests. There is no doubt that investigators will be more effective if their efforts are concentrated on the promising cases. Criminals strike repeatedly, and it makes more sense to catch them through their infrequent mistakes than to waste energy looking into their every depredation. And whether a crime is worth investigating is an evaluation easily made by the responding uniformed officers.

This kind of approach, however, places the chief in the dilemma of having to tell the vast majority of victims that the police are not going to investigate their cases because of the low probability of success (redlining)—a sure political loser.

Faced with these "discoveries," the researchers studied six cities to see what would work or what seemed to be working. They were Santa Ana, California; Detroit; Houston; Denver; Oakland; and Newark, New Jersey. Their report, issued in October 1985, cited many innovations, a lot of which had to do with modernizing the agencies through management reforms and establishing closer ties with the community.

The chiefs were found to be progressive, innovative, and talented, and high praise was heaped on their reforms and on the prospects of success. It was difficult, in the reading, to spot the sort of tough management reforms that puts the chief at odds with the union or the city council or the mayor. Putting too high a value on police efforts is a common failing of studies of police agencies that are groping with rising crime levels, when police activities are not nearly as relevant as, for example, the number of impoverished minority males in the population. But no one wants to admit the irrelevancy of cops to the rate of crime.

Over seven years after the publication of this report, the best answer to the hopes of progress so glowingly described in its pages is a simple recitation of the names of the cities studied, together with the mental images they inspire: Santa Ana, Detroit, Houston, Denver, Oakland, and Newark. That says it all.

LAW AND ORDER

Controlling and reforming the police must have as their purpose the creation of an agency that attacks the problems that are destroying our cities. The police must use legal and aggressive tactics that may be politically unpopular, especially in a time when the mayors fear urban explosions.

Aggressive tactics like the use of decoys, stakeout units, sting operations, undercover agents, and wiretap orders, can be almost too effective, in that they may produce a disproportionate impact on minority suspects. The policy has to be examined for racism, but the facts have to be confronted, too. One of the grimmer realities of American life has been the creation of life conditions that make criminality almost inevitable. Racism has made blacks frequently the perpetrators of street crime and all too frequently its victims. This circumstance cannot blind us to the need to punish, but it also imposes the responsibility of examining the conditions that make this behavior so prevalent.

Reforming the police will involve adopting tough policies of monitoring and control that will make the chief unpopular and which will involve clashes with the cops union.

CONCLUSION

We don't understand cops, but what is far more important is that we don't want to really control them or confront the tacit racist assignment we've given them. The Rodney King, Jr., and Don Jackson incidents and the parading of the Willie Hortons become the inevitable denouements.

Chapter Eleven

THE CRIMINAL
JUSTICE SYSTEM
The Courts, Laws, and Options

*The true administration of justice is the firmest pillar of
good government.*
—Engraved on face of the New York City
Criminal Courts Building

For the police chief to be understood, he or she must be
imagined as a balloon, in a room full of other balloons, rubbing
against each other and bouncing about, emitting occasional gas
and sometimes even exploding. The other balloons can be
labeled "the mayor," "the city council," "the press," "the police
union," "corporate interests," "community activists," "the people," "ad hoc coalitions," and "the criminal justice system."

In describing a system, the dictionary uses such terms as
coordinated, ordered, a unitary whole, correlated members, and other
phrases connoting various parts working in harmonious unison
to achieve the desired end. A cursory inspection of the daily
workings of the criminal justice system (CJS) reveals that the
term *system* is an oxymoron, as the reality shows an anarchic

group, at odds and in disarray, marching very roughly toward hazily conceived objectives that are often at variance with the purposes for which the agency was created. America's CJS is more like the bazaar at Baghdad than like the idealized vision of an integrated whole.

No single person is paid to oversee the CJS. No one is assigned to correct imbalances or grotesqueries. No official is charged with ensuring its efficient and cost-effective operation. The CJS is a disparate group of institutions, each with its interests and passions, and in which each is forced to work with the system's other parts. At the same time, each competes for the resources that spell life or grave illness for that agency. None of the parts ever quite die.

The CJS has permanent players and occasional intruders who may, nevertheless, participate critically in the system's functionings (one is forced to use the word despite its patent absurdity). The legislature comes to mind as just such an occasional, yet central, player.

Police administrators on the firing line of what has now been at least a thirty-year war with crime have become adept at shifting the public's ire onto other, less visible or vocal elements of the system. Judges have been frequent targets, condemned for liberalism by such hard-liners as the FBI's J. Edgar Hoover, who was not above twisting the workings of a police agency to his own private purposes.

JUDGES

The role of judges is rarely fully appreciated in the United States. They have been excoriated for softness during the same time that the prison population has tripled. Judges preside over the criminal justice process by overseeing trials, at which their functions are mainly to issue rulings on the admissibility of testimony or evidence. They declare a mistrial as a result of error and make explanations to, and guide, the jury, and they issue sentences. Judges interpret the law and generally serve as referees for the contending forces of prosecution and defense. Sometimes, when the accused waives the right to a jury trial, the judge sits as both the trier of facts and the interpreter of rules. The judge is there to guarantee the integrity of the process and to ensure the realization of that vaguest, yet most desired, of concepts known as justice.

It is ironic that the Earl Warren Supreme Court, which so professionalized the police by raising the standards of police performance and by insisting on punctilious observance of the processes outlined in the U.S. Constitution—a novel idea, to be sure, for most of this nation's history in the field of criminal justice (perhaps another oxymoron)—should have become the principal target of those searching for villains in the system's failures.

The Warren Court reformed the police by ensuring the voluntariness of confessions (the so-called *Miranda* rule). It began by insisting on the legal validity of the evidence being presented (the exclusionary rule) and went on to require accessibility to lawyers, prompt arraignment, and a speedy trial. These and other measures had the effect of transforming America's police into a corps of crime fighters who were much better trained, more legally aware, better prepared, and more effective.

We will see, though, that delivering substantive reform does not, by any means, ensure either credit, the absence of criticism, or even an acknowledgment of the reform's contribution to any positive result.

The Warren Court

No discussion of criminal justice in the United States during the hectic days of the sixties, seventies, eighties, and nineties could be informed without a reference to the U.S. Supreme Court during the Chief Justiceship of Earl Warren.

Before the first (in the 1961 *Mapp v. Ohio* case) of a series of landmark rulings that dramatically changed the way cops operated on the street, America's police were free to do pretty much as they pleased with no fear of reprisal.

Even the Feds, required to justify the legality of their searches and seizures, handed tainted cases to locals who would not be questioned about how they had come into possession of the contraband. The policy was hallowed by the somber term *the silver platter doctrine*, which failed to conceal completely the fact that the fancy name simply condoned police criminality. These convenient handoffs of tainted evidence existed from 1914, when the Feds were first required to demonstrate that their intrusions and confiscations had been done legally, until the Supreme Court decided to hold the locals to the same standards as the Feds.

After 1961, local cops would have to prove that they had recovered the evidence by using legal means, such as a warrant or consent. Police agencies the country over now had to acquaint themselves with such legal arcana as search warrants, wiretap orders, other court documents, and the requirements of the U.S. Constitution.

Prodded by the brilliant Justice William O. Douglas' wholesome suspicion of official power, the Warren Court insisted that it be demonstrated that confessions had been secured voluntarily and that the accused had had access to a lawyer—and quickly—in the same manner as better heeled white-collar and organized-crime predators. Police lineups were to be conducted with some regard for fairness, and the accused must be accorded the rights presumably guaranteed to every citizen.

Not surprisingly, these turned out to be wildly unpopular initiatives, as any extension of constitutional rights to society's pariahs were bound to be, and a serious movement to impeach Chief Justice Warren gathered powerful momentum.

Whatever one may think of the issues, the life tenure granted Supreme Court justices furnishes the independence that enables them to issue opinions that may run counter to the popular view, but that reflect their concept of the Constitution's requirements. It is worth noting that, more than thirty years since *Mapp v. Ohio*, the cries of having "handcuffed the police" have a hollow ring, given the arrest and incarceration rates that the CJS has been able to manage even while working within the very real strictures of the Warren Court's edicts.

It would not be too much to say that the Warren Court transformed policing in America, by erasing third-degree methods, eliminating illegal police raids, sharply reducing illegal searches and seizures, and ensuring some measure of protection of the rights of the least of our nation's citizens. And if there was any truth that court had grasped, it was that the rights of the highest are best secured by protection of those of the most scorned.

But because other courts have lacked the broad intellectual grasp, historical perspective, and depth of talent of the nation's highest court, new methods had to be found to bring fairness and consistency to the sentencing process especially.

Sentencing Guidelines

The police have generally succeeded in painting judges as the weak links in the criminal justice chain. Legislatures have buttressed the assault by passing sentencing guidelines, ratcheting the seriousness of some crimes (especially drug offenses) upward, and increasing the number of crimes receiving mandated sentences. All of these actions are aimed at reducing a judicial discretion perceived as having run amok.

And, indeed, studies have consistently revealed a crazy-quilt pattern of inconsistency in sentencing practices.[1] Typically, judges have been given identical cases and asked to furnish a sentence. The disparities have been so great—some

---

[1] William Zumwalt, "The Anarchy of Sentencing in the Federal Courts," *Judicature*, vol. 57 (October 1973).

judges releasing the suspect and others giving long sentences of incarceration—that a mechanism had to be found to reasonably limit judicial discretion. (These disparities have had the harmful effect of undermining inmates' faith in fairness and making them intractable after they have compared notes in prison.) A formula granting some leeway was devised that offered a range of sentence limits, depending on the suspect's record and the seriousness of the current case.

The guidelines also include the possibility of deviation, in exceptional cases, with the requirement that the judge offer a written rationale. It makes a lot of sense to insist on written justifications for official decisions, at all levels and in all agencies. In the case of too many decisions, no rationale is offered. Such a requirement would force bureaucrats to think long and hard about their decisions, would remove a lot of special dealing, would enhance public accountability, and would bring the openness of "sunshine laws" to bear on more government actions.

Sentencing guidelines also have the purpose of a more careful selecting of candidates for incapacitation, thereby targeting the serious recidivist while not overburdening already swollen prisons.

The reform was widely and vigorously opposed by judges, who saw it, correctly, as placing limits on their most important power: sentencing. One of the key characteristics of the CJS is how much power is concentrated in the hands of the various players and, of course, how jealously this power is guarded.

Technological Progress and Obstacles

Another reform resisted by judges is the adoption of a computer tracking system that follows a suspect from arrest to final disposition. Such a system holds the promise not only of controlling cases more efficiently as they go through the system but also of finally developing a system of criminal records on which the various agencies can rely. The resistance is a reflex (in that it is felt to be an intrusion onto sacred turf) and is also rational (in that it may expose inefficiencies, and worse, in a creaking system).

If a tracking system is adopted, every decision along the way will become a matter of continuous record, and judges, chary of criticism, don't want to be accused of springing killers on an unsuspecting public. Cameras in the courtroom and "Court Watch" programs (described elsewhere) also fall into the class of unwelcome intrusions.

In fairness, it ought to be added that judges' native caution has also produced such undeniable benefits as a general refusal to credit "lie detectors" and making their results inadmissible in court. Still, just like the rest of us, judges don't like folks looking over their shoulders.

DNA

The most recent and most important scientific controversy relating to the admissibility of evidence is the DNA question. DNA (deoxyribonucleic acid) is the basic building code for all chromosomes. The characteristics of DNA vary completely from person to person and are detectable in body fluids like blood or semen. They yield a recognizable genetic fingerprint.

An Ohio federal district court held an exhaustive review of the use of DNA in 1991 and found that DNA evidence, which would identify specific victims and suspects, was admissible. This landmark finding seemed to tip the scales decisively, but not conclusively, in favor of making DNA identifications virtually as persuasive as fingerprints.

The case for DNA's value was extended by the findings of two Yale scientists, reported in the February 1992 issue of *Science*, that genetic analysis can be used, with confidence, to establish identities.

The totally conclusive case, however, remains to be made.

On another technological front, the explosive growth of fiber-optic lines and digital signals has created serious complications in the execution of legally secured wiretap orders. What the issue comes down to is the need to coerce telephone companies—legally, of course—into rendering the necessary technical aid to the agency authorized to eavesdrop.

But technology will, as always, be found lacking if the appropriate human resources, as in the selection of judges, are not identified.

Selecting Judges

As with police chiefs, we discover that a key problem lies in the type of people selected as judges and in the processes of selection used. The systems vary, depending on whether the judge is to serve at the state, local, or federal level. The federal judges are generally regarded as the best because they are appointed by the president, following a filtration system that carefully screens the candidates. Additionally, in the late eighties, federal judges tended to be promoted from within, deepening the experience and professionalism of the federal courts, even as the bench assumed a much more conservative cast. Locally, selection may be through election, which largely means self-selection or party appointments of faithful hacks as a political payoff.

Women and minorities have not fared well in the process, whether elected or appointed. In the forty-one states using election, the system probably violates the provisions of the Voting Rights Act.

One study found the judges examined to be "assiduous, loyal and reliable party workers who made considerable contributions of time, money, or both, to their respective political clubs."[2]

---

[2] Alexander B. Smith and Abraham S. Blumberg, "The Problem of Objectivity in Judicial Decision-Making," *Social Forces*, vol. 46 (September 1967).

Wherever one looks in the CJS, the need for good management leaps out, usually from behind cries of being swamped with overwork and demands for additional help.

New York is the only state that requires the sequestration of juries in criminal trials. Court officers were paid more than $2 million in overtime in 1989 (the figure must certainly have risen since) for guarding jurors kept in hotels overnight. A bill to end mandatory sequestration was killed in committee by a 27 to 0 vote, following heavy lobbying by the court officers' unions.

Better Judges/Better Justice

The appointment of judges by the governor, with the advice and consent of the state senate or its equivalent, is favored if it is preceded by nominations by a distinguished panel of citizens and lawyers, from which the governor must choose. Tenure of about a decade has received general support because it affords sufficient time in office to promote independence without removing the prospect of accountability altogether. In this system, the reappointment process is identical to the original appointment process.[3]

But even promoting the selection of the ablest lawyers wouldn't produce the wise and experienced judges envisioned in the ideal we might call American justice. Judges must have the "street smarts" of a good cop and the understanding of a seasoned, thoughtful, and experienced citizen. Training and education have to be tied to any selection plan, which should be as assiduous in its search for excellence as the political clubs are in their search for party faithfuls to reward. And even the

---

[3] *The Challenge of Crime in a Free Society: The President's Commission on Law Enforcement and Administration of Justice.* Washington, DC: U.S. Government Printing Office, February 1967.

best judges can, for many reasons, go bad. An effective monitoring system is essential.

Judges are, like the police, instruments of justice, and their corps must necessarily be justly constituted. Thus there must be a fair representation of women and minorities in the judicial ranks.

In order for the courts to work, judges have to be fair, consistent, and effective. Bludgeoned by criticisms from all sides, they've turned pretty mindlessly Draconian in recent years, without making us safer. Neither greatly increased arrests nor swelling incarcerations have worked. The clear need is for both cops and judges to be more discriminating.

Judges need to separate the chronic recidivist from the casual criminal and must devise strategies of control that include jailing as well as possible alternatives to incarceration. They need to use the threat of a harsh sentence to modify behavior through such approaches as making release contingent on treatment. They need to intervene more frequently to curb abuse by prosecutors, cops, or any other organization in the system. Judges play a pivotal role in dispensing justice. They are uniquely positioned to detect flaws or abuses and must find the courage to assault them. Their performance in the area of addressing egregious abuses by cops and prosecutors has not been impressive.

The challenge is to jail those needing to be locked up and to ease the demands on the prison system by selecting other methods of control for the majority, who don't require confinement. Those methods include fines, restitution, community service, halfway houses, house arrest, and probation or other conditional releases. Innovative approaches will flow from a real interest in devising effective alternatives.

Judges, however, ultimately rely on what is brought before them by the prosecutors, who wield an enormous amount of power over what gets to the court.

ATTORNEYS

Prosecutors

Street criminals are introduced into the criminal justice system by the cops who arrest them. This arrest sets a process in motion in which a succession of players make critically important decisions about the fate of the case. The first of these players is the prosecutor, who decides on the charge, and even on whether to try the accused at all.

Street crime is prosecuted by local officials called *district* or *county attorneys*, who are, almost always, elected. Elections preclude the arguments surrounding the process of the selection of so many other members of the system because the voters make the choice, after what is usually a pretty energetic debate on the issues.

The power of the prosecutors can be summarized by a quote from former, and later discredited, New York Judge Sol Wachtler, who said they can "indict a ham sandwich." They can also prosecute or not or choose anything in between, from a plea bargain to a negotiated release to a no-holds-barred, out-for-blood trial.

I can recall, as chief of police in Minneapolis, bringing a stack of around five dossiers on unprosecuted murders to the county attorney. In every case, we had definite suspects and some evidence—enough to prosecute, in my opinion. All of the cases were potential losers; that is, we would probably secure indictments but convicting the suspects would be very chancy. No prosecutor wants to lose a highly visible case.

I agreed that the evidence was thin and that we might well lose, but I wanted at least to discomfit the suspects and bring them to trial. The prosecutor wanted more evidence, better witnesses, improved odds. I argued that the passage of time would only make things worse as witnesses disappeared or died, as memories faded, and as interest waned. He won, and the cases were not prosecuted. Trials would have been expensive and time-consuming, but the importance of the cases outweighed these considerations, as well as the risks of loss.

Later, however, in a notorious case involving a serial killer of native American women, I insisted on a prosecution despite thin evidence. The killer was picking the women up in bars, taking them to secluded spots, and mutilating them. In fact, we'd jailed the suspect on a vague charge of Social Security fraud. The county attorney was, again, very chary of taking on a losing case, but my threat of taking the issue to the press (the euphemism is "going public") moved him. He wouldn't prosecute just yet, but if I assigned some investigators to the case to secure more evidence, he'd go forward. The understanding was that he'd proceed with the case even if my sleuths failed to dig up additional evidence.

Fair enough. The assignment was made, and *mirabile dictu*, the detectives came up with important new evidence, leading to the conviction of the suspect. In this case, the county attorney had been right, and the result justified his caution.

Each of the segments of the CJS exercises enormous power and exerts it vigorously, while protecting it fiercely. The cop who defines a street guy as an "asshole" will find a way to arrest him; the judge who harbors a prejudice against muggers (a conservative judge has been defined as a liberal who's been mugged) will find a way to express it; and the district attorney with an ax to grind will discover the occasions to grind it.

The law requires probity, coolness, a healthy respect for the weight of the available evidence, and a willingness to follow what sometimes look like tortured processes.

I'd had cases in the Bronx in which the prosecutor was tempted by political pressures to indict a cop in the shooting of a Hispanic youth, to indict another cop in the shooting of a mentally disturbed male, in another, and to indict cops in a few other cases in which minority communities had taken a deep interest. He'd also been tempted to charge bodega (Hispanic grocery) owners who, fed up with repeated holdups, had bought illegal guns and shot robbers. In those cases, as police chief of the borough, I'd call the prosecutor and express my interest in the case, cajoling, pleading, and thinly threatening a nasty controversy if it didn't go my way. We didn't want "an ugly public row over this, did we?" It was easy for him to accommodate me by simply submitting the cases to a grand jury and manipulating the desired result. I never failed to get my way in the four hectic years in which the two of us functioned as chief and prosecutor, and yet, only a short while after my departure, he indicted the cop who shot Mrs. Bumpurs. In that case, there had been no one to call to warn him of the consequences of indicting a cop who'd been doing his job, and, I suspect, he had plenty of community leaders threatening reprisals if he didn't prosecute the officer. Deservedly, he lost the case.

Just as the cops practice "selective enforcement," prosecutors engage in "selective prosecutions." Each of the system's parts possesses, and uses, enormous latitude.

Tom Wolfe's novel *Bonfire of the Vanities*, which so accurately captured the reality I'd faced for four years in the Bronx, offers a glimpse into a prosecutor's office that reveals political slobberings over the prospect of prosecuting a rich, white Protestant defendant as a sop to the minorities sweating and suffering in that county. The anguish over the "piece-of-shit cases" that are their daily fare perfectly depicted the realpolitik of this arcane office.

Plea Bargaining

Plea bargains have earned the opprobrium of the public, but everyone in the system recognizes them as essential features of a court operation that can try only about 5 percent of the cases it handles. Without plea bargaining, the CJS would disintegrate. District attorneys are deal makers, and the real concern is that, under the intense pressure of the day's volume of cases, they too frequently make bad deals.

In the marketplace that is America's CJS, the actions of one player ripple through the labyrinth, affecting everyone. If the cops, for example, do the popular sweeps and roundups of junkies, the system floods and is forced to undertake hasty adjustments. Everyone has to work faster, and the rules have to be changed if a breakdown is to be averted. There is also a need—indeed, a fervent, if unexpressed, desire—to return to the somnolent rhythms of familiar routines. In those circumstances, the DA may be forced to take pleas of guilty in exchange for slaps on the wrist, just to clear the court calendar.

Contrary to popular belief, the prosecutor's job is not to seek convictions, but to promote justice. Theoretically at least, the prosecutor has an equal responsibility to exculpate as to convict. The public, however, is in no mood for mercy, and the prosecutors have to face them every four years or so.

We can further extend the marketplace analogy if we recognize the dynamics of the bargaining process. Everyone wants to start at the highest point, believing that to be the best way of leveraging the best deal possible. Thus, a prosecutor will frequently go for the most serious possible charge—even when it is legally unrealistic—in order to coerce a suspect into pleading guilty to a politically palatable lesser charge. That this charge may have little relation to the suspect's actual act doesn't seem to trouble the DA, but the fact is that introducing such mendacities cheapens the process and weakens any claim to serving the ends of justice. Such distortions breed contempt for the system in everyone.

If the jails are bursting—and they mostly are—judges have to take this into account and sentence accordingly. Their failure to do so has been another important impetus for such reforms as sentencing guidelines. Their failure to take capacity into account overwhelms an already strained corrections system. For all its desires to function autonomously, the CJS is decidedly interdependent.

Defenders

The Sixth Amendment of the U.S. Constitution provides that the accused in a criminal prosecution is entitled "to have the assistance of counsel for his defense."

The Supreme Court held in *Johnson v. Zerbat* (304 U.S., 358, 1928) that the federal government must provide counsel to the accused. Under the Fourteenth Amendment's requirement of due process, the Court later mandated that the states provide counsel for indigent defendants. The right extends not just to the trial, but to all the critical stages of the prosecution, from being identified as the target of an investigation to sentencing, and everything in between.

The Court's decisions inspired the growth of public defender systems in forty-three of the fifty states; the other states provide the services in other ways, such as through assigned counsel or contract systems. Although subjected to the same budgetary buffetings that slap the rest of the system, the promise of representation inherent in *Gideon v. Wainwright* (372 U.S., 335, 1963) and *In re Gault* (387 U.S., 1, 1967) has been largely met, quantitatively if not qualitatively.

The CJS is, of course, an integral part of American society, and as such, it mirrors the virtues and disabilities of the larger body. Just as there are crimes that are more "important" than others—because of the celebrity of the victim or of the suspect, or because of the unique nature of the event and the meaning it conveys to the citizens, or because of the wealth or power of the principals—some clients are more important than others. It always comes as a shock to Americans to discover that the poor and excluded fare no better in our courts than they do in corporate warrens, in other corridors of power, or on the streets of our cities.

Double Standards

Well-heeled defendants not only secure the best legal talent and fight the prosecution vigorously but get second and third bites at the apple with elaborate and costly appeals, which frequently enough carry the day. They also get to hire skilled investigators to secure evidence for their side and, increasingly, are able to employ experts who provide critical advice on the selection of juries, enabling their lawyers to pick those whose profiles fit the carefully wrought description of those likeliest to be sympathetic. They are also able to hire expert witnesses, whose testimony in a trial may be very influential with a jury.

Ralph DeLorean may have been videotaped doing what was alleged to have been a drug deal, but expensive lawyers convinced a jury otherwise. Max Von Bülow may have been convicted of drugging his wife into a comatose state, but his resources enabled him to hire Alan Dershowitz and overturn the judgment. William Kennedy Smith used investigators, jury selection experts, expert witnesses, and expensive counsel to gain an acquittal on a rape charge in 1991. When all else failed powerful convictees were able to secure pardons. If one imagines impoverished blacks in those cases, it will quickly become clear why prosecutors win the overwhelming majority of criminal prosecutions.

Right to Counsel

Access to and availability of lawyers, as a matter of the rights of indigent defendants, are a reform of recent vintage in terms of the full flowering of the constitutional promise. In 1963, *Gideon v. Wainwright* extended the right to all state defendants facing felony trials, and the following year, *Escobedo v. Illinois* applied the right of access to an attorney to a suspect in custody.

The quality, tenacity, and time commitment of the defense is distinctly related to the prospect of prevailing. To be viable, the defense has to search for exculpating evidence or supportive witnesses. Experts can make a huge difference. Jury selection may require hiring expensive analysts. Researching the law, the precedents, and the sufficiency of documents takes time and money. Assigned counsel—the Legal Aid or public defender lawyers—are certainly experienced, but they are harried, bereft of resources, and rarely able to devote the time and energy that an all-out defense requires.

The overwhelming majority of street criminals are poor and cannot afford to hire high-priced defense counsel. The criminal bar is not a practice that is widely lucrative; only a few really prosper.[4]

Starved for funds and attracting the lower tier of lawyers, the public-defender system mostly struggles heroically against powerful tides, but its presence has brought new vitality to the concept of representing the indigent defendant.[5]

Although it may be difficult to connect the existence of a vigorous defense bar with making our streets safer, it must be said that dispensing true justice and making the presumption of innocence real are indispensable ingredients in the achievement of urban peace. A society that works infamies—even against those accused of heinous crimes—cannot expect its citizens to put much faith in its processes. And the victims of such injustices develop a real, and deep, grievance that frequently finds expression in violent acts.

THE LEGISLATURE

If life is a game, its rules are made up at the state level by the men and women sent to the state capitols, with titles like senator, representative, and governor. The only real check, besides the rough and tumble of party politics, is judicial review to examine whether the laws passed conform with the reigning documents: the state and U.S. Constitutions.

[4] Sue Titus Reid, *Crime and Criminology*. New York: Holt, Rinehart & Winston, 1979.
[5] Anthony Platt and Randi Pollock, "Channeling Lawyers: The Careers of Public Defenders," in *The Potential for Reform of Criminal Justice*, Herbert Jacob (Ed.). Beverly Hills, CA: Sage, 1974.

"There oughta be a law" encapsulates the faith of Americans in simply passing a rule of behavior and letting its magic take effect.

Despite the central importance of the legislative process, few criminal justice tomes pay it much heed, and the President's Crime Commission (1967) mostly ignored it altogether. When it became unavoidable to make a reference to it, the reference was generally in the form of "revise the law on . . . " or "adopt legislation . . . " relating to drugs, or "clarify the law . . . " on eavesdropping, and so on.

The state legislature, as an elected body, usually reflects the popular will, and all too often, it panders to the public's worst instincts to curry political favor. The current rage is to be tough on crime and drugs and to pass mandatory sentences and increased penalties, which fly about legislative halls like confetti at a parade.

The Stampede to Toughness

The best example of the dysfunctions of mindlessly tough approaches was New York Governor Nelson Rockefeller's drug laws of 1973. A study four years later revealed that the attempt had failed to reduce drug use or drug crime.[6] Our own perspective on the appalling conditions in the state, two decades later, confirms the abject failure of the approach.

Caving in to public pressure may well result in counterproductive outcomes. The role of the experts is to inform the body politic of the complexities behind, and the ramifications of, tactics used to handle difficult social problems like drugs and crime.

---

[6] *The Nation's Toughest Drug Law: Evaluating the New York Experience.* Final Report of the Joint Committee on New York Drug Evaluation, National Institute of Law Enforcement and Criminal Justice. Washington, DC: U.S. Government Printing Office, 1977.

The passage of laws is not the panacea so many believe it to be, at least judging from the boiling waters of legislative assemblies. We have a plethora of laws, adopted ad hoc, without regard to an overall policy or a grand design. Changing a drug misdemeanor to a felony is popular work, but is it consistent with the overall drug program? Anomalies and absurdities are bound to creep in when issues are seized in midflight for their publicity value. The legislature might well turn its energies to weeding out archaic, unenforced, and unenforceable statutes that are breeding contempt for the whole process.

Minnesota's sentencing guidelines is a model of thoughtful, responsible, even unpopular, legislation that serves the very useful purpose of constituting truth in sentencing. Instead of blaring headlines about an accused facing "up to twenty years," which no one ever expects a prisoner to serve, the guidelines provide a realistic assessment of the true prospects in the case. The guidelines incorporate a decent regard for the available prison space and attempt to find useful alternatives to incarceration. That they have, since 1979, served the state splendidly (they have kept the prison population down and Minnesota ranks forty-ninth in per capita incarceration rates, while maintaining reasonably low levels of crime) has not diminished the enthusiasm of the Rambos for assaults on the provisions of these guidelines.

Legislatures must do the useful rather than the popular thing. Rockefeller's drug laws fed the public the red meat it clamored for, and on which it choked. The result was a bursting prison system and the Attica revolt, even though the actual uprising predated the passage of those specific laws. Minnesota's guidelines have provided an effective and thoughtful vehicle for the control of criminals beyond prison walls.

The Need for Patience and Sophistication

The guideline experience ought to tempt legislatures into building on the premise of treating serious chronic offenders more harshly, by building—after thorough research and study—a model that identifies the chronic recidivist and targets him for tougher penalties. I've repeated that this is a difficult problem, and open to error, but so are all other processes in this field; that is why it is dotted with such elastic and undefinable phrases as "probable cause," "beyond a reasonable doubt," "accidental," "justifiable," and even the concept of the "reasonable person" in judging the limits of an action. All a formula can really do is to maximize the prospect of making correct decisions and to build in safeguards that will reduce errors. Errors will occur in any human enterprise.

The Racketeer Influenced and Corrupt Organizations Act (RICO) statutes have proved very effective weapons against organized crime and offer a good example of the sort of innovative laws that legislatures can produce when they use experts and proceed thoughtfully. RICO may well prove a case of too much of a good thing, however, as prosecutors use it in cases that seem quite a distance from the intent of the framers of the original legislation. There are other effective tools awaiting wiser use.

PROBATION

The best and first hope of understanding the accused comes with the background report prepared by the probation officer to guide the judge in sentencing the convicted criminal. This is the first time that a real effort is made to examine the reality behind a face, a number, and a charge.

The probation report is an attempt to evaluate the accused—in terms of his work, school, family, military, criminal, and personal history—and to establish the treatment that, first, will offer the maximum protection for society and, second, will address the issue of applying a relevant sanction.

Complex human behavior, like crime, requires a relevant response. The consequence has to be appropriate if a wasteful or counterproductive result is to be avoided. In a very real sense, incarcerating a nonmenace is as dangerous as failing to imprison a chronic predator, because filling up scarce bed space will force the release of criminals who must be warehoused. And every criminal is free, some of the time anyway, so the point becomes to establish how much freedom is wise and whether it doesn't make more sense to supervise someone on the street, as opposed to springing him from prison, cold, onto an unsuspecting and unprepared populace, with no controls whatever.

Probation implies control. It includes monitoring and visits and verifications. It can involve drug test checks at treatment centers that report on attendance; the verification of employment, school attendance, or residence; and any other legal intrusion that helps establish the true activities of the probationer. The budget-crisis-inspired tendency to overload probation officers (POs) with huge volumes of cases has nearly wrecked the system. Such measures not only ensure the defeat of the program but risk permanently discrediting the process as unworkable.

The PO can verify restitution and can check to make certain that community service or other requirements have been met and that the conditions of release are not being violated. The PO is the monitoring agent for the broad range of alternatives to incarceration. There is little doubt that such alternatives have to be found and used more extensively, as our jails and prisons are reaching flood-tide conditions and are overflowing.

A majority—even an overwhelming majority—of sentences wind up in the supervised freedom called *probation*.[7]

WHY PROBATION?

In 1970, the American Bar Association supported more extensive use of probation because:

[7] Norman A. Carlson, "The Future of Prisons," *Trial*, vol. 12 (March 1976).

1. It provides freedom for the convicted, establishes the primacy of the law, and protects society.
2. It promotes rehabilitation by keeping the convicted in the community.
3. It avoids the negative effects of prison life.
4. It's cheaper.
5. It minimizes the impact on the offender's dependents.[8]

A Bureau of Justice Statistics report on a representative sample of 12,370 felons placed on probation in 1986 revealed that 43 percent had been arrested again, on other felony charges, within three years. Tighter monitoring might improve this figure, but it has to be recognized that failures will occur and that returning felons to criminogenic environments makes the promise of recidivism a self-fulfilling prophecy. Simply releasing criminals, without any sort of follow-up controls, would appear to be a lot riskier.

The supervision has to be real, and there has to be a willingness to sentence the offender to jail if there is a serious breach of probationary conduct. Consequence has to be the *sine qua non* of the probation effort.

PAROLE

Parole is a conditional release from prison to a supervised freedom. Frequently confused with probation, where there is no initial incarceration, parole has come into disrepute as a result of crimes committed by felons released by boards composed of hacks and cronies. Governors have been notably reckless in their appointments to such boards. Parole is a state function, and the board reviews cases to establish whom to release.

---

[8] American Bar Association, *Standards Relating to Probation*. Project on Standards for Criminal Justice, 1970.

Many parole board members have been found to be too ill equipped or inexperienced to judge when a convict may be safely released. Once again, we encounter the central importance of selection standards and practices, which have a devastating impact on the quality of the services rendered.

Decisions are often inconsistent or arbitrary, and some are guided by the notoriety of the case or political factors. There have been few evaluative studies of parole; nonetheless, its failures, as in the Willie Horton case, have produced horrific consequences. In some respects, the people in the best position to evaluate a convict's prospects for success in freedom are his keepers, the corrections officials, who do not usually participate in the decision to grant or withhold parole.

A system that needs all of the tools it can get can ill afford the loss of one (parole) whose successes are many and unheralded and whose failures are trumpeted from presidential campaign platforms.

OCCASIONAL PLAYERS

The fixed and permanent players are those who are directly and invariably involved in the process, from arrest to final release. The others flit in and out, depending on circumstances, although their role may be crucial to the event or to the system.

Such organizations as the American Civil Liberties Union play critical roles in defending constitutional rights—frequently in unpopular causes. Many cases are settled through civil suits. The press exercises enormous oversight power with its prying lens. Ad hoc groups may take an interest in a cause and influence the system—as abortion foes are attempting to do in trying to overturn the *Roe v. Wade* decision of 1973.

Groups such as the Society for the Prevention of Cruelty to Children vigorously pursue crimes against little ones. Minority groups may demonstrate for the establishment of a review board that will exercise real power over the police agency's disciplinary processes. Political bodies like investigative committees may be formed to examine aspects of the system, and these may go as high and as wide as a presidential commission on crime.

In short, the CJS has a fixed and permanent component and a shifting ad hocracy that can become an explosive variable. No one oversees the system as a whole or looks after its coordination. Any reform, such as computerizing the CJS process across agency lines, faces unexpected prospects and an uncertain fate, whatever its merit. The system resists both intrusion and turf invasions with equal vigor.

A smoothly functioning CJS is absolutely essential to any short-term strategy for combating street crime. Everyone agrees that sure detection, a fair and speedy trial, and swift and certain punishment for the guilty are the ingredients needed for any attack on street crime. The police must be reformed and managed more effectively. Judges must be more carefully selected and trained. Prosecutors have to make better deals. Defenders need more help. Probation and parole should be made meaningful by being granted resources and guidance, and corrections must manage its population more intelligently.

Today's mugging must be addressed, and the mugger must be punished. The long-term answer is to try to find out where he came from and to change the conditions that produced him. In between, we have to devise better methods of control.

Chapter Twelve

THE CRIMINAL JUSTICE SYSTEM
Corrections

My object all sublime
I shall achieve in time—
To make the punishment
Fit the crime.

—*The Mikado* (1885) W. S. Gilbert
and Sir Arthur Sullivan

Our society's attitude toward crime and criminals is often reflected in the words we use to describe treatments or institutions. Once we called them *penitentiaries* because that's where we sent sinners to reflect on their deeds and repent. Much was made of rehabilitation as reform swept our chain gangs and prison colonies. *Corrections* seemed a lofty enough term to mask our fears and vindictiveness. Gradually, as we came to recognize the threat posed by the chronic recidivist, we succumbed to the euphemism of *selective incapacitation*. That we haven't produced penitence, or rehabilitation, or correction, or even incapacitation has proved a frustration met with demands for still tougher penalties and more prisons.

Most of the innovations have focused on increasingly harsh

333

approaches, but an occasional effort has been made to head the developing criminal off at the pass.

SCARED STRAIGHT

One program, described by some as "Scared Straight," has young, redeemable first offenders taken to such places as Sing Sing prison to tour the facility and listen to inmates describe in graphic terms their experiences of gang rape, assaults, and other abuses. The objective is to scare the teenagers into going straight. The program is a part of a probation program. It has come in for some criticism, and some evaluations have questioned the worth of the approach, given the high failure rate of some of its participants. What its limits seem to illustrate is the complexity of human motivation and the need to devise a panoply of approaches, in the hope of reaching a few with one and a few with another, without really always knowing which will work with whom. Scared Straight is, like most educational programs, an act of faith rather than a measurable approach. Still, even if the success rate is low, it can be justified on the basis of its low cost.

Further down the line, the adoption of formulas or matrixes was seen as a way to bring uniformity to the justice process.

THE IMPACT OF SENTENCING GUIDELINES

If a formula could be found that would accurately predict rearrest, or recidivism, within three years of the current arrest, in 90 percent of the cases, would it be worth applying in sentencing decisions, if we know that 10 percent of those thus treated would be innocently victimized by the harsh sentence?

Although no such formula has yet been found, there is a real question about whether it ought to be used, even if it were devised.

Additional questions arise when noncriminal factors, such as unemployment, alcohol or drug addiction, education, and living arrangements, are factored into a recidivism-predicting equation simply because they are relevant to a person's prospects of future criminality. The question of race arises when blacks are disproportionately affected by such formulas. Is this race discrimination or does it simply reflect the reality that blacks commit, and are victimized by, more street crime? In this case, we would have a racial disparity based on real, rather than discriminatory, factors.

Attempts to devise a recidivism-predicting formula have resulted in accuracy levels that have rarely exceeded 70 percent, odds that are only a bit higher than the toss of a coin would produce. There is real doubt that this percentage can be improved.

The goal of sentencing is to fit the punishment to the crime, often referred to as "meting out just deserts." A secondary, but important, objective is to incapacitate the offender by keeping him off the streets. This second factor necessarily includes an assessment of a suspect's future actions and involves predictions, whether formulaic or subjective.

If the reality is that judges are now trying to predict an offender's prospects of future success (no recidivism) or failure (the commission of additional crimes), isn't it sensible to make reasonable attempts to devise objective formulas based on research, analysis, and observation? This is the real answer to the question of whether it is worth pursuing the search for a formula when the prospects of the development of a really good one (better than a 90 percent rate of accurately predicting future recidivism) are so dim. The fact is that seat-of-the-pants hunches are being applied now and will continue to be applied, so why not try for the best approach? The system invariably ignores the truism that neglect and poor practices constitute treatments, too.

The development of formulas will be useful in dealing only with populations that behave predictably and repetitively, like the chronic street criminal repeater. Murders, for example, may be aberrational acts that occur in isolation and are not likely to be repeated. Serial killers and single-incident mass murderers often have no prior criminal records, yet the seriousness of their crimes demands stern action. Criminology is speckled with such complexities, and they cannot be ignored.

One classification system devised by the U.S. Department of Justice for parole board use focuses on the seriousness of the crime for which the offender has been incarcerated, the likelihood of recidivism, and in-prison behavior. The latter point has always struck me as a particularly important, and invariably overlooked, factor, if sound evaluative and recording techniques are used by the prison administration.

This Justice Department parole system has led to an analysis of sentencing practices and to the discovery of wide and irrational inconsistencies, resulting in incomprehensible disparities. The discovery of the widely differing approaches of judges accelerated the movement to uniformity that resulted in the development of the sentencing guidelines that have been increasingly adopted in the 1980s and early 1990s. These sentencing guidelines offer a matrix of sentencing approaches that provide formulas, include ranges of time to allow some flexibility, and allow for exceptions, while imposing a requirement that the judge explain, in writing, his or her reasons for deviating from the formula's range. The guidelines take into account the prior record, the severity and nature of the current offense, and such other factors as prison capacity and provide a matrix that the judge consults, devising sentences accordingly. The result is a uniform and predictable scale that virtually eliminates sentence-shortening approaches such as parole.

The growth of these classification methods has extended into the field of probation, as more elements of the criminal justice system (CJS) attempt to discover the magic formula that will infallibly predict success or failure.

The system's struggle to find useful formulas to guide its actions is healthy and useful because it promotes speculation, thought, research, and analysis. Such examinations will encounter racially charged questions, such as why, when black males constitute 6 percent of America's population, they make up almost half the prison population. Such questions ought to stimulate discussion of the reasons and causes, rather than a dodging of the issue because it isn't politically correct to talk about such matters.

Formulas can be useful, but the search for justice's Holy Grail, in terms of a really relevant, applicable, and accurate system for predicting future behavior, must continue.[1]

Minnesota adopted sensible and restrained sentencing guidelines in 1979, which had the effect of tempering any legislative initiatives to increase the prison population by mandating that any law that increased the number of inmates had to be accompanied by either an appropriation for the additional prison space or a relaxation of other legal provisions that would release an equal number of prisoners. In this way, Minnesota avoided the prison flooding that has overwhelmed other states. Although there has been much bristling over these guidelines, they have effectively protected the state from horrendous prison overcrowding.

Minnesota has made wide use of such alternatives as probation, community service, fines, restitution, halfway houses, mediation, and work release. The legislative halls still thunder with cries for retribution, and some punitive drug legislation has been passed, but a restraining instinct that grasps the sense of complexity behind all the crime continues to serve the state well. Violent crimes increased 28 percent between 1980 and 1989 in Minnesota and this increase has added to the prison population, but the guidelines have prevented that wave from becoming a flood.

Although I support capital punishment, it is a measure of Minnesotans' collective sense of decency that they've lived without it for about eighty years with no enormous rises in crime.

[1] Joan Petersilia and Susan Turner, *Guideline-Based Justice: The Implications for Racial Minorities.* Santa Monica, CA: Rand Institute, 1985.

The challenge is to control the criminal population, and this control can take many different forms.

METHODS OF CONTROL

A quick review of the available offender control programs, nationwide, reveals the wide range of options and the large number of possibilities. Such a review immediately suggests the need for adopting many different approaches to meet the complexity in the population of criminals.

Supervised control ranges from nominal, or minimal, supervision, which may include a fine or victim restitution, to the field supervision of a criminal in once-a-day checks, which may also include restitution, training, or treatment. Control may involve intense supervision, or pretty constant monitoring, and may also include the other factors. Control may take the form of partial incarceration in a halfway house or residential drug treatment center, or by electronic supervision or weekend furloughs. At the top of the scale is secure confinement in a prison, which may still include carefully measured doses of freedom.

OFFENDER FEES

Having the offender pay for monitoring services, like probation, in return for the privilege of avoiding incarceration, is another expanding innovation in the CJS. Typically, the fees are used to pay for the costs of probation or parole but they have included jail and prison costs, too. Generally, they are charged for supervision or room-and-board rates or for such services as drug treatment.

Such fees, and civilly imposed support payments or judicially directed restitutions, offer another avenue for mitigating the impact of crime and bringing other consequences to bear on the issue of individual responsibility and accountability.

HUGE FINES

We love to read of famous white-collar criminals going to prison, but besides the political value and the secret titillations we derive, does this approach make much sense? Are such criminals dangerous to the rest of us? Might they not be more effectively used to society's profit?

A short period of incarceration, in such cases, is essential, to concentrate the mind of the accused and to ensure disgrace and humiliation. But the victims and the society might reap greater profit from bankrupting fines that truly exhaust the resources of the criminal and leave him or her broke, while affording the authorities opportunities for restitution to the victims. There would be the problem of locating all manner of concealed assets, but the threat of a long prison term would afford the prosecutor a lot of bargaining leverage. As white-collar prosecutions have grown, and with them seizures of assets, recoveries, and confiscations, a latter-day crew of bloodhounds has emerged, whose specialty is locating hidden assets. These investigators lend muscle to the fine-and-recovery effort. The political sensitivity of the issue, however, has largely precluded large-scale adoption.

A day fine program, in which a defendant is fined a day's wages (or a multiple of such earnings), maximizes the prospect of equalizing the economic impact on offenders.

Imprisonment has an important symbolic value, but the maximum social good might be garnered by a short jailing and a long commitment to atonement. The conviction of a successful prizefighter for rape might produce some social worth if he were jailed briefly and released on the condition that he raise, for example, $50 million to $100 million for the treatment and care of abused women.

OUT, BUT NOT FREE

No one doubts that many more offenders can be supervised through probation, much more cheaply, than through incarceration, but budget slashings and enormous increases in probation officers' workload have tended to render the probation process a nullity. These cuts have been undertaken mostly at the same time that huge sums have been found for prison construction, and it is worth mentioning that the administration in Washington, which can't find the money for social services, found billions for the construction of new prisons. One recent U.S. Attorney General derided the search for crime's social and economic causes, and his successor offered the simple formula of "more prisons or more crime."

Officials have found it easy and convenient to effect savings by failing to fill probation job slots and simply assigning more cases to the remaining staff. After a while, supervision becomes a perfunctory process, reduced to occasional phone calls and very rare visits. In those circumstances, offenders are bound to succumb to temptation and fail. The publicity surrounding such failures—when someone on probation or other conditional release has committed an atrocious crime—confirms the public's suspicion that we are too soft on criminals.

Some, however, have taken a different tack. The State of Georgia devotes about one fifth of the $500 million allocated to corrections to a probation system that uses house-arrest monitoring equipment and surprise visits with a Breathalyzer to check for alcohol violations. Georgia's system provides for a hierarchy of sanctions, from light to tight supervision. Under intensive monitoring, the convict must agree to hold a job, possibly pay a fine or perform community service, conform to a nightly curfew, and abstain from using drugs or alcohol. Probation officers pay surprise visits at least four times a week to check on alcohol use, and convicts must report at least twice a week for drug testing and counseling.

Electronic ankle bracelets and other monitoring equipment are available to control more serious violators. Those who violate conditions can be sent to a residential facility, for closer supervision, classes, and counseling, yet still report for work every day.

The most serious sanction, before being sent to a prison for permanent lockup, is a quasi-military detention center where the inmates are given uniform jumpsuits, march everywhere, snap to attention when a guard appears, and do road maintenance, park cleanup, and other public agency projects. They attend evening classes at day's end. This approach is more fully described in the section on "Shock Incarceration" below.

The recidivism rate is no greater among these probationers than among those incarcerated and released—and everyone gets out, sooner or later.

JAILINGS, PROBATION, AND PAROLE

The development of sentencing matrixes, called *sentencing guidelines*, to promote uniformity and truth in sentencing, and to regulate the rates of increase in prison populations, has led to the decline of parole—the conditional release of prisoners before the end of their sentence. Nevertheless, despite the diminishing popularity of parole, the enormously swelling activity of the CJS still led to a 12.1 percent increase in the number of parolees in 1989 over 1988, when there were a total of 456,797.

A study by the National Institute of Justice revealed that, by 1990, only 40 percent of prison releases were based on discretionary parole, compared to about 70 percent in 1977. Supervised mandatory releases constituted 30 percent in 1990 and fewer than 10 percent in 1977. Unconditional releases remained fairly even, at 14 percent in 1990 and 18 percent in 1977, and other conditional releases rose to 16 percent in 1990, from about half that total in 1977. The probation population (not incarcerated but kept under supervision) grew 5.6 percent, to 2,520,479, and those under some form of correctional supervision (in local jails or state or federal prisons, or on probation or parole) rose to over 4 million in 1989, or 1 in every 25 adult males. This number represents an increase of 34.6 percent from 1985 to 1989.

In New York City, it takes 14,000 employees to control the 20,000-plus inmates, but only 1,565 probation officers to supervise 60,000 adult and juvenile offenders. The public's preference for jails will doom any effort to incorporate useful programs into probation services or, indeed, to improve the quality or quantity of supervision over the criminals on the street. Every citizen seems to think tougher penalties and more prisons will enable us to build our way out of this morass of crime.

The nation's jails held 104 percent of capacity in 1990, an actual decline from 1989's 108 percent. There were nearly twenty million jail admissions and releases (almost evenly divided) for the year ending June 29, 1990, with males constituting 91 percent and blacks 47 percent of the total. Unconvicted inmates totalled 51 percent.

In Massachusetts, a study of such programs as furloughs, participation in prerelease activities, and being let out of a lower security facility, as opposed to exiting a maximum-security prison, revealed that these programs produced significantly lower recidivism rates.[2]

The key factors centered on maintaining or establishing such societal links as family, economic, political, and social roles through a gradual reintegration into society.

Were there failures? Willie Horton, for one. But the point has to be to maximize the odds rather than to try to establish a foolproof and infallible system.

Jail construction and its internal organization reflect organ-

[2] Massachusetts Department of Corrections, *The Effect of Community Reintegration on Rates of Recidivism: A Statistical Overview of Data for the Years 1971 through 1987*, July 1990.

izational theories and philosophies. High-rises tend to be more structured than lower, flatter, more open, spacious buildings. There is the issue of openness—with unarmed guards mixing with inmates (called *direct supervision,* and affording a much closer opportunity for interaction with and evaluation of inmates)—or more security-conscious tightness, with guards at glassed-in observation posts. Proximity to what is usually a central, downtown, congested court center often dictates the construction of a costlier high-rise.

Television monitoring and other surveillance techniques can reduce a problem more prevalent than the rare escape attempt: suicide.

NEW YORK CITY'S JAILS

New York City's inmate population grew from 7,000 in 1980 to 22,000 in 1990. Over $1 billion was spent on new jails, and the city corrections department's budget went from $120 million in 1981 to $800 million in 1990. Crime in the city rose 15 percent over that period, and murders reached a record of well over 2,000 in 1990. The spiral of violence continued its rise in 1991 and 1992.

The explosive growth in arrests created unimagined congestion and confusion. Corrections guards grew to fear contracting dread diseases, like AIDS or tuberculosis, in such confined quarters, and they staged militant blockades of Riker's Island in a contract dispute. Pregnant Legal Aid lawyers took leaves rather than expose their fetuses to disease risks. The danger of inmate violence and abuse rose exponentially—to the point where judges became reluctant to send tender young men to jail for fear they'd be gang-raped. A highly touted corrections commissioner was forced to leave amid charges of mismanagement and incompetence.

Current plan to build 5,500 new jail beds, for over $1 billion, comes to a cost of about $181,000 per bed, not including debt service and operating costs. Such costs don't take into account the value of the land, welfare payments to families, lost wages, taxes the inmate might have paid, or even potential restitutions to victims or the community. It would've been substantially cheaper to send the inmates to Harvard. This jail construction was proposed by the city's first black mayor, who'd said, during his campaign, that, if there were more social services, there might be less need for cops. In caving in to the quick fix of incarceration, Mayor David Dinkins illustrated the difference between candidacy and incumbency, although he seemed determined to make the latter a brief experience.

STRANGE JAIL SPACES

The expanding prison population has turned their housing into a growth industry. American businesses responded with typical élan to the challenge. Mark Correctional Systems of Maywood, New Jersey, has devised a computerized assembly line that turns out maximum-security steel cells, which contain seventy to eighty square feet of space and require only stacking and connecting to electricity and plumbing to become operational. The cells, which weigh six thousand pounds each, as compared to the thirty-two thousand of the standard concrete model, can be adapted for plumbing fixtures, doors, windows, bunks, desks, and wiring. They meet the specifications set by the American Correctional Association for maximum security.

Meanwhile, since 1989, a shipbuilder near New Orleans, Avondale Industries, is building a 47,325-ton barge that will house eight hundred inmates for New York City's bursting jail system.

In criminal justice, just as in every other activity, the talent and innovations go where the money is.

SHOCK INCARCERATION

The growth of innovative approaches illustrates the fecundity of the released imagination. Many of the ideas need work, and some may have to be abandoned altogether—the search for a panacea will founder on reality's shoals—but there is little doubt that fresh and varied approaches are desperately needed to cope with the ever-rising challenges of violence and crime.

Shock incarceration (SI) involves a short period of confinement—usually three to six months—involving "boot-camp" activities that include drills, labor, discipline, exercise, and other features of military life. Some programs include education, treatment, and vocational training.

The SI programs are usually reserved for young offenders who have committed the less serious crimes and who seem suitable for reform. The focus of the program is to disinter the buried hope of rehabilitation. It also seeks to deter, punish, and even incapacitate, while reducing prison costs—if it, in fact, does divert those who might otherwise be later sentenced to prison time. Practitioners have experienced, over and over, the effects of a natural law in the CJS, which forces clients into institutions simply because of their availability and existence. One result has been the immediate filling of space with inmates who might have been conditionally released.

Because society rarely affords employment opportunities to its ex-convicts, whether young or older, whether exiting prison or SI programs, it makes some sense to marry some such program as SI to a youth or adult national-community-service program, patterned after the Depression's Civilian Conservation Corps or Works Projects Administration, by way of supplanting the vanishing military as a job of last resort, and affording released inmates the opportunity for useful service. As matters now stand, all our inmates graduate into idleness and temptation that make a return to criminality inevitable.

Each innovation has to be very cautiously approached.

We're dealing with complex human behavior, and the preventive strategies will vary widely with the individuals involved. SI may work for some, Scared Straight may deter others, but some will be unimpressed by both. The more approaches available, the better, and these should be based on research, planning, and careful preparation. They should be thoroughly studied and evaluated.

THE TOUGH APPROACH

The prisons are flooded with inmates from low-level drug arrests, many sent there through tough and inflexible mandated sentences such as New York State's punitive drug laws of 1973, which, for example, required judges to imprison everyone convicted of a second felony within ten years of the first. And many minor drug offenses were elevated to felonies as a way of "getting tough" on drug dealers. Stephen Gillers, a defense lawyer who studied the laws' effects, dubbed them "Rockefeller's Folly," but the legislators, anxious to avoid the "soft-on-drugs" label, voted overwhelmingly for the legislation.

Generally, federal laws are even tougher than most state laws. The mandated sentences of the Feds, which allow for no deviations or use of discretion even in exceptional cases, often produce grotesquely skewed results. Thus, a woman who, for protection, had carried a gun in her purse for over twenty years, and who was sitting in a car while her friends bought marijuana, received five years in prison, with no chance of parole. She was prosecuted in federal court, whereas the fellow who arranged the marijuana deal, who was prosecuted in state court, would very likely serve no more than three years in state prison. The woman had never been previously arrested and was regarded as a religious, responsible churchgoer, retired postal worker, and devoted grandmother.

Fixed and inflexible sentences always produce anomalies because of the complexities of each separate case. Such approaches have driven the federal prison population from just over 44,000 in 1987 to almost 100,000 projected for 1995. And this number doesn't take into account such initiatives as those offered by New York's Senator D'Amato, described in Chapter 5.

Such tough measures force the CJS into dysfunctional adjustments. No drug suspects are willing to plea-bargain into such a sentencing buzzsaw, so they opt for trials, overwhelming the courts. Deals must be struck with murderers, robbers, and rapists in order to clear the trial calendars, or the charges against the drug operators must be twisted into something the system can massage. Today's anarchy in our prisons can be traced to such quick fixes as harsh mandated sentences for low-level drug users and sellers, although we'd prefer to think that it is entirely due to recently skyrocketing crime statistics.

The Attica Prison riot of September 9, 1971, took the lives of thirty-nine inmates and guard-hostages, and at least sixty others were wounded, shot by the invading force retaking the prison. This riot could be traced to the abuses produced by prison overcrowding. That Governor Rockefeller had, on that occasion, refused to go to the prison and negotiate with the rioters was of a piece with the tough stances being taken by officials, with predictable results. Tough stances surely have their place, but so do negotiation and patience.

Today the Attica Prison riot serves as a historic signpost, pointing to the dangers of acting on rumors and gossip and to the need for reflection, planning, and a balanced mediational approach to unprecedented and complex crises. Those charged with restoring order at Attica should have known, but didn't, that their only real control over events was limited to the "go" or "no-go" order they gave their minions. Once loosed, cops ordered to violence are simply an armed mob that sets on another mob. The directors' not knowing this produced fateful results. Over twenty years later, an agonized jury found

partially for the inmates in a $2.8 billion lawsuit brought by
1,281 prisoners.

The next twenty years saw such steadily worsening prison
conditions as to convince any observer that Attica's lessons
were a long way from having been learned.

THE LAW OF UNINTENDED EFFECTS
DRIVING PRISON OVERCROWDING

Prison systems tend to be capacity-driven in that the number of those incarcerated will swell with the availability of additional space if measures are not taken, in advance, to forestall
this result. Jurisdictions that build additional prisons soon fill
them to overflowing. The system is forever adjusting and adapt-
ing, and we keep forgetting how unrelated these adjustments
are to objective realities. Minnesota and North Carolina have
roughly equal per capita crime rates, yet the latter's rate of
imprisonment is five times greater than the former's, a fact
suggesting that the numbers in prison do not have a direct
impact on crime rates. Nevertheless, the building binge continues as America faces soaring crime rates in the 1990s.

We must be very careful, though, about concluding that
incarcerating criminals does no good at all—a thought made
tempting by such statistics. The point must be to incarcerate the violent recidivist needing incapacitation, and to devise alternative approaches for those representing lower risk
levels, without abandoning the threat of imprisoning them if
they fail to conform with the law. At this moment, the majority
of those imprisoned neither are there for violent crimes nor
pose a real threat to the public's safety. A huge number are first
offenders. Most could be released without material risk; could
be placed in monitored treatment, work, or educational programs; and would be making space for those who really should
be put away.

In a curious sense, the tremendous explosion in the prison

population, at a time when crime has not increased at anything approaching the increase in the rates of imprisonment (and the "lock-'em-up" binge has been going on for over twenty years now), illustrates the law of diminishing returns. If one concludes that imprisoning chronic, serious recidivists produces a high return in terms of future crimes prevented because of the prisoner's incapacitation, then, as the less serious offenders get locked up, the return, in terms of the numbers of crimes avoided through each incarceration, declines, until it simply isn't worthwhile to lock up the very casual and occasional nonviolent criminals who might be kept under control in another way. This is precisely the current case in America, but our obsession with Willie Horton drives us to think of every offender as being equally threatening.

POPULATION GROWTH

The prison population has enormously outpaced the rise in street crime in America, driven by fear and a demand for action. In 1970, there were just over 200,000 prisoners. The figure rose gradually to 250,000 in 1975, and to over 329,000 in 1980. The population then exploded, to 502,000 in 1985 and to 771,000 by December 31, 1990. The country's overall population will have increased by only 15 percent between 1980 and 1994, when it is projected that there will be 1,133,000 in prison.

Millions of Americans are arrested every year and are jailed before being brought to court. It is one of the ironies of our system that the overwhelming majority of persons behind bars, at any given moment, haven't been convicted of anything. They're either awaiting arraignment or too poor to make bail before trial. But it is the prison population—made up of convicted felons serving long sentences—that, appropriately, draws the lion's share of attention. Its growth, ironically, is not even distantly related to actual rises in street crime. We have enormously high levels of crime and violence, but the imprisonments are driven more by public attitudes than by statistical tables.

The membership of the prison population and their brothers in the ghetto are the groups of street criminals who are terrifying the nation. Their characteristics are centered on race, poverty, and addictions. They constitute an agglomeration scooped by a large and undiscriminating net that makes no real distinctions between menaces and low-risk criminals. The CJS reflects—even magnifies—the injustices and inequities of the larger society. The prisoners are the losers in the race toward the American Dream, but the contest was rigged from the start.

National Institute of Justice (NIJ) study revealed that, of the 450,000 inmates in state prisons in 1986, over 96 percent were male; almost 47 percent were black; almost 27 percent were eighteen to twenty-four; and almost 46 percent were twenty-five to thirty-four. Almost 62 percent had less than twelve years' education.

The crimes that most frighten the citizens are the stranger-to-stranger acts of violence that raise such flashes of recognition as "There, but for the grace of God, go I." Yet the reality is that the home is the most dangerous place and that those known to us pose the greatest threats to our safety. In all violent crimes, by state prison inmates, in 1986, for example, 16.6 percent of the perpetrators were close to their victims, 24 percent were known, and almost 60 percent were strangers. In murder 5.8 percent were close, 9 percent were known, and almost 12 percent were strangers. Blacks were more likely to engage in stranger-to-stranger violence (63.7 percent of the black inmates) than whites (54.7% of the white inmates).

The undiscriminating facets of the system are made worse by mandatory drug sentences that fill the prisons with first- or second-time offenders when we ought to be concentrating on the chronic predators. In 1986, for example, a survey of state prison inmates revealed that almost a fourth of the males were first-time offenders and three fourths had one or more prior convictions, a large number (almost 21 percent) having one.

Thus, a total of 44.2 percent of the violent male inmates had one prior conviction, or none.

An understanding of the involvement of alcohol and drugs in street crime is essential to the development of any remedial program. Another 1986 survey by the U.S. Department of Justice's NIJ, of state prison inmates who had committed violent offenses while under the influence of drugs or alcohol, revealed that more than half had imbibed or used.

The juveniles entering the system are mirror images of their older brothers in prison. The juveniles in state institutions in 1987 tended to be disproportionately (41.1 percent) black; undereducated, and overwhelmingly male.

Police agencies increased felony arrests 37 percent between 1985 and 1989, mostly for drug offenses. They have flooded the prisons with blacks and addicts, the uneducated, impoverished, unemployable, and probably even undangerous male members of the underclass, all the while citing "hamstringing Supreme Court decisions" and crying for more cops. Legislative mandates for tougher sentences—which were themselves responses to public pressures to do something about crime, drugs, and violence—have fueled the rise in incarcerations, together with tougher judges.

The ratio of black to white incarceration rates in 1988 was 6.25 to 1: 155 per 100,000 whites and 965 per 100,000 blacks. The Sentencing Project reported much higher figures in 1990, but the Department of Justice criticized it as "misleading for failing to take into account other countries' use of work camps and mental hospitals to hold persons we send to jail."

An ambitious building program has failed to keep pace with the increase, but a rapid succession of court orders to reduce overcrowding and other abuses have impelled the authorities either to release prisoners en masse, without regard for their level of dangerousness, or to build faster. One of the significant developments has been the use of special masters to oversee the orders of the court and help find solutions to prison congestion and the appalling conditions leading to riots, violence, and loss of control. These enlightened efforts, sometimes encouraged by such entities as the Edna McConnell Clark Foundation, have probably forestalled any number of prison riots and have forced the bureaucrats to retake control of their institutions. By 1988, there were forty-two states operating under court orders to reform their systems.

We like to style ourselves an easygoing, even naively merciful, people, but the statistics belie this popular myth. We do have more serious problems with street crime, drugs, guns, and violence than other countries, but we also imprison more people per capita than anyone else. A 1990 study by the Sentencing Project in Washington, D.C., had the United States heading the list of nations with 426 incarcerations per 100,000 population. South Africa was second with 333, and the then–Soviet Union was third, with 268. England was tenth with 97 per 100,000, and the Philippines was twenty-second, with 22. Japan's number was 45, and Turkey's was 96.

How can these numbers square with the tireless bromide that our criminals are getting away with murder? And how can we explain the related statistics that show us as having the highest percentage of children (17 percent) living below the poverty line?

Although our clearance rates are low, and most crimes go unsolved, the statistics illustrate that the cops catch up with everybody, eventually. The notion that the overwhelming majority of criminals don't get caught is refuted by a brief appraisal of our prison population. As we've noted earlier, the fact is that criminals commit many crimes before they're caught, but most of them seem to get caught—later, rather than sooner.

The Sentencing Project's 1990 report, *Young Black Men and the Criminal Justice System*, showed that one in four black males, aged twenty to twenty-nine, was in prison, in jail, or on probation on any given day. The over 609,000 black males under some form of criminal justice control far exceeded the 436,000 enrolled in higher education on that same day.

The exploding prison population has forced a search for alternatives. House arrest permits the offender to work, see his doctor, attend treatment programs, and see to other authorized business. He must, otherwise, remain within hailing distance of a monitoring box in his home, which picks up radio signals from a transmitter on his ankle. Any interrupted signal is picked up by the corrections department's computer, which checks the authorized absences and informs the probation officer when no permission has been granted. The judge then decides how to handle the transgression. This sort of monitoring lends teeth to the probation process.

A key point, in any such program, is to acknowledge the inevitability of occasional failures and the importance of striving for statistical, not absolute, measures of success. The approach requires the sort of moral courage that has, with disastrous consequences, been mostly absent from any discussion of criminal justice in this country.

Of the 47,812 men and women monitored in Florida, from October 1983 to June 30, 1990, 22 were arrested for murder. We might call this the "Willie Horton syndrome" in so far as that symbol may actually have been an isolated failure in an otherwise successful operation. The political heat surrounding Horton cowed those who should have been insisting on a rational overall evaluation of the program in which he'd proved such a notable failure.

PRISONS AND POLITICS

Governor Jim Florio of New Jersey faces the same political dilemma because his prison population rose from 5,800 in 1980 to over 23,000 in 1991 (140 percent of capacity), at the time of a budget deficit estimated at over $800 million. To avoid being called soft on crime, he hesitated to adopt the very recommendations suggested by his study group—that mandatory sentences, especially in drug cases, be revised and that alternatives to incarceration be used. About half the prisoners had been added as a result of drug laws that imposed tough mandatory sentences under the state's Comprehensive Drug Reform Act of 1987. California, whose prison population went from 22,000 in 1982 to over 100,000 in 1991, faced the identical quandary. Most other states were in the same boat.

And liberal black mayors, who had good reason to appreciate the plight of the ghetto dwellers, and who often eschewed such aggressive tactics as stakeout units, decoy and sting operations, and other approaches wrongly attacked as "entrapment," nevertheless found it expedient to cram the jails with drug users and dealers.

COUNTRY CLUB PRISONS

The use of a tiered system of low-, medium-, and high-security incarcerations also permits the system to respond with some sense of proportion. It is the deprivation of freedom that gives jailing its bite. The existence of harsh conditions simply dehumanizes the inmates, although, again, some will be cowed into submission.

The concern over our "softness on crime and criminals" has caused our officials to be very wary of creating "country club prisons," whatever their merits. Using a mixed approach would enable the system to control its inmates more effectively, to select the serious predators and menaces for special attention, and to promote more safety within the walls.

As with so many other issues surrounding criminal justice, the reality of "country club prisons" is precisely the reverse of public attitudes toward them. The truth is we need more of them, not fewer. The failure of our prison system lies in our overrelying on its promises and on our hesitancy to use methods now discredited as "soft."

The purpose of corrections is to protect society—statistically rather than individually. The purposes of imprisonment are to incapacitate, deter, punish, and rehabilitate. Imprisonment needs to be focused on the chronic recidivist. As we've noted earlier, many of the inmates are old enough to be considered safe for release, given what we know about the criminal career. It is mainly the province of the young. Increases in such tough penalties as isolation cells, the use of handcuffs and leg irons, and the restriction of privileges have now made prisons safer than our streets, even as they burst to overflowing, but it is a safety that rests on the use of oppressive measures that heighten tensions and frustrations.

The failure of our prison system has given rise to a "nothing-works" psychology that ensures the defeat of any hope of searching for useful approaches. Complex human behavior, which crime surely is, needs to be addressed with complex solutions. Each crime and each offender pose unique problems and opportunities for the system. Our society has to understand the complexities sufficiently to allow for the use of such sensible alternatives as fines, restitution, community service, treatment, halfway houses and other residential facilities, house arrest, several levels of probation, parole and conditional releases, mediation, and other forms of punishment and control. Our corrections system is costly, wasteful and inefficient—and a perfect reflection of our panic and our insistence on quick and easy answers.

Two decades of Draconian approaches have only made us less safe.

MEASURES OF DESPERATION AND EXASPERATION

Impatience and frustration have led inevitably to embracing simple, direct, increasingly harsher solutions. In the July 16, 1991 issue of *USA Today*, the Chicago police chief called for the adoption of tough techniques as are featured in Chinese prisons, where sanitary facilities are a bucket and prisoners are given a bowl of rice and a bottle of tea daily. He also called for random searches and permission to use illegally gathered evidence in court. He was flying in the face of appalling incarceration rates, and the rising homicide rates in his own city. That the chief was black illustrated the complexity of the situation and the pressures working on police executives.

The chief later complained that his remarks had been taken "out of context," but he nevertheless continued to defend China's tough approach, even to drug dealers.

The description of the lives of Chinese prisoners was a description of the harshness meted out to those sentenced to death, which can happen to embezzlers and other non-violent criminals, and which includes little food, a lot of lice, and coffin-sized punishment cells. Nevertheless, Chinese citizens alarmed over what they perceive as a crime wave complain of coddling prisoners. The Parade of Execution is often conducted with police vehicle sirens at full blast, intended to cow the populace into compliance with the law. The prisoners' hands are bound with rope and nylon chord circles their necks to enable an armed officer to fasten the prisoner tight, for the bullet, and to preclude the crying out of any revolutionary slogans.

Statistics are unreliable, but crime in China is generally held to be increasing. This rise is attributed to the liberalizing policies which began in the late seventies, although reversed later, and increased traffic in drugs. The nation is still regarded, by visiting Americans like the Chicago police chief, as remarkably safe.

Throwing everyone in jail appears to be as effective as throwing no one in. If the system is overloaded, it becomes unable to discriminate between menace and sensible risk. Jailing everyone has not reduced U.S. crime or the population of criminals. The overwhelming majority of prisoners could probably be monitored and controlled through much cheaper and more effective strategies without a significant increase in crime levels, but this approach would produce the occasional individual failures with which no politician wants to be associated.

PRISON ABUSES AND THE BATTLE FOR CONTROL

Although the authorities seem to have wrested control of the prisons from the inmates in recent years, greatly reducing the numbers of murders, assaults, and other indices of inmate control, horror stories continue to surface. A *New York Times* op-ed piece on October 22, 1990, reported the case of a nineteen-year-old farm boy, sentenced to one year for possession of marijuana, who wrote "Help me, Help me" on a psychiatric evaluation form. He'd been sexually assaulted every hour on the hour, for forty-eight hours, by inmates in a facility designed for 120 and holding 465.

For too many black men living in conditions of racism, poverty, and exclusion, a prison sentence becomes an inevitable rite of passage, much as college becomes the expectation of the white middle class. Those with nothing to lose have little to fear.

CAPITAL PUNISHMENT

All that can be said about capital punishment has probably been said. It seems likely that killing the Ted Bundys will deter a minority of other criminals, and it certainly kept Bundy from striking again. It is awful for the state to kill, and mistakes are possible, but punishment, generally, does deter, and rewards do inspire positive behavior. Neither works everywhere and with everyone, all the time. The human animal is conditionable, but complicated.

To say that capital punishment doesn't deter others is to say that the example of punishment has no value for the onlookers. This view flies in the teeth of all human experience. It's not the same as saying, however, that inappropriately harsh punishments have much value. Punishments have to be relevant, meaningful, proportionate, and timely if their example is to be of value in having the desired deterrent effect.

Not all murderers, or even a majority, will be deterred, but nothing like all murderers face even the long-shot prospect of execution. It has normally been reserved for the cruel, calculating, often repeat killer, whose acts have offended the public conscience beyond the impact caused by the vast majority of homicides. The murders of such repeaters as Ted Bundy serve as paradigms that illustrate the dangers lurking in our streets.

It's absurd to say that, if all murders aren't deterred, capital punishment can't be a deterrent. The fact is that some are logically bound to be deterred.

The recent history of executions in America began in 1976, when the U.S. Supreme Court reinstated the death penalty after it was satisfied that factors of racial bias had been addressed. Through 1990, 143 prisoners had been killed by the state. Their average stay on death row had been seven years and eleven months.

As 1990 ended, there were 2,356 prisoners awaiting death in thirty-four states. Almost 99 percent were males; 58.4 percent were white and 40 percent were black. All had been convicted of murder. Although thirty-six states have the death penalty, it has been applied differentially, with Texas (33), Florida (21), and Louisiana (18) leading the list since 1977. Amazingly, California has had 247 prisoners awaiting execution since 1989 yet had not, since 1976, put a single prisoner to death.

From 1976 to 1990, a total of 1,335 prisoners had had their sentences commuted or reduced, had been resentenced, or had died. These represented over a third of the total admissions to death row (3,451). The ratios of whites to blacks held constant in admissions, reductions, and executions.

The number of executions has gradually risen since the process resumed in 1977. The current cycle began with 5 in 1983 and climbed to 21 in 1984, then declined to fewer than 20 in 1985 and 1986 before rising to 25 in 1987. There were 11 in 1988, 16 in 1989, and 20 in 1990. The poor fare no better in capital cases than they do in any other human enterprise in this country, but special pains have been taken to ensure that blacks are not disproportionately executed.

The U.S. Constitution clearly includes the possibility of the state's taking life because it speaks of persons not being deprived of life, liberty, or property without due process of law. Such wording obviously implies the prospect of taking a life.

Opponents and proponents frequently cite studies and statistics, but none of these are persuasive when we see, for example, that North Dakota, with 9 murders in 1991, is the safest place in America—and it has no death penalty—and that Washington, D.C., with about the same population, had more than fifty times that number of murders: 489.

Killers do escape, as Ted Bundy did, or are released, as happened to mass murderer Arthur Shawcross. They kill again.

Other countries are abandoning the death penalty, but they don't suffer the levels of violence that we do, and the stranger-to-stranger killings here are rising as the clearance rates are declining sharply. Clearly, we need to deter the small percentage of calculating murderers who weigh the risks.

Prisoners on death row fight furiously to avoid execution. Little thought seems to be spent on victims, past or potential future ones, by opponents regularly conducting anti-execution rallies outside prison cells.

Often the argument over capital punishment drifts into an attack on punishments, and we have to grasp that this is a key component of social control. There is a real danger in broadening the reach of capital punishment beyond killers, however. Executions should be reserved exclusively for murderers. Capital punishment is central to the concept of individual responsibility and accountability. Death, by the state, is used to deter, and to dispense retribution.

Safeguards have to be introduced to reduce the possibility of error. There should be a separate hearing for a death penalty, in which the guilt of the accused is established beyond the shadow of a doubt. Those under eighteen at the time of the crime and those mentally deficient or otherwise impaired should not be executed.

The incredible delays and costs can be mitigated by making the process more efficient and speedy.

In the final analysis, the rightness or wrongness of the issue becomes a personal and subjective judgment.

Will we ever know whether capital punishment deters?

Will we ever know which act of love or charity has changed a life?

We're not likely to learn, in any sharply defined sense, although there remains the hope that deep and relevant research will lead to better answers than we can offer today.

A more relevant question is: How is the human animal's behavior shaped and conditioned, if not by positive and negative actions? Because capital punishment is the ultimate negative sanction, it seems silly to hold that it has no power to influence a calculating observer's actions. Didn't the tough kidnapping laws and the high rate of arrests in such cases influence a dramatic decline in such crimes? Although many might argue that the execution of the Lindbergh kidnapper, Bruno Richard Hauptmann, was barbarous, how many would say it failed to deter others? And the evidence against Hauptmann was very serious.

It doesn't seem likely that concentrating on any single strategy, punitive or humanitarian, will safeguard society. Both altruism and repression have their place, and both need to be included in any approach intended to correct the offender and to safeguard society.

Chapter Thirteen

SHORT-TERM ANSWERS

A journey of a thousand miles must begin with a single step.

—Lao Tzu (sixth century B.C.)

In the final analysis, everybody says, "Sure, sure, attacking poverty and racism and making certain everybody has a stable, wholesome upbringing may reduce the number of criminals, but how do I stay safe today?" Trying to answer this question should not divert our gaze from the longer term issues that hold the promise of a saner, safer society and that constitute the *sine qua non* of societal stability.

Trying to ensure the safety of one's person, property, or loved ones has to be seen as simply increasing the odds of being safe. It is foolish to think that crimes can be avoided altogether. Victims have been gunned down while engaged in the most routine and familiar pursuits, or while they were in bed. Any place can be burglarized; the only question is of the level of difficulty of entry. All any of us can do is reduce, not eliminate, the risk of victimization.

A BRIEF REVIEW

Even short-term strategies must involve fierce exertions if we are going to slow and reverse the negative momentum that has, since the early 1960s, gathered so much force and made us all so much less safe.

The family has to be strengthened. Whereas 1 in 20 was born out of wedlock in 1958, by 1988 the figure had increased to 1 in 4, and it is, of course, much higher for poor blacks. The general absence of fathers has proved a burden to the teenaged mother, her child, and society.

The decline of the cities and the problems of racism have greatly accelerated the rise of violence, addiction, homelessness, and crime.

The tendency of politicians to run with popular programs, irrespective of their worth, has precluded the development of carefully wrought legislation that would help promote family stability and economic independence.

The general absence of corporations from participation in the battle against social problems has contributed to their spread.

The sporadic and ad hoc involvement of nonprofits has led to uneven progress.

The gross inefficiencies of the criminal justice system (CJS) have weakened its ability to deal with the criminal population in a discriminating and effective way.

Even short-term solutions have to contain the promise of real progress. Our panic flight and feverish search for safety have repeatedly tempted us to embrace the palliatives offered by cynical politicians anxious to exploit their main chance.

Safety must begin with each of us.

When the personal efforts to ensure safety fail, the system
has to take over.

THE ROLE OF THE CJS

Although the CJS is basically locking everyone up and
stuffing the jails and prisons to bursting, and although punishment does work, together with rewards and encourage-
ments, as a way of influencing human behavior, it has to be
admitted that tough law-and-order enforcement will not, by
itself, produce the desired results. It has now had a good
twenty-year run, at the least, and the principal value of the
tough effort has been to prove that exclusive reliance on its
efficacy is foolish and wasteful. This proof should not tempt us
to abandon tough measures; rather, it should influence us to
meld hard approaches with other strategies that will enable us
to apply a broad and deep variety of treatments to the differing
challenges that crimes and criminals represent.

The CJS is saturated to overflowing and threatens to suffer
a nervous breakdown, if not a total collapse, although its justly
fabled capacity for adjusting has managed to fend off the
prophecies of doomsayers for many years. Massive numbers of
arrests of the minions of the drug world have filled the prisons,
bringing the law of diminishing returns into play. As more and
more small fry are caught, the system's ability to distinguish
and address the serious, chronic predators is diminished.

The creation of a president's commission on crime, to undertake a well-financed study of crime, its causes, and its possible cures, using a broadly multidisciplinary approach, holds
out a hope of developing a strategic plan to guide the nation's
faltering War on Crime.

Experimenters, practitioners, scholars, researchers, and
thinkers, from across a broad spectrum of disciplines directly
and indirectly tied to crime, criminals, and the factors imping-
ing on them, need to compile information on what is known,

what has been tried and has worked or failed, and to provide a reasoned program for the future conduct of America's War on Crime.

Such a study effort would require the expenditure of perhaps $30 million and eighteen months of time, but much more than that is now being utterly wasted, and billions more appear to be headed for the black hole of uncontrolled and unfocused expenditures by the CJS. The document produced by such a commission not only would contain recommendations for action but would also, if it received the publicity a good report would command, educate the American public on the complexities driving street crime, and on the need to develop sophisticated responses to its challenges.

In the meantime, the CJS, usually a local, fragmented affair, desperately needs better management, more effective coordination, closer cooperation, and a clearer sense of mission, much more than it needs the one thing it insists on clamoring for: more resources.

What Cops Might Do

The crisis in the police world is one of management. Police agencies neither produce good managers nor are particularly pressed to do so. Most city managers, councils, and mayors know little or nothing about the selection process of perhaps, their key appointee, the city's police chief. The selection is usually made behind the scenes, on the basis of the advice of key insiders, whose central concern is the political fallout likely to result. It is said that one shouldn't watch either laws or sausages being made, and I not only agree but would add the selection of police chiefs to that short list.

In a city where municipal labor unions help a mayor get elected, they are likely to participate in the selection of key department heads. The appointment of a search committee is often window dressing to cover the selection of a predesignated favorite. Unions pursue the interests of their members, not the people's good.

Police departments are frequently agencies that are bloated with high-ranking officers; that practice wasteful fiscal approaches such as overtime expenses, rentals, and equipment purchases; that pander to powerful police unions; and that are run by untrained executives whose reflex response to problems is to ask for more resources—and who are neither selected nor rewarded for managing sparely, productively, or efficiently. Management is not one of the talents found in many American police executives, nor is it frequently required by those who hire them.

In narcotics enforcement, for example (as we saw in Chapter 8), the easy approach is simply to make more arrests and thereby reduce the pressure of the public's demand for action. Task forces that aim at the higher-ups, using lower levels as informers, securing wiretap, bugging and search warrant orders, and other costly, time-consuming, and complicated measures, are not especially popular with influential figures trying to get the drug dealer off their block.

In a very real sense, the problem of dealing with all street crime can be reduced to the absurd choice between whether the police do the highly visible thing of getting that drug seller out of the neighborhood or whether they interdict his supply by striking at the higher, and much less visible, levels. The political payoff, in the short run at least, lies with the buy-and-bust jump collars on the street.

Political considerations are deeply involved in the question of whether such aggressive crime-fighting techniques as decoys, stakeouts, and stings, which disproportionately arrest and sometimes kill black members of the underclass, should be used at a time when blacks are gaining political leverage in the nation's urban centers.

Politically Sensitive Approaches

There is no inconsistency between aggressive law enforcement and respect for civil liberties. The police have every right—indeed, the duty—to adopt proactive crime-fighting techniques that replicate the victimization patterns in their communities and deflect the attacks onto waiting cops. Proactive sting, stakeout, decoy, and related strategies have been vitiated because of their disproportionate impact on blacks, but that's who the criminals and the victims are. The spurious issue of entrapment has been raised to befog the question and shift the focus of the argument.

Policing need not see its choices as sailing between the passive Scylla of Detroit or adopting the myopically aggressive activism of the Charybdis of Los Angeles. A sensible mean can be found that uses tough law-and-order approaches without injuring citizens' rights.

Sting, decoy, and stakeout operations work very effectively. They have been among the most innovative approaches conceived by the police in recent years. Abandoning them, as most major cities have done, for unstated but clearly understood political reasons not only weakens the crime-fighting effort but discourages the search for inventive solutions to the crime problem and helps create more cynicism among the cops. And the abandonment has been a silent and secretive one that the public isn't even aware of. It hasn't included the drug users and dealers because the political heat has been too intense.

Redlining

The police must experiment on, research, and become aware of successful techniques tried elsewhere and remain receptive to new ideas. Such programs as "crime stoppers" enable the police to involve citizens in helping solve crimes, through publicizing the offense, seeking informational calls, and offering anonymous rewards. Analyzing the areas (hot spots) that create problems and developing approaches to the problems enables the police agency to center its energies on the city's trouble spots. Even redlining (the practice of not investigating unpromising cases) will free an agency's energies to focus on more solvable problems. Such ideas as community-oriented policing should be melded with the priorities of fighting crime more effectively, responding to emergencies faster (and screening out responses to un-needed calls), and retaining control of the streets through aggressive traffic enforcement.

The police have to be controlled and directed. The key lies in the selection of a tough, experienced, knowledgeable chief executive who is determined to provide better police service through an agency that is disciplined, trained, and supervised.

Weeding out the unfit—the "thumpers and thieves"—has to be seen as a top organizational priority. It is critical that the cops understand the agency's priorities, its value system, the primacy of the law, and the consequences that follow deviations from policy. Although no administrator in his or her right mind would say so, the truth is that police officers wield great power and the use of this power is most effectively channeled into legal lanes through the employment of sanctions that make it clear that violations will be punished severely. Although police departments must be led through positives such as clean, energetic leadership, viable salaries, and reasonable benefits and other rewards, incentives, and recognitions, the entire effort must be undergirded by a strong sense that criminal actions and willful violations will be harshly dealt with.

The workers have a right to unionize to secure wages and benefits, and to be protected from the arbitrary and capricious acts of irresponsible or feckless managers, but they should not be managing the police enterprise, as they do too often in too many cities.

The police union represents labor, and the chief represents management, and the relationship is adversarial and must be honorable. There must be trust, discussion, and openmindedness, but there must be tension, too, as well as a recognition of the different roles each has to play. One of the serious litmus tests of police leadership, which establishes whether the chief serves the convenience and comfort of police colleagues or the interests of the people, lies in the police union's attitude toward the chief. A vote of confidence should raise the antennae of public suspicion, and an assault on the chief should not be automatic cause for alarm.

Police agencies are rarely understood by public officials, the media, or the citizens, yet everyone is confident she or he knows these secretive arms of government. The most important element of control is knowledge. Those who would direct or guide police operations, through such measures as policy directives or the rendering of judgments over police actions, must develop a firm understanding of these complex and largely unknown organizations.

Reforming police agencies holds out the very real hope of creating a force that will provide more safety at less cost, through efficiency, modernity, responsiveness, and effectiveness. Better management is the key.

A more effective police agency will be feeding a more manageable product—the arrested suspect—to the rest of the system.

Prosecutors

Most prosecutors in America are locally elected district or county attorneys who must face the voters every four years or, like Thomas E. Dewey of New York, escape into higher office. As elected officials, they are, of course, vulnerable to the vagaries of public opinion, and few items will sway the voters as readily as a low batting average of convictions in criminal cases. This vulnerability persuades many prosecutors to make bad deals with accused offenders and makes them timid about prosecuting cases that look as if they may prove losers. The effect of this hesitancy is to enable serious criminals—including murderers, as we've seen—escape even the inconvenience of a trial because of the prosecutor's fear of failure.

Because prosecutors work closely with the police, they will rarely, if ever, bring even egregious cases of police perjury, the securing of evidence illegally, or other wrongdoings to the attention of the police administration for investigation and follow up action. Thus, a major monitoring tool for curbing police abuses atrophies for lack of use.

Prosecutors have as great a duty to exculpate as to convict, but in today's panicky law-and-order climate, this is not a responsibility that is taken very seriously.

As elected officials prosecutors don't like assuming the risks connected with programs that do anything but put the offenders away. Alternatives to incarceration are not popular with DAs.

Prosecutors are slow to respond to such needs as getting drunk drivers off the road or coercing batterers of women into treatment, because these are regarded as low-level, low-visibility cases—frequently involving citizens with whom middle-class prosecutors can identify and who have resources with which to fight the charges—and because of the inconstancy of many complaining witnesses. Fierce public pressure, from feminists and such groups as Mothers Against Drunk Drivers, has had to be applied to prod the prosecutors into responding.

Prosecutors should focus their energies on major offenders and target them for intensive attention, whatever the current charge. The system easily affords this sort of elasticity. We did hold a serial-killer suspect on an obscure Social Security fraud charge in order to give us time to secure additional evidence on his murders. The prosecutor is a key figure in identifying and going after the chronic recidivist.

The need is to reform from within and to manage better, according to a carefully wrought set of priorities. Simply lavishing resources on any agency will merely result in overlaying and masking inefficiencies that are bound to surface, and more seriously for having been given time to spread.

Defense

The defense bar is an area of which it could be said that they have, indeed, been starved of resources. Who wants to allocate funds for the benefit of the criminals everyone hates and fears?

Defense is as unsexy as probation. Yet, if our democracy is to have any meaning, the rights of the least have to be assiduously protected if the rights of the rest are to be preserved. The resources must be allocated to ensure the sort of defense that gives weight and meaning to the presumption of innocence on which our system rests. At this moment, the scales are widely off balance, in favor of the prosecution. This imbalance may comfort readers, but I've seen corrupt and brutal systems at work, and they not only fail to deliver more safety but actually function far less effectively because so much energy is being diverted to criminal or improper pursuits.

The defense bar is in a position to observe the conduct of the police in court and needs to be invited to report evidence of police wrongdoing. This is another potentially promising area of review, but, usually because of the police administration's failure either to encourage or to welcome such reporting, it is rarely, if ever, used. And, of course, the judge and the DA have usually observed acts of wrongdoing by the cops and refused to report them—and they'd have a lot more credibility with the chief than the public defender.

The defense counsel is also an officer of the court, though, and, as such, is charged as much with the task of promoting justice as with the responsibility for an effective defense. These aims must be seen as complementary, not as in conflict. If there is credible evidence of guilt, the approach must be to get the best possible deal—consistent with the needs of the accused and the safety of the public.

The public and its officials will have to recognize the defense bar as being an essential link in justice's chain. Our democracy's worth is established as much in its courtrooms as in any other conceivable arena. It is essential that we do justice in those halls, and this absolutely requires the provision—as the Supreme Court has held—of effective measures of defense for the accused.

Judges

The key question on the effectiveness of the judiciary centers on the selection process. Integrity, wisdom, knowledge of the law, and experience in life are only a few of the important characteristics needed by jurists. Yet they are frequently selected only for party fealty and are routinely elected by unknowing voters.

The federal judiciary is widely regarded as superior because of the filtration process leading to appointment. Bar associations comment on fitness, U.S. senators from the candidate's state put their imprimaturs on the choice, selection committees of respected lawyers prepare commentaries, editorialists express opinions, and the whole process is very much more visible than that in other selections. The president makes federal court appointments after screening by the Senate, which has the benefit of a thorough FBI background investigation.

The preparation of a list of recommended candidates, by a select committee of the local bar association, from which the governor would make a selection, for a long-enough term (ten years or so) to ensure tenure and independence—these are some of the features that ought to accompany the state and local appointment process. A select committee of citizens would also serve to get public interest and involvement into the process. The state senate's judiciary committee, or its equivalent, should examine each judicial nomination and put the matter to the larger body, following the committee's recommendation, for an "advise-and-consent" message to the governor. Reappointment could be subjected to a process that included a governor's designation and another review by the senate committee and another senate vote.

Judges need to be trained better. They rarely have the experience, in any phase of the CJS, needed to make knowing judgments. Prior employment in both defense and prosecution—to ensure a wider grasp of the functions of each, to lift the status of both, and to ensure a wider supply of workers—ought to be an important prerequisite for a career on the bench. Lawyers who aspire to judgeships should be tracked into prosecutors' and Legal Aid assignments.

Judges are, like prosecutors and defenders, uniquely positioned to observe police performance in the critical areas relating to arrest, testimony, the presentation of evidence, and other key activities. Moreover, they have the power to act, on their own initiative, and to contact police administrators, with an assurance that they will be heard and heeded. This is another area of control that isn't used as often as it should be. Judges simply don't see their role as including the supervision of police behavior.

Sentencing guidelines came into wide adoption precisely because of the deficiencies of judges that stem from the process of their selection. The studies undertaken in this area offer eloquent testimony to the need for training and for applying more rigorous standards of selection. The judges also have to focus on recidivists, and in order to do this, they must know what they're looking for. The probation officer's report can be an invaluable guide in this effort, if it is used. In common with much of the rest of the CJS, judges have proved stubborn resisters of reforms.

Computer technology is now at a point where it can be enormously useful to the CJS, yet many judges see it as an unwarranted intrusion into their activities. The fact is that such a monitoring device could reveal inefficiencies in the court's processes by pointing out delays, adjournments, or accommodations to favored lawyers that affect the efficiency of the operation. The defensiveness that attends the adoption of computerization needs to be seen as working counter to justice's interests.

Judges ought to welcome such scrutiny as "court watch," where volunteers sit and observe and comment on the behavior of the principals. Cameras in the court serve the same salutary supervisory purpose. Citizen interest and involvement should be encouraged and welcomed, as should any attempt to open up the process and reform its workings.

The key to crime deterrence lies in swiftness of apprehension (the police role) and the certainty of punishment (the prosecutor's and judiciary's assignment). Speedy justice has long been seen as an essential concomitant of any valid system. It is embodied in the axiom "Justice delayed is justice denied." Judges should move to realize this objective by resisting measures intended to exhaust the prosecution's witnesses or otherwise defeat the process through trickeries, delays, and circumventions.

By extending all rights to the accused, a judge preserves the rights of all of us. We have seen that the historic and sweeping reforms of the Earl Warren Supreme Court, in terms of demanding that the police scrupulously observe the law as they enforce it, have actually helped to professionalize America's police and to make them much more efficient, rather than "handcuffing" them, as some critics have held. The cops have greatly increased their ability to detect and arrest offenders and have stuffed America's prisons while following rules they have denounced as onerous.

Judges are key players in our nation's system of justice. If they are carefully selected, trained, monitored, evaluated, and guided, they can enhance the speed and quality of our court operations without additional expenditures and without sacrificing the interests of justice one whit.

Corrections

Jails and prisons definitely have important roles to play in attacking crime, but they have to be a part of the plan, rather than the one and only answer. Incarceration should be high on the rising scale of sanctions that have to make heavy use of alternative measures.

Probation, if properly supervised, is a powerful monitoring tool, and the offender is freed to function normally. This is a revocable privilege that can be a lever to exacting such responsible behavior as getting a job, remaining drug-free, and assuming responsibilities. Community service, restitution, mediation, fines, house arrest, and the use of halfway houses should be important features of the system.

Overwhelming the CJS with volumes of arrests merely ensures its malfunction and results in producing less safety, not more, as the system is unable to discern the real menaces and treats all offenders perfunctorily. Trying to build our way out of the crime dilemma has proved a futility—and a costly futility at that.

We should not blanch at the prospect of boot camps or country club prisons, recognizing that it is the deprivation of freedom that counts. It makes sense that we use various levels of security, that dangerous felons be kept separately from less dangerous ones, and that behavior in prisons help determine the duration of incarceration and the sort of supervision one graduates into on release.

Using dramatic confrontations such as "Scared Straight" may help youngsters decide to opt for more wholesome futures, as may using ex-addicts as lecturers. New ideas should be encouraged and explored. The system needs additional strategies and more options. It must abandon the idiot notion that mindless repression and singleminded toughness are the only answers.

A key challenge is to identify the chronic criminal repeater, who represents such a safety menace. Maintaining complete, and better, records and encouraging research into the question may help in the development of a more useful predictive scale. Building a comprehensive presentence report should be the first step in a continuing process of creating a cogent and meaningful dossier on an offender. The purpose must be to establish the prospect of responsible future behavior, recognizing that some risks are being and must be run.

Everybody gets out—more or less—but the question of when ought to be based on the risk represented by the offender to potential future victims.

The function of corrections is to correct, that is, to exact acceptable performance. There is an element of punishment and there should also be prospects for rehabilitation, through such programs as drug or alcohol treatment, literacy and other educational approaches, and vocational training. The offender has to be deterred from future criminality, and deterrence is best accomplished through the kinds of punishment that people want to avoid, and through the kinds of satisfactions that encourage better future behavior. The serious recidivist needs to be incapacitated. This is a key feature of any crime reduction strategy because of the disproportionate contribution to the crime rates by a small minority of repeaters.

And some must be executed.

It is as fatuous to hold that the death penalty doesn't deter as it is to say that punishment has no persuasive power over human behavior. Obviously, only a small minority of killers would be put to death, but these would be the cold, cruel, calculating murderers who represent such a danger to innocent, unsuspecting, and, frequently, helpless victims. Executing a killer at least reassures the rest of humankind that this person, at any rate, will pose no future threat to anyone.

A comprehensive menu of weighted sanctions would bring order to the mélange of ad hoc approaches now posing as a corrections system. But the folks in charge have found it more convenient to furnish facile responses.

POLITICS AND POLITICIANS

What is America's number one problem?
And who is in charge of attacking it?

The second question is easier than the first: The politicians are charged with leading us in the assault. Fitfully, belatedly, and reluctantly, to be sure, they've led us to such battles as the ones relating to civil rights, feminism, nuclear war, the environment, consumerism, the Vietnam war, and, earlier, education, poverty, housing, unionism, and other social struggles. Over recent decades, the principal worries have centered on either war or the economy.

It is worth noting that the Vietnam war, a source of enormous public anguish in the sixties and seventies, took over 50,000 American lives, in about 12 years, or somewhat more than 4,000 per year. In 1991 over 24,000 Americans were murdered in our internal war with ourselves.

Segmenting the issues invites us to fragment the questions into insignificantly small units, but if we lump crime, violence, drugs, and guns into one category—a not altogether unreasonable bundling—we should get a very high reading on the public's Richter scale of concerns. Still the debate seems to center on one and then on another of these interrelated issues.

I would place the issue of violence first on the nation's agenda of problems.

Our nation's leaders—in the White House, the governors' mansions, the mayoral offices, the legislative halls, and the court rooms—have mostly failed either to articulate the problem or to address its challenges.

By failing this test, they endanger all of us.

State Legislatures

Foreign visitors are always struck by the fragmentation of America's CJS. Usually, they are accustomed to a centrally directed effort, from the nation's capital, and are invariably stunned by the irrelevance of Washington, D.C., and the centrality in the process of mayors, city councils, and state legislatures.

American police agencies receive their marching orders—

in the form of the laws to be enforced—from their state capitals. Unfortunately, these are often places housing generally unsophisticated and not always extensively educated citizens, not to mention their normally having a total lack of experience with the CJS. The result is often a desperate grasp at the popular, flashy ploy that will get the legislators a headline and reduce the public pressure for action. Instituting death penalties, mandating sentences, and escalating drug misdemeanors into felonies are virtually irresistible temptations. Anything that smacks of softness on crime, whatever its inherent long-term merit, is eschewed. We've seen this tendency even in the nation's capital, the place to which we send our ablest politicians.

The adoption of sentencing guidelines; the use of alternatives to incarceration; treatment, education, and prevention approaches to narcotics use; and any of a host of other useful long-term and substantive crime treatment or crime prevention reforms—all are usually smeared as "liberal" and are consigned to perdition. Schemes involving housing for the homeless, rights for gays, welfare for the poor, health care for the uncovered, and education for the excluded are received with little patience.

The pressures accompanying dizzying levels of crimes and violence have turned our legislatures into groups of nervous panderers eager to offer politically correct responses to complex problems, whatever their prospects of success. Our willingness to accept simple, ready answers ensures that these are just what we will get.

State legislatures and similar bodies will have to find the courage to vote against crime bills that eviscerate the U.S. Constitution, and that still don't deliver additional margins of safety. They will have to vote against drug bills that won't work, and that have been demonstrated to be unworkable. They will have to learn to develop systemic responses to the challenge of crime; that is, they must not only pass laws that they think will really help to solve a crime problem but also assess the impact of the law on the various elements of the CJS.

Failing to take account of the impact has resulted in prisons bursting with low-level drug dealers and users while leaving no room for dangerous criminals. The system's adjustments will, in the circumstances, force it to make bad deals with the recidivists, who don't face mandated sentences. This is a prime reason for the disrepute of plea bargaining among our people.

In the final analysis, we, the American people, receive the government we demand and deserve, and we are not going to deserve very good government if we continue to insist on quick and easy fixes to the crime problem and to accept simplistic answers from those seeking our votes.

Despite the farcical aspects of the "I'm-going-to-outspit-you-on-the-toughness-on-crime" debate in the nation's capital in 1993, by both parties and their most prominent leaders, they have shown a capacity, occasionally, for thoughtful, responsible, workable legislation in the crime area.

RICO

The legislature and the executive have occasionally shown they can devise effective legal solutions to seemingly intractable problems of corruption. These rare initiatives invariably follow careful preparation, long study, and expert assistance. These isolated instances do prove that legislatures can overcome their inherent indolence and work to produce real results. The adoption of such statutes as RICO (the Racketeer Influenced and Corrupt Organizations Act) has provided law enforcement with a very valuable tool with which to attack organized crime.

In 1988, the U.S. government filed a civil RICO case against the Teamsters, alleging that this vast national union of 1.55 million members had been run as a lucrative racketeering enterprise, a private bank to finance hidden investments in Las Vegas casinos. The union, rather than fight a government that regularly (following a lead established decades earlier by the activism of then-Attorney General Robert F. Kennedy) sent its leaders and high executives to prison (four of the Teamsters' recent presidents had been jailed or indicted, and all but 7 of 150 charged union officials had been convicted), agreed to a consent decree that permitted court-supervised secret elections of union officers by the entire membership, for the first time in the organization's history.

The result was the democratization of a union that was described by the *New York Times* on December 16, 1991, as one "run mostly by thieves for the past 40 years," and that had the power to strangle the nation through its control of our delivery systems. The election of a maverick in 1991 signaled the victory of the reform forces and the beginning of the process of making the Teamsters a clean and responsible arm of labor.

The irony—there always seems to be one—was that an administration that had been notably reluctant to take energetic positions on domestic issues, and that had benefited from the support of the old-line Teamster leaders, had intruded so vigorously into this particular domestic issue.

The courts will have to make sure that cops and prosecutors don't overuse RICO to the point of abuse. Cops and prosecutors are notably wont to overuse strategies that work, and there has been some straying from the legislation's original intent. It is probably too much to ask that the DAs practice some self-restraint, and this is why reliance on the courts will have to do.

Such initiatives as RICO do, nevertheless, point clearly to the potential good inherent in legislative power and its ability to produce socially useful long-term approaches.

National Service

America's kids—especially its poor kids—are all dressed up with no place to go. The shrinking of the military leaves

fast-food restaurants as the only viable means of mass employment. Constructive alternatives have to be found.

The national government has to create a menu of choices
that offers the chance of meaningful employment and career
development to kids now dropping out of school and dropping
into drugs, violence, and crime. Such a menu should include:

1. The military.
2. A police corps modeled on the ROTC, which would pay
   for a four-year college education in exchange for four
   years of service as a cop.
3. A Civilian Conservation Corps type of service for our
   parks, roads, and forests.
4. A teaching corps similar to the police model.
5. A Peace Corps for international assignment.
6. A public health, medical, and emergency corps.
7. An urban conservancy corps to work on urban problems like cleaning up the inner cities.
8. Some other form of public service employment that
   either offers a job after high school or exchanges college
   tuition for four years of paid service.

The issue of voluntariness versus compulsory service has
to be addressed, and powerful arguments could be made for
the latter, but the option probably must be a voluntary system
that is so attractive it will prove irresistible to our youth.

Mayors and Governors

The key executives of government, especially as related to
crime and violence, are the CEOs of states and cities, who
dispense resources, make appointments, contribute to the development of legislation, and shape policies. That mayors and
governors have normally had little knowledge of criminology
has resulted in the perpetuation of a confused, overwhelmed,

unbalanced, and generally malfunctioning CJS. The easy answer has been to pass tougher laws, build more prisons, hire more cops, and get tougher judges. The usual suspects get collared in the roundups, and it is clear that exclusive reliance on toughness hasn't worked.

No one is paid to think of the system as a whole. Mayors and governors are centrally positioned to provide a systemic approach. Appointing an adviser or coordinator with real power over resource allocations and appointments would result in a more responsive and effective CJS.

The War on Crime is being lost, in the short run, because of the public's panic and the surrender of elected officials to it. The result has been toughness, all around, that attacks the symptoms—addiction, crime, and violence—while utterly ignoring the causes. The best hope rests with thoughtful, painful, responsible long-term approaches, but something has to be done for the present to reduce the fever.

Once the CJS has been brought into play, the patterns of criminal behavior have been set, the criminal has been shaped, and the crime has been committed. By then, it is really too late to think of prevention. We have to look upstream for the development of strategies that prevent the cycle of criminality from being set in motion.

GUNS AND DRUGS

The proliferation of weaponry lends efficacy to every evil impulse. The toll exacted by our murderous firepower would be not only insupportable, not just unthinkable, in other nations but would actually be more than enough to cause the expulsion of any national administration if it were the result of a war. Lyndon Johnson was ousted from the presidency largely because of casualty rates in Vietnam that were fractions of our routine daily body counts.

The murders are bad enough, but the assaults, rapes, robberies, and lesser crimes have become so commonplace as to scarcely warrant any public attention.

In recent years, progress has been made toward a saner national view of firearms, especially the concealable variety, but it is no exaggeration to say that the problem's surface has barely been scratched. We should be striving for national legislation that would severely restrict the availability of handguns and easily concealable firearms. The few permitted should be licensed to those who have demonstrated a need for and a proficiency with the weapon, and the weapons should be registered and strictly regulated.

Existing weapons that become illegal must be surrendered, and the owners must be compensated by the government, at market value, for confiscated weapons. Following an amnesty period of eighteen months for weapons that would be strictly described and carefully defined by the law (to cover, in general, the firearms that can be readily concealed on the person), the possession of such weaponry should constitute a felony. The penalties should be incorporated into the sentencing guidelines of the federal government. In this case, as in all others, mandated sentences must be avoided.

The National Rifle Association (NRA) has long held that any attempt to control instruments of murder will start us on the "slippery slope" to banning all firearms. It is essential that the legitimate concerns of responsible gun owners be addressed and satisfied.

The NRA's "slippery-slope" position can be outflanked by protecting Americans' rights to the ownership of such long guns as shotguns and rifles. There is, of course, the issue of registration. It makes a lot of sense to maintain serial numbers and central records of these devices for the purpose of tracing and recovery, if they should be used in a crime or should be stolen. We do, after all, license and register motor vehicles without impeding the rights of ownership, and the state's obligation to protect its citizens through registration and documentation needn't conflict with such rights.

Semiautomatic assault weapons, such as those described in Chapter 7, and machine guns should be banned outright.

Every knowledgeable observer of America's street crime carnage places gun control high on the agenda of any items calculated to create a safer society. Drugs are the other factor in the equation.

DRUGS

Chapter 8 attempted to illustrate the enormous contribution of illicit narcotics and alcohol to our high levels of street crime and violence.

The connection between drugs and street crime is deep and wide. Boasts by the Bush administration and its drug czar that we were making headway in the War on Drugs ignored the appalling and alarming facts surrounding addiction among the poor and excluded, who are frequently also the victims of racism. Our lack of a focused and unified national strategy precludes our making any progress in this war, as different jurisdictions go their disparate ways in pursuit of an elusive victory.

Addiction is complex human behavior that cries out for understanding and for the development of responses that reflect a grasp of the profundity and variability of the problem. Sophisticated, carefully wrought approaches are needed.

Causal factors have to be understood if addiction is to be prevented. The educational program must reach the hard-core users who have not, thus far, been influenced by programs that seem to be reaching the educable.

Treatment must be made available for every addict who seeks it and for every addict coerced into it.

Enforcement is certainly a critical component of the approach, but it must focus on the higher-ups: the exporters, importers, distributors, money launderers, and others at the upper end of the industry's hierarchy. Addiction to illegal narcotics is both a supply and a demand problem, and interdiction strategies must include everything and everyone between the grower and the user.

The various approaches to the narcotics problem have been discussed in detail. Legalization is morally bankrupt and strategically wrong. A second currency makes no sense. Military interventions would be suicidally counterproductive. The obvious fact is that panaceas haven't worked and won't work, which is not to say that debating all the approaches may not lead to new, and useful, programs.

The creation of a president's commission on crime would at least ensure comprehensive analysis and discussion and the formulation of recommendations, based on research and experimentation, that could be followed. Such an approach would also bring in other, related and essential, disciplines, like health, medicine, and social services. Other nations, like the Netherlands and Colombia, are profiting from such thoughtful approaches.

A task force on drugs could be a large subordinate unit of a president's commission on crime, which would undertake a sweeping look at American street crime, in all its facets.

The large and growing expenditures on the War on Drugs are ominously reminiscent of the former escalations in defense spending. Focusing the lion's share on enforcement—cops, prosecutors, judges, jails, and the like—is worse than a mistake; it is counterproductive, because it tends to ignore prevention, education, treatment, and research into any of these areas. At the very least, there ought to be a greater balance in the allocation of resources among these competing needs.

Abolishing the drug czar and closing the entire office would prove a brilliant demonstration of the government's willingness to become more efficient. Centering efforts in the Drug Enforcement Agency would focus responsibility for the War on Drugs in one arm of the government.

The problem of street crime will not, and cannot, be solved

while the drug epidemic rages among the underclass. Drugs and alcohol constitute the only mechanisms available to escape the awfulness of daily life in the ghetto, and until these life conditions are addressed and ameliorated, we can look forward to a continuation of drug and alcohol use. The short-term answer must lie in the development of a national strategy to combat the scourge of drugs along a broad front that brings varied disciplines into the fray.

Although the CJS plays a central role in the War on Drugs, it is madness to leave the conduct of the struggle entirely in its hands. The corporate sector has a large and varied role to play both in a positive sense, such as in Honeywell's New Vistas High School, and in the negative sense of engaging in a partnership with the CJS to keep drugs out of the workplace and joining in the war on crime generally.

SHOPLIFTING

Many drug addicts, particularly women, support their habit by shoplifting, which has become a serious problem for retailers. The adjustments have escalated to the point where customers are admitted into shops by electric buzzers, having passed inspection by the shopkeeper within. Liquor store owners have created vaultlike fortresses, from behind which they transact their business to combat robberies.

Theft, the most frequently occurring of the Uniform Crime Report's Part I crimes, has particularly bedeviled large department stores, many of which have adopted such security measures as affixing devices on merchandise that, if not removed by the cashier at the time of sale, trip an alarm at the store's exit, alerting security personnel. The apprehension is made outside the building or premises, to establish criminal motivation. Customers can always claim they are still shopping if intercepted within the store and then must pay for the merchandise before leaving.

Major retailers have had to establish policies about dealing with shoplifters. With corporate lawyers playing increasingly critical roles in such enterprises, the urge to caution increases exponentially. This caution frequently results in not pressing criminal charges, but merely intercepting and questioning the shoplifter, recovering the merchandise, and warning the person not to return to the store. This strategy is felt to forestall the possibility of a lawsuit.

The fact is that an aggressive posture, predicated on sound legal reasoning and reasonable actions, proves the best defense. Making an arrest on the basis of evidence and articulable grounds is the best hope in deterring thefts. Even if the shoplifter is acquitted, a lawsuit for false arrest can be defended, assuming there were reasonable grounds for the arrest in the first place and the defense is pursued energetically. Cases should not be settled on the basis of cost-effectiveness, and arrests should be made for thefts. Arrest need not mean automatic incarceration, but it ought to be a negative consequence that educates the offenders.

Ours is still a civil and criminal justice system in which people entering the process with clean hands can expect to emerge unscathed.

Shoplifters, like everyone else, act on the basis of information, and theirs ought to be that this retailer is tough, prosecutes criminally, and defends lawsuits energetically. Such organizations as gossip tabloids, which engage in sensational disclosures that are sometimes of dubious veracity and that seem libelous, have discovered that vigorous legal defenses frequently preclude judgments. Too many organizations, like major retailers, insurance companies, and others, have found it too easy to settle questionable cases and pass the costs on to the consumer—whether these costs result from thefts or out-of-court settlements. The short-term costs may indeed be lower, but the long-term costs are usually higher and certain to continue.

In our increasingly cashless society, thieves are discovering the need to strike quickly when credit cards are stolen. It is imperative that the system adjust to ensure the immediate reporting of a credit card theft and the apprehension of persons presenting such cards for merchandise or cash. The "eating" of stolen cards by banks' automatic teller machines is another effective way of interdicting such thefts.

Chaining property, driving with car doors and windows locked, removing tempting articles from view, marking property, and using security measures will all help, but only in the short run and only until circumventing methods are devised by the criminals. Striking at the causes that drive people to such desperate straits holds out a surer promise of the long-term prevention of such crimes.

Business must also awaken to its responsibilities to attack embezzlement, fiduciary betrayals, fraud in all its forms, and other sorts of white-collar crime. Our corporate heads have proved, in the main, very reluctant dragons in pursuing crime in the executive suites.

In order to succeed, any short-term attack on the many faces of crime is going to require an interdisciplinary approach and the involvement of various professions and groups.

HEALTH, MEDICAL, SOCIAL, AND OTHER SERVICES

The need for political will and a determination to do the right thing, to take risks, to acknowledge failures, and simply to respond commonsensically to challenges has never been greater, nor have these qualities ever been in shorter supply. Tragedies that strike from the blue cannot be averted, but too many events cast their shadows before them, and a demoralized system shuts its eyes to the clues.

Willie Horton may well have been an example of a statistically successful operation in which he represented the inevitable, and expectable, failure. The political will to assert this possibility was clearly lacking.

The murder of 22 innocents in Killeen, Texas, on October 16, 1991, by a maniac with a Glock-17 semiautomatic pistol, with a minimum magazine of seventeen bullets, would not have happened in any other industrial democracy because of controls over such weapons. Given the political courage to ban such killing machines, such crimes are preventable.

Myryam Orellane was charged with battering her child to death on October 4, 1991. She had left traces of abuse that the authorities chose to ignore or dismiss. The dead child had come to the notice of officials as being abused, but they'd done nothing.

Accountability has to be restored to the system. Bureaucrats have to be prodded to act, to take risks, and to be rewarded for trying. We are rapidly constructing a system in which no failure can be safely acknowledged—in a world in which failure is inevitable. What was lacking in the Orellane, and similar, cases was any evidence of responsiveness or interest, and this cannot be excused.

The involvement of social-services, health, educational, medical, and related authorities in the battle against crime has been largely ignored, despite its deep relevance. No progress can be made in the effort to reduce violence as long as this exclusion continues.

Foundations and universities can encourage the research and support the experiments needed to develop new approaches.

The short-term crisis facing the CJS is one of management, political courage, and perspective. Lavishing resources on cops and prisons will only tempt officials to waste them, as they are doing now. These officials, as well as the other members of the system, need to be held to stricter account for the performance of their agencies. The public's perspective will have to be broadened to include an appreciation of the complexity of the issues and an awareness that the answers will require subtlety, sophistication, analysis, and study. Reliance on demagogic approaches and mindless actions have to be recognized as leading to frustration and defeat.

The War on Crime will not, and cannot, be won through short-term measures, but many more successful battles can be waged in this arena, and more tragedies avoided, if we adopt sensible measures to make the CJS work more effectively.

Chapter Fourteen

LONG-TERM ANSWERS

*I believe in one God and no more, and I hope for happiness
beyond this life. I believe in the equality of man and I believe that religious duties consist in doing justice, loving
mercy and endeavoring to make our fellow creatures happy.*
—Thomas Paine (1737–1809)

Are we witnessing the decline of the Great American Experiment?

Is the "malaise" a former president spoke of, less than
twenty years ago, overtaking us?

Have we become an economically, racially, and morally
bifurcated society?

Have we lost our way, and is the rise in addiction, gun-
play, crime, and violence a mere symptom of deeper problems
signaling decay?

In short, is the fate of our nation tied to the question of
how we deal with the domestic problems surrounding family
and city, poverty and racism, and the violence and social
dissolution they are producing?

I believe the answer to all these questions is yes, and that a failure to undertake a debate on the issues, or to develop an action program, will spell curtains for our nation.

SOCIETY

We, as Americans, are jointly involved in an enterprise known as the United States of America, and we are, collectively and singly, responsible for its direction and fate. The country's course is set by the millions of decisions made by each of us as we vote, divorce, hire, spend, save, play, or work. The sum total of our choices guides the ship on which we all sail.

Our current choices center on hedonism, oppression, racism, and self-centeredness. Our generation's approach might easily be defined as the NIMBY (not-in-my-backyard) factor. And many who didn't start out as NIMBY-ites have lapsed into this attitude out of frustration and fear.

As America headed into the third century of its noble existence, the gathering darkening clouds had one common characteristic: They all bore the label *domestic* rather than *international*.

Although inflation has been tamed from the appalling levels of the late seventies to around 3 percent in 1991, unemployment affected over 15 million Americans who were seeking just part-time jobs or full-time employment or who had just given up. Food stamp recipients numbered almost 23 million, and almost 36 million persons, under sixty-five, had no medical insurance. The budget deficit soared to an incomprehensible $400 billion in 1992, and the number of homeless was variously estimated at between one million and three million. The chasm between the contented and the disaffected continued to widen.

Americans have fatuously dismissed the underclass with comments about shiftlessness, welfare, pregnancies, and crime, while ignoring the thousands who repeatedly flock to any promise of employment. The press has been notably derelict in communicating the pathetic enthusiasm with which the poor embrace even the chanciest opportunities to work.

The great money shifts of the 1980s had centered on moving wealth from black to white, from young to old, and from poor to rich. The cities smoldered with violence, crime, and social disintegration. A definite elite could be identified in educational indices that revealed our best, and richest, students as being at the top, with the rest lagging behind.

The easy temptation was to blame our leaders, but they turned out to be our mirror images.

Altruism Index

Many small towns have a thermometer painted at the approaches, to indicate the status of a charity drive. The goal is at the top, and a red line shows the movement toward it. The point is to fill the empty space and even, perhaps, to produce an overflow.

I think of such a thermometer as that hamlet's altruism index: its willingness to share with its less fortunate inhabitants.

America's altruism index, in terms of the wealth and attention we contribute to the health, education, employment, housing, and welfare of our underclass, is barely visible. The "thousand points of light" seem to have gone out, if they'd ever actually been turned on.

The Racial and Economic Chasm Grows

The growing economic disparities—between white and black, young and old, urban and suburban, overclass and underclass—is consigning large numbers of citizens to lives of hopelessness and failure, in the midst of plenty and of clear windows affording views of that plenty. Those who have nothing to lose risk little by breaking laws that they see as latter-day fetters on their wrists.

The overclass's absorption with self and pleasure guarantees the continuation of selfish and dangerous policies of non-sharing. The upper fraction takes home the lion's share of our economic pie, and those at the bottom fight over meager crumbs. It is the inequity and injustice that breed frustration, anger, and criminality.

It is easy to see the nineteenth-century selfishness of England's rich and the plight of its poor through the eyes of Dickens, and it is equally easy to see how a bit of altruism might have helped, but we are somehow incapable of applying that lesson to our own country and own age.

We congratulate ourselves that we've fought the War on Poverty and rue the judgment that poverty won, but we believe it. We also believe that we've fought a War on Drugs, and that drugs won.

Both propositions are dangerously wrong.

Our War on Drugs has been a cynical, superficial, demagogic effort that was never properly waged or thoughtfully addressed. Its failure has demoralized us, and we confusedly look for quicker fixes, thereby making things worse.

The War on Poverty was characterized by a lack of planning and by a naive faith in money and in the good instincts of both clients and administrators. This war was also declared lost and was abandoned in mid-effort, by a leader who'd come to make the rich richer, at the expense of the poor. The remarkable thing is that any good emerged from the War on Poverty at all, yet studies have demonstrated that the levels of poverty in America were declining under that war's fitful assaults. Instead of looking at the balance sheet, we've focused our gaze on the poverty pimps, who have made it so easy for the rest of us to abandon the effort. By concentrating on the failures we are able to justify abandoning the effort.

The war on racism ended at the courthouse door. We failed to recognize that economic, social, and even cultural barriers would be raised and widened to maintain extralegal forms of the subjugation of blacks.

The huge and burgeoning amounts of crime, violence,

addiction, gun trafficking, and social dissolution in our cities will not decline unless we undertake a massive individual and national effort on a scale that embraces the notion that the nation's survival hangs in the balance.

It's easy to forget the power of one determined individual. We've largely lost sight of the citizen who can make a difference. We need to be reminded of the potential inherent in every human and in the power of the people to change the nation's course, as they did in the civil rights struggle, the Vietnam war, the pacifist and antinuclear movements, the environmentalist and feminist battles, the consumer movement, and such early ordeals as those relating to education, welfare, unionism, housing, health, and, yes, even Social Security.

Many groups such as Mothers Against Drunk Drivers or those fighting handgun violence began because of one person's determination to turn a tragedy into something constructive.

Galvanizing this hidden force, and the idealism that resides in every breast, holds the promise of moving neighborhoods forward. The bovine sense of helplessness that attends so much of modern life works to defeat the dreams of achievement that a focused individual can realize. A prerequisite is the determination to turn a negative into a positive and to turn passivity to activism.

Society is nothing more than the totaled actions of a series of individuals, each adding to and shaping the general tendency.

THE INDIVIDUAL AND THE FAMILY

Our search for villains overlooks our own complicity. Ignoring the socratic injunction to examine oneself leads to disaster. We are offended by reminders of our straying from the basics—family, love, work, planning, generational responsibilities, and concern for others—and we enjoy (the word we use to describe every experience) those who amuse, entertain, or dis-

tract us. Sports, drugs, gambling, and good times have become
the embodiment of the American Dream.

Individuality

We divorce too frequently and too frivolously. We allow
our feckless rulers to choose themselves, forget that they're
repeating our messages to us, and decry the circumstances that
force Hobson's choices on us. We rail over a tax system's
impact on our lives that, in reality, actually oppresses the black
and the poor, and we mutter imprecations over the feckless
poor and speak of bootstrappism when we've removed the
economic ladder's bottom rungs and promoted dependency.

We resist public housing, halfway houses, or homes for the
retarded in our neighborhoods. "Not in my backyard" is what
property-value-conscious Americans are shouting, and not with
my tax dollars, either. Americans flee to the suburbs and abandon the cities and try even to take their jobs with them, along
with the schools, the cops, and the other services.

And yet, if the existentialist message holds that the individual is central, and that his or her actions matter, why
can't we extend the demand for action to the underclass? The
answer lies not in their poverty, but in their race and in
the particular history associated with it in America. American
blacks simply had their history, culture, language, religion, and
all other factors related to their origins erased, so that they
have been disabled from using the opportunities of bootstrappism. This dilemma must be confronted and debated before we
can get on with assimilation and insisting on self-development
and self-reliance.

We insist that more cops be hired and prisons built, but we
congratulate ourselves that the problem of crime has been
studied to death and that we now need action.

We don't ask for the reason behind the absence of black
faces in our corporate boardrooms, universities, clubs, homes,

or offices, but we insist that they be stuffed into our prisons, and we ensure that they'll be huddled over grates in our nation's capital and in every city, and that their young men and women will fight our wars.

We feel powerless but take no action. Bombarded by stimuli, we rise only to the most tempting bait and change channels when we're no longer amused. Rome had its bread and circuses, and we have our welfare doles and TV. It's easy for us to see how a people lost their way and worshiped golden idols, but it's hard for us to see our own moral bankruptcy and hedonistic searches for pleasure.

We will have to become better citizens before ours can be a safer nation.

Education

In education, the chasm between rich and poor widens, with fateful consequences for the excluded and for the society that they will influence. Nowhere is the sense of a divided and selfish society more clearly, and dangerously, etched than in the issues surrounding how we educate our young. Politicians who choose to remind us of the injustices are severely punished.

National leaders can blather all day long about lifting America's educational standards and performances, but the hard question centers on government's willingness to equalize the underclass's resources. New Jersey tried to shift resources from its richer to its poorer schools, and the result was a legislative overturn in state elections, and a U.S. senator's nearly losing his job, and the mangling of the career of the governor who'd proposed this piece of social equity.

It will take more than money to turn out an educated citizen, but the current maldistribution of resources ensures the underclass's failure.

As a consequence of the difficulties surrounding equalization factors, the debate has concentrated on the edges, such as lengthening the school year, adopting national tests to establish levels of achievement, and decrying the effects of blasted families and too much television.

Strong and devoted families, with a reverence for education's wonders, a willingness to work with the schools, and the existence of high expectations, need to be wedded to discipline, structure, and a return to such basics as math, science, and literacy in order to turn out an educated citizen. Ghetto schools need more money. Higher teacher competence, less television watching, more reading, and supportive friends are also essential ingredients for success.

Television may well be the most powerful potential educational tool, but it has been trivialized and turned into the enemy of learning by its surrender to entertainment and profit.

The first, and most critical, factor in building a safer society remains the central organizational unit: the family.

The Family

The family must be strengthened, and that strengthening must begin by honoring a solemn commitment to stick by your partner, for better or worse, in sickness or in health, till death do you part. What can anyone's word be worth who breaks such an oath? How seriously can we take the assurances of parents that they'd "do anything" for their child if they can't be bothered to remain in that family and see their parental responsibilities through? Obviously, intolerable conditions of danger, abuse, or grotesque excess have to be addressed through divorce, but we ought not to expand these definitions to include frivolous concerns about pleasure, fulfillment, or simple dislike.

Ethics, values, and morals are taught in the home. Safe sex cannot become a substitute for caring or intimacy. Pill popping and drinking will become the models if that is what the kids observe.

America's fate will be decided in the fate of its families

and in the fate of its cities. And much of what takes place in both will be decided in legislative halls and executive suites.

OUR RULERS

It may be fashionable to scorn government, but it steers our ship and we ignore its operations, or its promise, at our peril.

We can be sure that special interests, lobbyists, and other opaque forces have greased the access to the rulemakers in life's game. Purchase of office has become the American style of government. Rich citizens finance their costly campaigns with personal wealth and thereby secure political power.

A cordon of narrow, special, selfish interests surrounds our elected bodies. Not only are the people kept from getting through the door, but it is their interests that must be sacrificed for the profit of those with the keys. A brief examination of the savings-and-loan scandal or of the Bank of Credit and Commerce International (BCCI), or a quick scan of the financial pages of the daily newspaper, will make the issues graphic.

At the upper reaches, we see criminality in the boardrooms, and at the lower levels we note a rising tide of criminality being fueled by official indifference to the forces shaping these criminals.

The Government

We always forget that we are ruled by our government. The allure of public life is the power of office. The great questions of our age are decided by our rulers—in court houses, legislative halls, and executive suites. And yet we continue to act as if our rulers were buffoons whose antics are not worth noting, and whose identities are interchangeable and irrelevant. We forget that our wealth is distributed, in the form of taxes and disbursements, by our government, which also decides how much is to be spent where. The government sets the rules for our game of life, and it establishes and enforces the penalties for any breaches of these rules.

We insist on behaving as if government had no role to play in our national life, and we repeatedly send rulers to Washington who have run against government involvement in our lives. And then they shelve this fiction and pander to our worst instincts by bashing the poor, inviting us to wallow in paroxysms of self-pity over our tax burdens, and exhort us to support enormous defense complexes and pursue dubious international adventures, while ignoring the cancers of crime, racism, and poverty consuming the nation's innards.

Our government could pump up the altruism factor by pushing for a latter-day Civilian Conservation Corps that would use the energies of our ghetto youth and by undertaking other, similar programs to help the underclass lift itself out of its misery. The decline of the military as a source of underclass employment will greatly exacerbate the crisis of inner-city youth. The government must become the employer of last resort and provide more generous unemployment benefits.

Washington could develop welfare programs that ensured a decent level of life and could build in factors of accountability that would ensure that those receiving aid performed responsibly, in return, and made real efforts to improve their lot. These efforts would include attending school, receiving training, trying to get work, raising children responsibly and limiting their number, and otherwise conforming to recognized standards of acceptable, responsible behavior. Those who made no effort would suffer the consequences of economic sanctions in the form of reduced benefits, evictions, and other reductions or withdrawals of support. The social contract must involve societal help—in the form of government subsidies—and the *quid pro quo* of responsible behavior by the recipient.

There isn't even any reason why welfare recipients shouldn't be required to keep clean and orderly homes, why men and women cannot be coerced or induced to respond more respon-

sibly to the conditions they have created, or why standards of
behavior recognized as the basics of a decent and responsible
style of life cannot be demanded or imposed. Those who receive help have a responsibility to function in socially positive
ways, and those who escape their responsibilities have to be
coerced back into working on the problems.

Scandinavia's gradual withdrawal from its heavy immer-
sion in welfare statism will be trumpeted, by many, as a sure
sign of the system's unworkability. We must study it, to be
sure, and we will probably learn that anything, taken to excess,
will experience difficulties, but this knowledge shouldn't tempt
us to throw the baby of hope out with the bathwater of dependency and indolence. The government has to come to see the
internal threat of crime and instability as being as dangerous to
our existence as the former "evil empire"—and allocate resources accordingly. There is no real need for new, much higher
taxes, but there is an urgent need to recognize the domestic
threat that poses such a danger to our national survival. (Although I'd argue that we could easily be taxed more, the focus
ought to be on shifting resources from external to internal
defense, on managing the government more efficiently and
taxing the underground economy more efficiently.)

There must be a way out of poverty and misery, and there
must be sanctions for those who choose negative paths.

WHENCE THE WILLIE HORTONS?

Finding the answer to how to create a safer America begins
with a question. If we are arresting all the street criminals
and incarcerating and otherwise controlling them in enormous
numbers, where do all the Willie Hortons come from?

Allowing that a much better job could be done, in the
short run, to make the system both more effective and more
efficient, the obvious implication of all that you have read here
so far is that our criminal population is growing at a much

faster rate than our CJS's ability to cope with the volume. The recidivists are created by social and economic forces over which CJS has no control.

It seems indisputable that there is something in our national makeup that is producing criminals at a very rapid, and increasing, rate, and that the kinds of suppression undertaken over the past quarter century haven't worked.

Imprisonment and Crime

More than tripling the prison population and greatly increasing arrests, jailings, probations, and other forms of control—of both young and old defendants—did not prevent 1990 from producing a record number of murders, following highs in the previous four years. The total was exceeded again in 1991. All the arrests, imprisonments, and other modes of oppressing crime had failed to stem the flood.

Most experts agree that the availability of guns and the thirst for drugs are powerful factors in our extraordinary levels of crime and violence, but they don't explain why white middle- and upper-class America doesn't participate in street crime to the degree and extent that black underclass America does. The issues of race and poverty simply aren't addressed, and the reason is that we might be forced to do something about them if we recognized their existence.

Despite floods of arrests and imprisonments the street criminals keep coming. If everybody's been arrested, where do the new criminals come from?

Arresting low-level users and dealers—and imprisoning them for long periods—is less effective than targeting importers and wholesalers of narcotics. If our social and economic systems make criminal behavior inevitable, we must look to those conditions, and their correction, as the only viable hope for long-term results.

If the street criminal is typically male, black, poor, addicted, uneducated, unemployable, born to a teenage single mother, persistently abused and neglected, and made to feel separate and inferior, then the obvious place for any prevention program to begin to address all these problems is upstream. By the time the CJS gets into the act, the criminal has been formed, and the crimes have been committed.

The social contract has to include the punishments we've been altogether too willing to apply, but it must also include more generous approaches if it is to complete the equation needed for enhanced safety.

Economic Justice

Capitalism has proved itself the most ingenious wealth-producing system ever devised, but it distributes the created wealth with manifest injustice. Capitalism creates wealth through the merciless competition of the marketplace, where only the fittest survive. If the wealth is distributed on the same basis, then only the strong prosper, and the weak are destroyed. Altruism—the concept of being one's brother's keeper—requires that the mercilessly competitive marketplace be humanized through distribution schemes that, while rewarding energy and strength, create floors beneath which the weaker cannot fall. One of the critical functions of government—and one that our current rulers have largely abandoned—is to tame and direct capitalism to the service of the nation, rather than only to enhancing the lives of the privileged few.

Once again, we are forced to face a really painful prospect: We may need to adopt some of the distributive features normally associated with socialism. It might just turn out that the Golden Mean works here, too, and that the answer lies in taking an eclectic approach and adopting the best features of both capitalism and socialism and melding them into a functioning system. This is another good illustration of politically incorrect thinking.

Whether we like it or not, only the government can produce the unprofitable housing needed by the large numbers of homeless. And only the government can create a national health system that will provide the needed coverage, in the same way that it has provided income to the elderly. Only the government can provide an educational plant that serves the poor, a welfare system that attends to the needs of the excluded, and job programs that offer hope to all our citizens, as well as the other programs that ameliorate the harsher aspects of a competitive culture that can exploit and crush its weaker members, even as its energies produce untold wealth.

The government, having offered help and hope, must also offer sanctions and supervision to those who will insist on going a negative way, and it must do so more efficiently. Nothing much will happen until our politicians develop a managerial perspective.

A society needs to protect itself from the criminals and malefactors in its midst. But a juster society can incarcerate, control, and, yes, even execute its members if it has openhandedly offered the means of rescue.

The government will do what we, as citizens, ask it to do, as it has done in settling wars, trying to clean the environment, extending rights to citizens, protecting consumers, and even, haltingly, resolving the abortion issue. It has also pandered to our nastiest appetites when it senses that that is what we want. We are going to have to want something better if we hope to survive. Our government, uniquely, is us. That is a thought that troubles many citizens a great deal—and it should—but it happens to be inescapably true.

In order for our society to undertake such vast structural changes as are envisioned here, we will have to begin a national debate on the pertinent questions and gradually arrive at a consensus. Fortunately, we are provided with at least the potential of such a forum every four years in presidential elections, and more regularly, if less importantly, in other local, state, and national races.

Does this mean that, if we were to buckle down to solve these problems, we'd face that horror of horrors: bigger government? It might mean that, but not necessarily. A central question rests on our getting better housing, roads, and infrastructure and on our shifting our resources from external to internal defense. For one thing, corporate managers have discovered that, by flattening the organizational pyramid and freeing up the workers to perform, they've done away with layers of functionaries. How much worse is our present bloated government bureaucracy, where stultifying layers of officials lie in wait to swat every initiative? Restoring autonomy and local control, and choices, to local schools, for example, would help nullify the paralyzing grip of central boards. This example extends throughout the government at all levels. Housing and social services should be provided locally. We must also recognize that, among the industrialized nations, we are taxed less, produce fewer services, and are the richest. We need only look at the most egregious examples, our corporate CEOs and their salaries, to see the grotesque anomalies we've allowed. We should not attempt to legislate corporate salaries, but we can pass laws relating to corporate democracy, accountability to shareholders, the responsibilities of directors, and similar matters.

At the other end, we have the ghetto dwellers who resort to crime as an inevitable response to the conditions of their lives. The War on Poverty must be refought. The dilemma of racism must be attacked. The struggles will be, in the first place, costly, and, in the second, painful. There is something in the human condition that seems to require pain before catharsis, and the heat of the crucible before steel can emerge. The pain, blood, sweat, and struggle of birth becomes a metaphor for life.

It is natural and understandable that we should seek to avoid such pain, but the alternative is the decay that now accompanies our present comfort, and that will, sooner or later, erase that comfort, too. There is a sure sense of national disquiet over our current drift.

Poverty and racism are the big agenda items. Ignoring their primary role in the crime equation, as we currently do, absolutely ensures a continuation of the rise in the appalling levels of urban violence we are experiencing.

It is totally absurd for us to take the position, as we have done now for the last decade or more, that the government can't do anything right, that the less we have of it the better, and that we cannot, and ought not, assign any significant task to it. Such a foolish view ignores the central reality of history, that people need instruments for regulating their daily lives and that this need has increased with the growing complexity and interdependence of modern societies.

Job Corps

We have accepted the myth that the War on Poverty was fought and lost and that we have to find another way out of this morass. We choose to ignore that war's successes and the need to tighten controls and accountability. Head Start is one prominent legacy of the effort.

President Lyndon B. Johnson began the War on Poverty in 1964. The effort was diminished by the demands of the Vietnam war and then by the 1968 election of President Richard M. Nixon, but the definitive end of the struggle came with the election of President Ronald Reagan in 1980. Today, there are about five million impoverished young men and women who are uneducated, unskilled, undisciplined, unsocialized, and unincluded. They are frequently addicted to drugs or alcohol, commit crimes, and become our future criminals.

One remnant of the War on Poverty is the Job Corps and its 106 campuses across the nation, which try to salvage the worst-off of the sixteen- to twenty-two-year-olds. It served 62,000 per year in the early nineties.

The Job Corps is a mix of vocational training, boarding school, and boot camp. Its record of performance has converted some of its severest critics, yet President Reagan tried to eliminate it altogether, twice.

The statistics are impressive: Almost 73 percent of Jobs Corps members have never been previously employed. More than 50 percent are black, and over 40 percent come from welfare families. Over 83 percent were, in 1990–1991, high school dropouts; the national total of dropouts was just over 12 percent. The program is clearly reaching the right candidates. This program takes the toughest losers and gives them structure, discipline, direction, and hope. Those who demand specific answers to what to do about our lost youngsters can be confronted with Head Start and the Job Corps as examples of programs that work.

Job Corps enrollment typically lasts ten months and has the high-school equivalency diploma as a goal. It engages with unions and the construction and other industries for jobs, and it contracts with private groups to run its residential centers. It is expensive, at $18,000 a year per student in 1992, but a Harvard education, or prison, costs more. It focuses, typically, on entry-level jobs in accounting, construction, building maintenance, office work, food service, health care, and transportation. It teaches hygiene, grooming, social skills, and how to be polite. It includes counseling on addiction and parenting.

The students receive housing, food, and medical care free; are paid $40 to $100 per month; and are given "readjustment money" when they leave, from $450 to $3,600, depending on their length of stay. Graduates can be funneled into programs like vocational training centers, where they are taught carpentry, construction trades, TV repair, automobile maintenance, and other service skills that enable them to get meaningful jobs.

The Job Corps has had its failures, but it has compiled an impressive record of success as measured by the graduates who have got jobs and become productive citizens.

Each ingredient—individual, family, government, corporations, and nonprofits—is, to a greater or lesser degree, essential to the outcome of a safer society.

GOOD CORPORATE CITIZENS

Many of our capitalist enterprises proudly style themselves "good corporate citizens" while polluting the earth or plundering resources. One might well ask, "Citizens of where?" The multinational status of many businesses transforms them into international colossi.

We have, however, seen examples of good corporate citizenship, in which the pursuit of corporate profit has melded with the obligation to do some good.

Mr. Lang, a graduate of a Harlem high school and a successful entrepreneur, started a national movement by offering to pay the full college tuition of any student successfully completing the course of high school study.

Granville Academy, founded in 1983 in Trenton, New Jersey, offers free courses in finance and computers to teenaged minority youngsters, as an adjunct to its formal school programs.

Although the merciless efficiencies of capitalism are an integral part of it, the opportunities to temper these with programs that promote society's well-being cannot be ignored.

City Pride

To some degree we've lost our way—misplaced our once-fabled faith in Yankee ingenuity and our plain determination to get the job done.

When Pittsburgh's last commercial bakery closed in 1989, displaced workers banded together and created City Pride Bakery, which planned to produce fresh bread for local supermarkets in the store's own wrapper. Before opening in the spring of 1992, it had more than enough contracts to guarantee a profit.

The factory is staffed by those most needing work. It is union-ized and offers high school courses, free child care, and subsi-dized lunches.

The organizers obtained federal grants for job training, as well as loans and grants from the state, county, and city, and hired a management team, developed a business plan, and received private investments from church groups, banks, busi-nesses, and individuals. The total start-up cost exceeded $7 million. The 100 employees own 10 percent of the business, and the hope is to increase the number of workers to 300 by 1997.

There are ten thousand employee-owned companies in America, examples that are waiting to be replicated.

The Role of Business

The triumph of capitalism internationally and the probusi-ness euphoria and policies in Washington since 1980 have boosted corporate status. Our faith in government has plum-meted. Most of us have got a good deal richer over that period, yet most of us would deny it and would decry high taxes.

International competition, especially from Japan and Ger-many, has made us protective and tolerant of those who gener-ate the wealth of our nation, but that sympathy hasn't entirely blinded us to the need for controls.

To a diminishing degree, we also curb capitalism's energies in the areas of monopolies and attempt to regulate essential services, like transportation and communication and utilities, because we cannot be placed at the tender mercies of the marketplace by monopolies in these areas. The democratic in-stinct justly fears the corrupting temptations of power. Control-ling multinational corporate giants, which can shift resources and operations globally, is certain to be one of the great con-cerns of the twenty-first century, but we have to concern our-selves, here, with more immediate issues of survival.

We are also justly concerned about the quality of the many

products offered for our ingestion, and we insist that the government evaluate and pass judgments on our foods and medicines. We even outlaw some altogether, such as narcotics, and sometimes delay the entrance of medicines into the marketplace out of this feeling of a need to protect the people. So, despite what we might call the late-twentieth-century unleashing of capitalism, corporate enterprises are still subjected to controls and monitoring.

The growth of the faceless multinational corporation is blurring businesses' connection to local communities as they adopt international perspectives. Thus, a homegrown company like Pillsbury, with family roots deep in Minnesota, is bought out by Grand Metropolitan, whose ties to any locale are as amorphous as its name.

Corporations pay lip service to being "good corporate citizens," but the phrase has a hollow ring in the ghetto. In fact, the central and overriding concern is the balance sheet: corporate profit.

Corporations should be lobbying the government to create tax incentives to establish enterprise zones in the ghetto, which would bring jobs and hope to its residents. They ought to be promoting internships, summer jobs, and similar programs for poor minority youngsters who need work experience and opportunities. Corporations ought to be contributing to the efforts to feed the hungry, shelter the homeless, and employ those seeking work—all of this activity within the rubrics of *performance* and *accountability*. Here, as everywhere else, standards have to be established and met, and unacceptable conduct should be punished. There is no free lunch, for anyone, nor should there be, but it seems indisputable that America's businesses have utterly failed to exhibit the qualities we might define as encompassing "good corporate citizenship."

There should be a compatibility between profit and altruism. Corporations have adjusted to a myriad of challenges, including corporate affirmative action programs, the feminist movement, and stiff competition, both internally and externally. Indeed, it could be asserted that capitalism's energies tend to be revitalized by challenges, and that it grows torpid and inefficient in the absence of such "unwelcome" stimuli. Both the human and the corporate organisms need to be discomfited in order to thrive.

The first requisite for corporations is to recognize the threats that poverty and racism pose to their existence. The decline of our cities threatens the viability of American commerce. Many corporations have already fled to the suburbs and exurbs, while others remain in refurbished downtowns, with sanitized corridors to permit ingress and egress. The building of fortresses, in the suburbs of the city, does promote safety, but sooner or later, those within discover that true safety comes from having a stable and pacific countryside.

Corporate America has mostly exempted itself from the great national anxiety about crime and its causes, but the underlying forces feeding and creating violence will require deep and broad attacks by all of society's elements. The nation's businesses have, willingly or not, been dragged into participating in resolving the great questions of the age: civil rights, the ecology, the Vietnam war, or whatever travail happens to be currently burdening the national psyche. They cannot be granted a pass on this issue. Their participation—in creating jobs and hope for the underclass—is too critical to be denied. The resolution of our internal problems of crime, riots, addiction, gun battles, and social dissolution will require the involvement of all of society's sectors. It really is a war, and it's going to take a war footing to restore peace.

THE NONPROFIT AND FOUNDATION SECTORS

American genius has produced many incredibly useful social tools that are not the less valuable because of their simplicity. Foundations that have been created to promote society's well-being, and that are protected from taxes in exchange for their nonprofit status, are examples of the genre. Other nonprofits, like the Project for Pride in Living in Minneapolis, stand out as paradigms of the operational projects that provide jobs, housing, and services for the downtrodden.

Role confusion lies behind many failures. Just as we have confused the role of government by resisting its legitimate, and needed, intrusions in our lives and have failed to maximize the societal involvement of our corporations, we haven't grasped how the focusing of the resources and talents of foundations on the internal problems of racism and poverty might help. Foundations have provided the funds, inspiration, and talent to solve many problems through research and study. In the main, they have been absent from the social arenas that spawn dissolution and crime.

Around 1970, the Ford Foundation did create the Police Foundation, with a $30-million ten-year grant, to undertake research in the police field, but following the initial enthusiasm, Ford has mostly sidled away from this effort. Except for that notable effort, and some projects by the McKnight Foundation and the Edna McConnell Clark Foundation's work in corrections, there have been very, very few involvements of foundations with the CJS. More important, however, foundations have not been particularly visible or active in combating the underlying causes of crime in America.

A notable exception has been the McKnight Foundation, which has an exemplary record of support for programs relating to housing the poor, teaching parenting skills to young mothers, and creating jobs and education programs for the hard-to-employ. It has extended grants to localities to spark local initiatives. These efforts have been accompanied by hard-headed insistences on accountability and performance-in-kind. Progress has been monitored. Sites and programs have been personally inspected, and results have been demanded. Frequently the grants have required a match from the government—as a test of commitment—and have covered only a start-up period, after which permanent sources of funding must be found elsewhere.

Under such pressures, successful programs have thrived and the failures have been buried. The Project for Pride in Living, mentioned earlier as a paradigm of this type of program continues to be supported financially by McKnight.

The corporate tie becomes clearer when the name of this foundation is traced to one of the founders of 3M (once known as Minnesota Mining and Manufacturing), William McKnight, and the continuing work of his daughter, Virginia McKnight Binger, and then of her children.

McKnight serves as a model of socially conscious foundations, committed to addressing the problems besetting its neighbors, and yet it has not ignored the essential (and easy-to-ignore, as "frills") arts, which inspire and define us as a people, or the medical questions relating to improved health. In order to accomplish these goals, there had to be a view and a focus; the foundation's leaders recognized the overriding problems of society and moved to help.

Today, there isn't a program in Minnesota that helps the weak and poor that doesn't have this foundation's fingerprints on its history, whether in the inner city or in the farm communities. Many of its efforts constitute seed money or loans or require matching funds and contributions, thereby encouraging others to support the effort—a pretty sure test of the program's viability.

Foundations can ensure the existence of important services in the bleaker areas of the city by subsidizing activity centers for youths who would otherwise be hanging out and creating problems. Such centers could offer athletic programs or programs in dance and the other arts, as well as crafts programs.

Neighborhood centers could offer programs for seniors, single parents, and others. Pillsbury House offers educational programs, art and craft classes, social events like a potluck meal, Bingo, medical and child-care services, and support and counseling sessions of all sorts, as well as theater events. Such efforts build community cohesion, channel energies into useful lanes, and enrich lives.

My experience of urban life has convinced me that the money is easier to find than the selfless and dedicated people needed to create the vision and bring it to fruition. Yet, without the resources, the devoted participants and leaders will not appear. Money is the fuel that drives the engine; it enables visionaries to breathe life into their dreams.

We are the enemy. Our obsession with pleasure and recreation, and our indifference to the plight of the black and poor, are producing the crime and violence we so eloquently deplore. It is all very well to attack The Monster endangering our lives, but we are going to have to look behind it, for the Dr. Frankenstein who created it. In the case of crime, violence, and riots, it may be the blacks who flail about, but it is the rest of us who created the conditions that made those flailings inevitable.

The malaise settling over the nation is terminal.

Our slide into decadence and despair will be accelerated by the absence of the challenge formerly represented by the Soviet Union, which kept us frightened and alert. No longer afraid, we can lapse into greater orgies of self-indulgence. The sort of moral regeneration needed will involve a full-fledged attack on racism and poverty. It will require such wisdom and altruism as will enable us to see that we need to be taxed more heavily; that we need to share, not keep; that we need to remember the words on our Statue of Liberty's base about succoring the huddled masses and not ignoring our poor; and that, rather than circuses, we need the stimulus of challenge and struggle that a real War on Crime and its causes will bring.

How do we restructure a society so that families will stay together and its citizens will rediscover the joys of service, in which the rich are poorer and the poor richer and where everyone has a chance to be educated? How can we help people find work or protect our citizens from attack?

Imperfections will always abound, but ours accelerate and

threaten our survival. The domestic crisis contains the threat of annihilating our society. The problems can be summarized in the difficulties surrounding four words: *family, city, poverty,* and *race.* Left unaddressed, these four latter-day Horses of the Apocalypse will crush us under their hooves.

Nothing less than an all-out effort to bring social, racial, and economic justice is going to save the noblest experiment the human animal ever devised.

The alternative is to witness the end of that glorious moment known as the American Dream.

INDEX